T0320377

The Collapse of Development Planning

THE POLITICAL ECONOMY OF THE AUSTRIAN SCHOOL Series
General Editor: Mario Rizzo, New York University

Although long associated with a deep appreciation of the free market, the
Austrian School has not been fully recognized as a unique approach in
analyzing the role of government in the economy. A major contribution
of the Austrian School was to demonstrate, as early as 1920, the impossibility of economic calculation under socialism. Recent events in the former Soviet Union and Eastern Europe have dramatically illustrated the
cogency of this argument. In more recent times and in contrast to conventional static analyses, Austrian research has been concerned with the
impact of government control on entrepreneurial discovery. To what
extent does the impact of such control go beyond the firm's static pricing
decision and reach into the very discovery of new opportunities and hence
the transmission of knowledge in society? Austrians are also concerned
with the dynamics of state intervention—the degree to which one intervention induces further interventions and, conversely, the degree to
which one decontrol "necessitates" further steps in the process of deregulation. Finally, the Austrian School is firmly committed to the value-
freedom of economics, that is, the separation of the analysis of policy
consequences from the moral and political values inherent in the *advo-
cacy* of particular economic policies.

The Collapse of Development Planning

Edited by
Peter J. Boettke

NEW YORK UNIVERSITY PRESS
New York and London

NEW YORK UNIVERSITY PRESS
New York and London

Library of Congress Cataloging-in-Publication Data
The Collapse of development planning / edited by Peter J. Boettke.
p.   cm. — (The Political economy of the Austrian school)
Includes bibliographical references and index.
ISBN 0-8147-1216-9. — ISBN 0-8147-1225-8 (pbk.)
1. Economic development.   2. Economic development—Case studies.
I. Boettke, Peter J.   II. Series.
HD75.C645   1994
338.9—dc20   93-51051
                         CIP

New York University Press books are printed on acid-free paper, and
their binding materials are chosen for strength and durability.

Manufactured in the United States of America

10   9   8   7   6   5   4   3   2   1

This book has been sponsored in part by the Austrian Economics
Program at New York University.

Contents

Acknowledgments   vii

1. Introduction   *Peter J. Boettke*   1

I. Theory   13

2. Money and Capital in Economic Development
Parth J. Shah   15

3. The Theory of Economic Development and the
"European Miracle"   *Ralph Raico*   37

II. Case Studies of Planning   59

4. The Political Economy of Development in Communist
China: China and the Market   *Jan S. Prybyla*   61

5. The Failure of Development Planning in India
Shyam J. Kamath   90

6. The Failure of Development Planning in Africa
George B. N. Ayittey   146

III. The Record on Foreign Aid and Advice   183

   7. The World Bank and the IMF: Misbegotten Sisters
   David Osterfeld   185

   8. Does Eastern Europe Need a New (Marshall) Plan?
   Steven Horwitz   210

IV. The Political Economy of the Asian Miracle   229

   9. Industrial Policy as the Engine of Economic Growth in
   South Korea: Myth and Reality   *Young Back Choi*   231

   10. The Political Economy of Post–World War II Japanese
   Development: A Rent-Seeking Perspective   *Shigeto Naka,
   Wayne T. Brough, and Kiyokazu Tanaka*   256

V. Market Solutions to Economic Development   287

   11. Privatization and Development: The Case of Sri Lanka
   Manisha H. Perera and Mark Thornton   289

   12. Financial Reform and Economic Development: The Currency
   Board System for Eastern Europe   *Steve H. Hanke and
   Kurt Schuler*   310

   Contributors   327

   Index   331

Acknowledgments

First, I would like to thank my colleagues in the Austrian Economics Program at New York University, Israel Kirzner and Mario Rizzo, for their critical input and support. Financial assistance from the Sarah Scaife Foundation for general support of the Austrian Program is gratefully acknowledged.

Second, in thinking about development economics I benefited greatly from my stay at the Institute for the Study of Economic Culture, Boston University, and the seminar there in which I participated. I would like to thank Robert Hefner and Peter Berger for including me in the program at ISEC. Also, I benefited greatly from my participation in a Liberty Fund Conference on Banking and Development organized by Lawrence H. White and George Selgin.

Third, the project was completed while I was a 1992–93 National Fellow at the Hoover Institution on War, Revolution and Peace at Stanford University. Dr. Thomas Henriksen, the director of the National Fellows Program, and Ms. Wendy Minkin, the administrator of the program, create a wonderful environment in which the fellows can work and learn. Ms. Jennifer Medveckis provided helpful research assistance. Financial support for the 1992–93 academic year from Hoover and from the Earhart Foundation is gratefully acknowledged.

Fourth, Mario Rizzo, the general editor of the New York University Press series on the political economy of the Austrian School, was supportive of the project from the beginning. Niko Pfund, the acquisitions editor at New York University Press, was also a source of encouragement and guidance. In addition, I would like to thank Despina Papazoglou Gimbel of New York University Press for her work on copyediting the manuscript and overseeing the publication process.

Finally, I would like to thank my wife, Rosemary, and our two sons, Matthew and Stephen, for their patience and loving support.

The Collapse of Development Planning

1

Introduction

Peter J. Boettke

Prior to the twentieth century, economic development was primarily thought of as a question of the institutional infrastructure of a society. Adam Smith's *An Inquiry into the Nature and Causes of the Wealth of Nations* ([1776] 1976) set the general tone for economic discourse on the determinants of prosperity for about one hundred years.[1] Smith argued that economic development was the result of expanding the division of labor within society. This expansion was due to the adoption of certain political, legal, and economic institutions and practices. Private property rights, monetization, the elimination of trade restrictions, etc., sustained specialized production and exchange, and as such led to the increased substitution of market forces for centralized decision making within the economic affairs of society. The division of labor, Smith pointed out, was limited by the extent of the market. Expanding the market allowed individuals to capture the gains from specialized production and exchange. In short, the source of economic development and prosperity was the adoption of institutions and policies that approximated the system of "natural liberty"—i.e., the limited government, night-watchman state of classical liberalism.

As the fate of classical liberalism as a political and economic doctrine waned in the twentieth century, the focus of attention with regard to economic development shifted. Questions of institutional infrastructure were replaced by those dealing with the appropriate policy mix to be implemented by the state to achieve economic development. Discretionary planning replaced the concern with rules and institutions.

Three developments in thought and history worked to undermine the emphasis on institutional infrastructure: (1) the formalist and positivist revolution in economics, (2) the Bolshevik Revolution and the rise of socialism, and (3) the Keynesian revolution in macroeconomics. Each of these three shifted attention away from *governance* to government activism.

The marginalist revolution in the 1870s was a great advance in economic understanding. Unfortunately, the formal properties of the logic of choice tended to distract theoretical attention from the institutional context of choice. The great advance of marginalism was the development of a universal theory of human action to aid our understanding of economic behavior. But, despite the formal similarity of the choice problem across time and place, the fact remains that the institutional context of choice changes the margins on which economic decisions are based. Unfortunately, the preoccupation with equilibrium states that soon came to dominate economics after the 1930s completely eliminated institutions from mainstream economics. What emerged was a theory of choice within a vacuum.

Oskar Lange, for example, argued that economics was a universal science, applying to socialist as well as capitalist economies. One might not disagree with Lange on this point, but within Lange's comparative analysis of capitalism and socialism the formal similarity of the choice problem was transformed into a study of the static allocation problem. In fact, Lange explicitly assumed away the importance of institutions in economic interaction, and, thus, in the comparison between socialism and capitalism ([1939] 1970, 61–62).

Lange was not alone is this assessment. As brilliant as they were, and as much as their own work remained rich in institutional analysis, Joseph Schumpeter (1942) and Frank Knight (1936) concurred with Lange. Leading thinkers were led into this error, as F. A. Hayek pointed out, because of the preoccupation with equilibrium states that the formalist revolution engendered (Hayek [1945] 1980, 91).

Positivism also contributed to the shift of focus away from institutional infrastructure by delegitimizing the study of ideology as an important component in social theory. Political, legal, and economic institutions are sustained on the basis of ideological systems of thought. Out of fear of ideological campaigns, positivism sought to eliminate all nontestable empirical propositions from science.

Combine the formalist preoccupation with equilibrium with the positivist disregard for ideas, and the kinds of questions that Adam Smith raised about the nature and causes of economic development and lasting prosperity are eliminated from the field. The natural tendency of neoclassical development economics was to ignore political, legal, and economic institutions, and instead to search for measures of development. The question of the institutional infrastructure of sustainable development was considered to be unscientific. Measurement alone equals science.

The Bolshevik Revolution and the rise of socialism also transformed the way scholars approached economic development. After the initial failure of the policies of War Communism (1918–1921), the Bolsheviks introduced a partial liberalization known as the New Economic Policy (1921 28). This partial liberalization led to a relative recovery of the Russian economy from the disaster of War Communism. The New Economic Policy, however, did not produce the desired results in terms of industrialization and agricultural development, as it suffered from internal contradictions which made official market exchange an insecure outlet due to arbitrary intervention (see Boettke 1990, 113–46; Boettke 1993, 25–30, 96–99). Net official marketings of grain, for example, in 1926–27 were only 50 and 57 percent of their pre-World War I level, although grain output for that period was almost equivalent to pre-World War I levels of output.

Lenin's death in 1924, along with these uncomfortable results of the New Economic Policy, led to a protracted debate among Soviet economists concerning the path to be followed in industrial development. The debates and controversies of the 1920s contain much that is of importance to economic and intellectual historians (see Erlich 1960 and Boettke 1990, 147–91, for a summary of the terms of the Soviet debate). As Alec Nove has pointed out, modern "development economics could be said to have been born here" ([1969] 1984, 129).

The Stalinist model of industrialization emerged out the 1920s controversy, and the Five-Year Planning System was born. Forced industrialization and collectivization, it was argued, were necessary to transform a backward economy into an advanced industrial power which could simultaneously defend itself against hostile capitalist encirclement and serve as a beacon to the modern world. The early reports of success from the Soviet government (at the same time that the Great Depression had destroyed faith in the market system in the West) were reinforced by the outcome of World War II. That the Stalinist model had prepared the Soviet Union to defeat Nazism became the standard justificatory explanation for forced industrialization and collectivization of agriculture. Whatever cost the Soviet policies of the 1930s imposed on the people, it was argued, the avoidance of economic crisis as the Great Depression and the victory over Nazism justified the expense. A new path to economic development had been discovered, a new world had been created. No longer was the world divided into developed capitalist countries and underdeveloped noncapitalist countries, now the classification included the First World (capitalist developed economies), the Second World (socialist developed economies), and the Third World (underdeveloped economies).[2] Development was no longer synonymous with capitalism.

The Keynesian revolution also contributed significantly to the shift of focus in development economics. First, the Keynesian theory reinforced the socialist viewpoint that capitalism was inherently unstable. The Great Depression, for example, was a consequence of aggregate demand failure which periodically results from chaotic and irrational investment decisions. Free-market competition could not be relied upon to self-correct for the systemic consequences of errors committed by private economic actors, let alone promote stability and security. Keynes argued that *laissez-faire* was dead as a legitimating ideology. In 1933, he went as far as to argue that the great social experiments of the time in Italy (fascism), Germany (national socialism) and Russia (communism) could point the way to the future of economic policy. Country after country had abandoned the old presuppositions of classical liberalism. Thinking men and women in Great Britain and in the United States would strive to find a hybrid of their own which combined the successful aspects of these modern economic policies with the successful components of their bourgeois political system. *Laissez-faire* liberalism was no longer a serious force in the world of ideas (Keynes 1933).

Second, the aggregate techniques developed in the Keynesian revolution provided economists with a way to measure economic development. Economic development became synonymous, as H. W. Arndt (1981) pointed out, with measured growth in per capita income. This equating of economic development with neoclassical growth theory had severe consequences for the theoretical foundations of development economics. The preoccupation with "growth" and "long-range" economic planning were reminiscent of the debates of the Soviet economists of the 1920s. This was not a coincidence. The development of the Harrod-Domar model of economic growth was directly influenced by the Soviet debates.

Evsey Domar remarked that the 1920s Soviet journal, *The Planned Economy*, was "a valuable source of ideas" for the development of his own approach. Soviet society represented a sort of economic laboratory where the social scientist could examine "his whole intellectual apparatus in light of a social and economic system sufficiently different from ours to make the experiment rewarding, and yet not so different to make it impossible" (1957, 10). Domar's model was an elaboration of the theory of growth worked out by the Soviet economist G. A. Fel'dman. In extending Fel'dman's model, however, Domar replaced the Marxist concern with capital proportionality with Keynesian aggregation. As a result, modern growth theory was completely separated from the traditional concerns of capital theory. But capital theory, properly understood, provides the basis for the microeconomic foundations for macroeconomic analysis. Without these foundations the theorist is left with a world in which there are either no market problems (the Walrasian world of general equilibrium) or no market solutions (the Keynesian world of aggregate demand failure).

Neither theoretical world does much to advance our understanding of real existing economies and the preconditions for their economic development (see Garrison 1984).

Modern development economics incorporated all three trends, each tending to reinforce the others. The formalist and positivist revolution demanded measurement, while Keynesian techniques of aggregation supplied the needed tools for measurement. The socialist idea of the chaos of capitalism received additional support from Keynesian theory. Moreover, the Soviet experience seemed to lend credence to the notion of comprehensive economic planning, while the Keynesian theory of demand management provided a policy technique for noncomprehensive planning of the economy.

Economic thought in both East and West accepted the idea that government management of the economy was the way not only to run a modern economy, but to transform a backward economy into a modern one. Alternative models of government management of economic development were exported from the First and Second to the Third World.

The hegemony of this paradigm for economic development has been seriously challenged by intellectual developments and political events in the past two decades. The Keynesian model fell out of vogue in the 1970s; then, in the mid- to late 1980s, the communist model of political economy collapsed. The traditional Keynesian model was proven to be logically flawed and empirically weak. The protracted stagnation of the British and United States economies, combined with high inflation, represented a serious anomaly in the Keynesian system. The rejection of the Communist Party throughout East and Central Europe in 1989, and the abolition of the Soviet Union in 1991, called into question the desirability of the Leninist political system. The terrible economic conditions in every one of the communist countries was witness to the folly of economic planning. Moreover, the record of the exported models of government planning for economic development in Africa, Latin America, India, etc., is conspicuously lacking in any success story.

The glasnost revelations from inside the former Soviet Union during the Gorbachev period are particularly relevant since they radically question all previous estimates of Soviet economic performance throughout its history (see Boettke 1993, 12–45). These revelations did not simply demonstrate the systematic falsification of statistics by the Soviet government, but Soviet economists were critically assessing the accuracy of even CIA statistics on Soviet economic performance. Living standards in the former USSR, as Grigory Khanin and Vasily Selyunin (1987) pointed out, had been falling for decades. But this decline was not grasped by the CIA. In 1986, for example, the CIA estimated that Soviet per capita GNP was about 49 percent of that in the United States. The revised estimates now put that figure at about 25 percent. Had the CIA figures been accurate, the Soviet economy would have been a maturing industrialized economy. The revised estimates, however, now reveal that the Soviet economy provided a standard of living to its citizens equivalent to that of a well-developed Third World economy.

Not only were the growth rates challenged, but all the success claims of the Soviet model were brought into question by Soviet scholars and intellectuals. Western historians, such as Robert Conquest, had for a long time exposed the extent of Stalin's crimes against humanity. Conquest's books, such as *The Great Terror* and *The Harvest of Sorrow*, were quite well known among intellectuals within the Soviet Union as they had circulated *samizdat* for years. Moreover, literary works by writers of the stature of Aleksandr Solzhenitsyn, Vasily Grossman, Anatoli Rybhakov, Arthur Koestler, and George Orwell had exposed the absurdities and tragedies of the Stalinist system—and these works were also well known within the Soviet Union. But these works were not part of the *official* culture and history of the Soviet people. There is, though, something vitally important about the transformation of historical conscience from a *sub rosa* existence to legitimate inquiry.

With the advent of glasnost in the late 1980s, Soviet intellectuals reclaimed their history and their literary culture. *Samizdat* periodicals ceased as the "thick" journals, such as *Novy Mir*, carried article after article which tore asunder one icon after another of Soviet history or published excerpts from long-suppressed novels. Classic books which had only circulated underground were now published in new editions above ground. The full extent, for example, of the planned loss of human lives from collectivization and political persecution in the 1930s under Stalin's direct orders began to be unearthed from under the debris of state propaganda and censorship (see, for example, Medvedev 1989).

Even the Great Patriotic War (World War II) did not escape scrutiny. The 1939 Stalin-Hitler Pact was officially acknowledged. The murder of Polish officers at Katyn was debated and finally confessed. Soviet officials admitted that Stalin's purge of the Red Army's generals just before the outbreak of war cost the Soviet army dearly. Without the assistance of its Western allies, the Soviet Union might very well have fallen to Hitler. Moreover, the embarrassing fact to Soviet leaders that many peasant communities, for example in the Ukraine, welcomed Hitler's troops as liberators from the oppression of Stalin's collectivization became part of the legitimate historical record. It was not the Stalinist model that provided the resources or unity of will to defeat Nazism, but rather the ultimate resolve of the Soviet people and the assistance of the Western allies. The Stalinist model, in fact, had made the Soviet Union highly vulnerable to Hitler's attack by crippling the Soviet economy and breaking the spirit of millions of Soviet subjects.

The sacrifices of the Soviet people were real, but what success story could this model claim in terms of enhanced consumer well-being or an improved way of living? There is a Soviet quip which captures the failure of the Stalinist model for economic development. It goes as follows. The problem with the First World is that you cannot breathe because of the industrial air pollution. The problem with the Third World is that you cannot drink the water because of the lack of sanitation. Unfortunately, in the Second World, as a consequence of the Soviet model of development, you can neither breathe nor drink.

All of this demands a reevaluation of the economic development literature. The Soviet model no longer represents a viable alternative. A new agenda for studying development economics must be forged. As the major opponent of the original Keynesian and socialist challenge, the Austrian School seems a natural place to look to for an alternative model of economic development. In addition, the Austrian School rejected the formalistic and positivist revolution in economic thought. In the Austrian tradition, economic development was never confused with measured rates of growth. To understand economic development, what is needed is not more elaborate formal models of growth or better techniques for measurement, but more detailed historical studies of the pattern of development across countries and periods. These studies, however, must be informed by a theory of economic and political processes which is rich in institutional analysis. In other words, what is required to forge a new agenda in development economics is a return to Adam Smith's concern with institutions and their impact on economic behavior. Economic development can be seen as part of a general theory of economic processes and social evolution.

The Collapse of Development Planning explores the theoretical arguments and historical experience concerning the effectiveness of economic development policy, including foreign aid programs. The chapter on money and capital in the theory of economic development provides an overview of the analytical issues involved in any examination of the pattern of development of an economic system. The historiography of the rise of the West introduces the central political, legal, and economic institutions that contributed to the rise of capitalism and liberal democracy. The case studies of development planning in China, India, and Africa, and of foreign aid programs (including the Marshall Plan) illustrate the importance of the insights derived from Austrian economics for understanding the historical record of government activism in development policy. The political economy perspective on the Asian model, and the discussion of market solutions to economic development questions explain the relative success of an alternative nondeliberative planning path to economic development.

Not all of the authors in this volume would consider themselves "Austrian," but each of the contributions focuses on political, legal, and economic institutions, their impact on economic behavior, and their role in the discovery and use of dispersed knowledge. In that sense, it is accurate to refer to this collection as "Austrian." It is too subtle a distinction for present purposes to elaborate on the differences between Austrian economics and Neo-Institutionalism (see, e. g , Eggertsson 1990). Despite their differences, Austrians and Neo-Institutionalists share a basic perspective on the approach to the study of society. Depending on how one draws the line, either Austrian economics could be viewed as a subset of Neo-Institutionalism or Neo-Institutionalism could be viewed as a subset of Austrian economics (see Langlois 1986). What was important for the present project was to begin to forge a new agenda for development economics that will focus scholarly attention once again on the institutional infrastructure of economic development.

While scholars working explicitly within the Austrian tradition have addressed development issues before in individual articles or in dissertations (most notably Irigoin 1990), this volume represents the first collection and book-length treatment of the subject from a modern market process perspective. It is offered to the community in the spirit of critical rationalism, and with the hope that it will stimulate some to challenge the insights offered, and others to mine the Austrian paradigm for insights into the pressing problems of the political economy of economic development that confront us throughout the world today.

Notes

1. I have benefited from useful conversations on the topic of economic development with Robert Conquest, Thomas Metzger, Ramon Myers, and Hilton Root. In addition, I would like to thank Ralph Raico for helpful comments on an earlier draft. The usual caveat applies.
2. P. T. Bauer has argued that the term "Third World" emerged merely to represent those countries receiving foreign aid from the developed world. My classification does not intend to challenge Bauer's etymological accuracy. Rather, I am just pointing out that a new classification scheme emerged to reflect the perceived fact that capitalism was no longer the only path to industrial development.

References

Arndt, H. W. 1981. "Economic Development: A Semantic History." *Economic Development and Cultural Change* 29 (April): 457–66.

Boettke, Peter J. 1990. *The Political Economy of Soviet Socialism: The Formative Years, 1918–1928*. Boston: Kluwer Publishing.
——— 1993. *Why Perestroika Failed: The Politics and Economics of Socialist Transformation*. London: Routledge.
Domar, Evsey. 1957. *Essays in the Theory of Economic Growth*. New York: Oxford University Press.
Eggertsson, Thrainn. 1990. *Economic Behavior and Institutions*. New York: Cambridge University Press.
Erlich, Alexander. 1960. *The Soviet Industrialization Debate, 1924–1928*. Cambridge: Harvard University Press.
Garrison, Roger. 1984. "Time and Money: The Universals in Macroeconomic Theorizing." *Journal of Macroeconomics* 6 (2): 197–213.
Hayek, F. A. [1945] 1980. "The Use of Knowledge in Society." In his Individualism and Economic Order, 77–91. Chicago: University of Chicago Press.
Irigoin, Alfredo. 1990. "Economic Development: A Market Process Perspective." Ph.D. diss., Department of Economics, New York University.
Keynes, John Maynard. 1933. "National Self-Sufficiency." *Yale Review* (Summer): 755–69.
Khanin, Grigory, and Vasily Selyunin. 1987. "The Elusive Figure." Novy Mir, 2 (February). Translated in *The Current Digest of the Soviet Press* 39, no. 25 (1987): 10–12.
Knight, Frank 1936. "The Place of Marginal Economics in a Collectivist System." *American Economic Review* 26, no. 1 (March): 255–66.
Lange, Oskar [1939] 1970. *On the Economic Theory of Socialism*. New York: Augustus M. Kelley.
Langlois, Richard, ed. 1986. *Economics as a Process: Essays in the New Institutional Economics*. New York: Cambridge University Press.
Medvedev, Roy. 1989. *Let History Judge*. Revised ed. New York: Columbia University Press.
Nove, Alec. [1969] 1984. *An Economic History of the U.S.S.R.* New York: Penguin Books.
Schumpeter, Joseph. 1942. *Capitalism, Socialism, Democracy*. New York: Harper and Row.
Smith, Adam. [1776] 1976. *An Inquiry into the Nature and Causes of the Wealth of Nations*. Chicago: University of Chicago Press.

I

Theory

2

Money and Capital in Economic Development

Parth J. Shah

A quick glance at my Austrian library (a rather complete collection if I may say so) fails to pick up any work with "economic development" or "economic growth" in its title. Despite being part of the modern economic science since its inception, as a coinitiator of the marginalist revolution, do Austrians have nothing to say about ancient problems of economic growth and development? Fortunately, a slight reflection proves the impression of the quick glance misleading.

Austrians did not have to create a special discipline of development economics for two reasons: first, their conception of the nature of the economic problem facing society; second, their articulation of the nature of the economic theory of economy-wide phenomena (the domain of *macro*economics).

Following Lionel Robbins ([1932] 1984), mainstream economics still[1] sees the economic problem facing an individual or a society as that of allocation of scarce resources among alternative and competing ends. In this view, the field of economics is a problem or a set of problems of rational choice among scarce resources of land, labor, and capital; and economic development, therefore, becomes a special type of problem of allocation and accumulation

15

of resources, especially of the produced means of production (capital), and so the subject is given a special and distinct treatment. The very word "problem" implies the existence of some "solution."[2] One effect of this perspective is the apparent appeal of government planning to achieve the goals of development. Under Robbins's vision of economics, economic development is seen as a problem that can best be solved by methodical and detailed rational planning.[3]

At least since Hayek's "Economics and Knowledge" ([1937] 1980), Austrians have defined the scope of economics as that of explaining creation, dissemination, and use of knowledge in society—that of coordination of individuals' articulate and inarticulate knowledge. Hayek in his the "Use of Knowledge in Society" ([1945] 1980, 77–78) provides a summary statement:

The economic problem of society is thus not merely a problem of how to allocate "given" resources—if "given" is taken to mean given to a single mind which deliberately solves the problem set by these "data." It is rather a problem of how to secure the best use of resources known to any of the members of society, for ends whose relative importance only these individuals know. Or, to put it briefly, it is a problem of the utilization of knowledge which is not given to anyone in its totality.

The problem is of coordinating individual plans reflecting decentralized decision making on the basis of dispersed knowledge. The price system provides information as well as incentives to act in ways so as to bring about meshing of individual plans. The price system performs its function well within the framework of private property and contract law (Mises 1981). Legal, political, and economic institutions and policies that allow the price system to operate and thereby foster coordination would lead to development: Development is simply a result of successful coordination.

Differences in the conceptualization of the economic problem by Robbins and Hayek lead to divergent views on the nature of economic development and the appropriate means to achieve it. Robbins's vision considers development as a *problem* to be solved by methodically planned allocation of resources. Hayek's vision contemplates development as a *process* to be fostered by the institutional framework of private property, the price system, and the rule of law.

The second reason for Austrians not to have a separate discipline of development economics was their view of the domain of macroeconomics. Macro theory must tackle both "the market for money" and "the market for time," individually and in their interactions.[4] Austrians deal not only with money (changes in its quantity, origins of such changes, and their differential impact on various prices) but also with the time element as expressed and embodied in the capital structure of the economy. Capital theory, therefore, is very much at the heart of Austrian macro theory. The mainstream, on the other hand, has (arbitrarily) barred considerations of capital and its structure from its macro theory and thereby been compelled to deal with the topic largely as part of growth or development economics.[5] Mainstream macro theory handles only liquidity and labor-leisure preferences; Austrians include time preference also.

Though Austrians did not see any need for a separate discipline of development economics, they have offered and can offer useful analyses and insights on the issues related to economic development. I will first set the stage by briefly outlining the Austrian subjective view of economic development and then tackle the main theme of this chapter: the role of money and capital in economic development from the Austrian and mainstream perspectives. After discussing the differing views on money and capital, the question of how money (or rather credit) gets converted into capital is raised. The banking system plays a pivotal role in this conversion process—the process of financial intermediation. This is especially true in underdeveloped countries where other types of capital markets are largely absent or are in rudimentary form. The people in the banking system who evaluate and decide on loan requests by firms—"bankers"—significantly determine the extent and nature of economic development. (Consumption loans are rather infrequent in underdeveloped countries.) Cameron (1967, 1972) and Goldsmith (1969) provide detailed historical accounts of the vital role played by the financial systems in general and the banking systems in particular in the growth processes of now developed countries. McKinnon (1973) and Shaw (1973) outline a theoretical framework explaining the vital role of financial intermediation in development.

The banking system and bankers, especially in underdeveloped countries, are major players in channeling money, credit, and capital. In the last part of this chapter, various views—Austrian, Schumpeterian, and mainstream—on the role of bankers are examined and a modified Austrian (Neo-Austrian?) view is defended. The mainstream views bankers as bureaucrats, the Austrians as tellers, Schumpeterians as surfers, and Neo-Austrians as equilibrists. Discussion of these alternative conceptions not only clarifies the role of bankers and financial intermediation in development but also identifies appropriate institutional arrangements within which bankers can perform that useful role. It is argued that free and competitive banking is such an institutional arrangement.

A Subjective View of Development

Standard textbooks on development economics typically define development in objective, quantifiable terms as growth in per capita real income or accumulation of means to produce such income growth (Todaro 1989, 83–86, for example). Realizing obvious pitfalls of such an aggregative view of development, they have moved on to defining development as elimination of absolute poverty, income inequalities, urban migration and congestion, unemployment, and underemployment. At times, achieving human dignity, self-esteem, and freedom are included among the goals of economic development. This proliferation of development objectives has had two important effects on the field. First, blurring of the boundary between development economics and traditional political economy since concerns about income inequalities, urban congestion, and underemployment are global, not limited just to less developed countries (LDCs). The second and more important effect has been growing confusion about appropriate policies and planning models. A given policy has a differential, and frequently opposite, impact on different development objectives. This has led to unending debates on balanced or unbalanced growth approaches, industrialization or emphasis on the agricultural and primary commodities' sector, import of technology or growth of indigenous technology, export promotion or import substitution, and so on.

In the coordination paradigm, Austrians focus on individuals and their subjectively perceived means-end framework—purposive human action (Mises 1966). In this framework, economic development means expanding the range of means available to individuals to achieve their desired ends. Economic development, Austrians argue, would be as natural in a society that facilitates coordination as its individuals' desire to better their lives. Adam Smith ([1776] 1976, 2: 49–50) has captured the spirit of this argument succinctly:

> The natural effort of every individual to better his own condition . . . is so powerful a principle that it is alone, and without assistance, not only capable of carrying on the society to wealth and prosperity, but of surmounting a hundred impertinent obstructions with which the folly of human laws too often incumbers its operations.

Development, Austrians conclude, is an unintended consequence of successful coordination. Voluntary exchange within the framework of private property and common law—catallaxy—guarantees the best opportunities for individuals to maximize their welfare (Skousen 1991). Coordination occurs through norms and practices, traditions, and institutions; through actors' "institutional matrix." The focus on coordination naturally draws attention to a wide variety of formal and informal social, legal, and economic institutions within which people act. Instead of a defined list of goals and their target levels, with specified policies to achieve them, Austrians favor a broader approach to development—a "comparative institutions approach." This approach (along with methodological individualism and subjectivism that underlie it) provides a unique theme to evaluate the role of money and capital in economic development.

Money and Development

The issues discussed in this area are standard: degree of monetization of an economy, role and optimum rate of inflation, and use of monetary policy to achieve sustained development.

Monetization: Why? And How?

Most LDCs have a sizable barter sector. In India, for example, the barter sector is estimated to have contributed 31 percent to net national product in 1955 and about 21 percent in 1975 (Laumas 1990, 377). Monetization of the barter sector substantially reduces search costs by eliminating the need for the double coincidence of wants and the precise timing of transactions, and diminishes storage costs since money can act as a temporary abode of purchasing power instead of commodities. Use of money saves real resources and stimulates the development of banking and credit mechanisms. These arguments for monetization are standard and to increase monetization inflationary policies are typically suggested.

An Austrian understanding of the role of money and money prices in a market economy argues against such inflationary policies. In addition to minimizing search and storage costs, use of money and money prices enables individuals to accurately calculate opportunity costs of their actions, and profits and losses of their enterprises. Money prices transmit information about relative scarcity and consumer preferences in one segment of the economy to the rest of the economy and thereby perform an integrating function. The prices simultaneously provide appropriate incentives to optimize the use of scarce resources and facilitate efficient allocation of resources throughout the economy. (See Hayek [1945] 1980) on the significance of the price system as a communication network.) Inflationary policies and unstable money distort the calculation, integration, and allocation functions of money prices and thereby impede monetization.

Monetization increases as an economy progresses from production for use to production for profit, as it moves away from self-sufficiency and relies more on the market for its provisions. Production for profit encourages the division of labor and specialization which reinforces the benefits of monetization. The routine attempts at self-sufficiency in LDCs generally retard the division of labor and specialization and thereby the degree of monetization.

Role of Inflation and Monetary Policy

"[I]t is the teaching of this *Treatise [on Money]*," Keynes intoned, "that the wealth of nations is enriched, not during income inflations but during profit inflations—at times, this is to say, when prices are running away from costs" (1930, 2: 154). Keynes's interpretation of the economic growth of Europe downplayed the role of thrift and endorsed inflationary policies: "It is unthinkable that the difference between the amount of wealth in France and England in 1700 and the amount in 1500 could ever have been built up by thrift alone. The intervening profit inflation which created the modern world was surely worth while if we take a long view" (1930, 2: 163). Development economics did not escape the Keynesian revolution that swept the profession (Bartlett 1992). Inflationary policies are advocated not only to keep "prices running away from costs," but also to monetize barter LDC economies, direct resources toward modern emerging industries, and most importantly to raise revenue to finance government projects directly through printing press and indirectly by slow repudiation of government debt.

The development literature is replete with debates about the optimal rate of inflation. As the costs of inflation were seen largely as a tax on nominal cash balances, the benefits of inflation seem to outweigh the costs. Like any tax, as the tax rate (inflation rate) goes up, the tax base (nominal cash balances) would shrink and hence the elaborate estimations about optimal inflation rates for various LDCs (Todaro 1989, chapter 17).

The Austrian understanding of the role of money prices in calculation, integration, and allocation (as discussed above) argues for first-order costs of inflation. Erratic inflations diminish money's medium-of-exchange function and compel people to spend more real resources for exchange activities, thereby reducing resources available for the production of goods and services. As that understanding was elaborated upon (see especially Leijonhufvud 1981 and Levin 1982), it was generally recognized that the costs of inflation were more than just "shoe-leather costs." Debates switched from optimal inflation rates to optimal monetary policy rules (under the phrase "discretion or rule?") and then to optimal monetary constitutions (Dowd 1989, chapter 3). Proposals of fixed money supply growth, nominal income or price level targeting, and free banking based on gold or a commodity basket emerged.[6] It is beyond the scope of this chapter to establish the proposition that a free banking system provides the most permanent and stable solution to problems of erratic inflations and to macro maladies induced from the side of money.[7]

Before leaving this topic, one more rationale for inflationary policies deserves our attention. This rationale is particularly relevant to the issue of development and has been supported by two otherwise rival groups: Keynesians (Tobin and Solow) and Monetarists (Patinkin and Friedman).

Money and Capital: Complements or Substitutes?

Monetary growth theorists (including Tobin, Solow, Patinkin, and Friedman) have argued that money balances and capital are substitute assets, and so by (moderately) increasing the inflation rate and thereby reducing the real rate of return on cash balances, government can induce people to hold more real capital.[8] Inflation, therefore, helps divert people's fetish for liquidity toward real capital formation.

McKinnon (1973) contends that in developing countries where capital markets are incomplete, money and capital serve as complimentary assets. In the case of incomplete or repressed capital and credit markets, a typical situation in LDCs, lumpiness or indivisibilities of investments make cash balances and real capital complementary assets. Inflation that reduces the real return on cash balances also retards real capital formation. Shaw (1973) reaches a similar conclusion through his debt-intermediation view of money.[9] Numerous empirical studies of LDCs support a McKinnon-Shaw complementarity hypothesis (Kapur 1986; Fry 1988). Inflation does not promote real capital formation.

Capital and Development

The significance of capital and its growth for economic development is beyond question. The issue that separates the Austrian and mainstream perspectives is the conceptualization of capital and the capital-using economy; or the why and how of the role of capital in development.

Carl Menger (1976) visualized the economy as made of various orders of goods, lower-order goods being consumer goods and higher-order goods being capital goods; and economic process as the conversion of higher-order goods into lower-order goods. Higher-order goods are valued for the lower-order goods that they help to produce. A capital-using economy, therefore, is a continuum of various orders of goods; such an economy has a specific structure of capital.[10] Capital goods are characterized by different degrees of complementarity and substitutability, and cannot be viewed as homogenous.

Bohm-Bawerk (1959) identified the principle of the "productivity of wisely chosen roundabout methods of production" to explain the usefulness of higher-order goods. Production of higher-order goods requires sacrifice of consumption of present goods, that is, it requires savings, and the extent of savings depends on the time preference of individuals. The rate of interest is the manifestation of this time preference; it is the price of a factor of production that may be called "waiting," as only with a lapse of time can higher-order goods can be converted into lower-order goods. A competitively determined market rate of interest guides entrepreneurs in deciding in which stage of production (or which order of goods) it will be profitable to invest. If people have lower time preferences and so are saving more and the interest rate falls, entrepreneurs would extend the length of the structure of production, that is, invest relatively more in higher-order goods.[11]

This Austrian "time-structural" conception of capital was attacked early on by J. B. Clark and later by Frank Knight. The Clark-Knight conception of capital was that of a "homogenous blob" with a flexibility of "putty clay" (perfect substitutability and no complementarity). They likened capital stock to a reservoir where water flows in (production) and out (consumption), but the reservoir itself remains a permanent quantity. Knight contended "all capital is inherently perpetual" (quoted in Skousen 1990, 68). Clark and Knight viewed production and consumption as synchronized and simultaneous, and denied that any waiting was involved in the production process. "Today we work, and today we eat; and the eating is the effect of working" (Clark quoted in Skousen 1990, 29). The Clark-Knight "stock-flow" view of capital was in direct contrast with the Austrian time-structural view.

The Clark-Knight concept of capital was later formalized in the Harrod-Domar growth model. The model treated capital as perfectly homogenous, symbolized by the letter K, putting aside the Austrian distinction of various orders of capital goods, the significance of their relative prices, and various degrees of complementarity and substitutability among capital goods. All that mattered for economic growth was the stock and productivity of capital, and not how the heterogenous capital goods were created and employed to form an orderly structure of production in a market economy in congruence with people's time preferences.

Focus on the stock of capital and explicit neglect of the structure of capital, coupled with Keynes's paradox of thrift (popularized by the famous example of a thrift campaign on a banana plantation) and the contentions that private investments are driven by "animal spirits" and engulfed in the "dark forces of time and ignorance," and that liquidity preferences and not time preferences determine interest rates, paved the way for the larger role of government in saving and investment decisions. "Perhaps the ultimate solution lies in the rate of capital development becoming more largely an affair of state, determined by collective wisdom and long views" (Keynes 1930, 2: 163).

Austrians emphasize both the stock as well as the structure of capital. It is the structure of capital that determines whether it is employed according to the preferences of individuals in the economy, that is, whether it is socially productive and whether it can be sustained over a period of time.

Financial Intermediation: The Significance of Bankers

Financial intermediation is typically achieved through capital (equity) and credit (debt) markets. Developing countries, which McKinnon aptly describes as "fragmented economies," possess incomplete and imperfect capital markets; generally "thin" markets lacking in a requisite array of financial instruments to meet the varying needs of customers in terms of maturity, liquidity, denomination, and risk sharing. Economic growth in developing countries is, therefore, substantially financed through credit markets.

One can even link the nature of financial intermediation with the level of economic development. In primitive economies, firms rely on self-financing and outside finance is available only on the basis of personal relationships. Developing economies have well-heeled formal (or informal when formal markets are repressed) credit markets and embryonic capital markets. Developed economies have access to almost complete and rather well-performing credit as well as capital markets. In fact, in developed economies financing of production is done largely on capital markets while that of consumption is on credit markets.

Within credit markets, the banking system plays the central role in financial intermediation in developing economies. Marshall, in his *Industry and Trade*, praises the nineteenth-century German banking system and the bankers for courage and foresight in financing new products and technologies. Cameron (1967, 1972) provides persuasive evidence on the crucial role played by banking systems in the early stages of industrialization of the West. He argues that whenever banks have been left free, they have generally performed a growth-inducing role and have hardly ever been a hindrance to economic growth. Recent case studies of newly developed countries also indicate the pivotal role played by banking systems (and monetary policies) in economic development. (See Lau 1986 for the analysis of South Korea and Taiwan.)

Pure Intermediation and Creative Intermediation

Banks are unique among financial intermediaries because only they perform two functions simultaneously—those of providing a payments system and financial intermediation. The monetary nature of banks' liabilities and their power to create payment media distinguish them from nonbank financial intermediaries. Focusing on the ability to create payment media or purchasing power, we can differentiate financial intermediation into two categories. One, pure intermediation done by nonbank intermediaries (merchant banks, investment banks, insurance companies, mutual funds); second, creative intermediation of banking systems.

It is the extension of credit by banks above the actual amount of savings done in an economy which seems to symbolize the dynamic process of economic growth. "The creation of purchasing power characterizes, in principle," Schumpeter argues, "the method by which development is carried out in a system with private property and division of labor" (1955, 107). He further states:

> The banker, therefore, is not so much primarily a middleman in the commodity 'purchasing power' as a *producer* of this commodity ... [H]e has himself become the capitalist par excellence. He stands between those who wish to form new combinations and the possessors of productive means. He is essentially a phenomenon of development ... He makes possible the carrying out of new combinations, authorizes people, in the name of society as it were, to form them. He is the ephor of the exchange economy. (1955, 74).

Whether banks ability to create purchasing power would be used in ways that are socially productive depends on the institutional structure of the banking system: the incentives and information which guide the decisions of the people operating the banking system. The role of bankers in the process of creative intermediation deserves more attention and analysis. The term "banker" must be understood in a functional sense and not so much in the sense of ownership; bankers are the people evaluating and deciding on the financing of projects, which could be those submitted by others (loan applications), or their own (in absence of any barrier between commercial and investment banking).

One way to begin appraising the significance of bankers in creative intermediation and thereby in economic development is to analyze various existing views on the role and function of bankers—views from (the mainstream) development economics, from the Austrian School, and from that pioneer of developmental analysis, Schumpeter. Given the shortcomings of these three views, a modified Austrian (Neo-Austrian) view is outlined.

Bankers as Bureaucrats

Much of development economics suffers from what Deepak Lal (1985) has called "dirigiste dogma." The mainstream believes that the price mechanism or the market economy must be superseded by direct government controls; that government must formulate a "development strategy" in terms of macro accounting aggregates such as investment, savings, essential consumer goods, and balance of payments; and that free trade is not only irrelevant but detrimental to development. In this development model dominated by central/indicative/informative planning, the role of financial intermediaries is simply that of carrying out the dicta of the planning boards. In most cases, banking systems are nationalized or subjected to such detailed regulations and controls that they are turned largely into plan-implementing agencies.[12]

To control the allocation of resources to sectors and industries chosen in the "development strategy," LDC governments have established sector- or industry-specific development banks, have fixed credit targets, and have put ceilings on deposit and loan rates of interest. Only imagination seems to be the limit for creating development banks: Industrial Development Bank, Agricultural Development Bank, Small Business Development Bank, Handicraft Development Bank, Rural Development Bank, and the list goes on.

Under government domination, prices in the credit markets, especially interest rates, do not reflect underlying economic scarcities and preferences. Governments routinely keep interest rates below market-clearing levels and then ration credit to favored sectors of the economy, creating a situation of financial repression and dualism. Interest rate ceilings also cause disincentives to save, lower the amounts of deposits available to banks for intermediation, and drive the growing sectors of the economy not favored by the government to informal credit markets (Chandavarkar 1987). Government-mandated low interest rates create a bias in favor of capital-intensive projects in countries with an abundance of idle labor.

Under the mainstream model of development, bankers do not play any significant independent role in financial intermediation.

There is very little room for individual bankers to exercise discretion among projects to be financed. Bankers are nothing but another bunch of bureaucrats.

Bankers as Tellers

Within the Austrian school, two rather different views of banking dominate. One, led by Murray Rothbard ([1962] 1970, 698–708), advocates 100 percent reserve banking and considers any type of fractional reserve banking as fraudulent. It contends that any old quantity of money is sufficient to lubricate transactions as long as the price level is free to adjust. The other view of free-banking theorists, led by Selgin, White, and Yeager, contends that with appropriate operational definition of the monetary unit, fractional reserve banking could provide a stable monetary environment. After fixing the unit of account, banks can be left free to adjust the supply of money, or rather media of exchange, to the demand for them.

Both groups have largely focused their analyses only on one function of the banking system, that of the provision of payment services. The question of financial intermediation and the role of bankers in that process have not received much attention from either group.[13] In terms of our distinction of pure and creative intermediation, they implicitly seem to highlight only pure intermediation and dismiss or reject the other.

Though Austrians have always emphasized the role of entrepreneurs in economic coordination, bankers are hardly ever used as models of entrepreneurship. One area where bankers do receive some attention is the Austrian business cycle theory. In the theory, when a central bank augments the pool of reserves or lowers the discount rate (strictly speaking brings the market rate below the natural rate of interest), bankers predictably respond by expanding credit and obliging the economy "to bite more than it can chew." Lowering of the interest rate makes investments in higher-order goods more profitable than those in lower-order goods. The resultant lengthening of the structure of production cannot actually be sustained since real savings have not changed ("money is masquerading as savings"). The artificially induced boom ultimately comes to an end.

In the Austrian business cycle theory, given the supply of credit (as determined by the central bank), bankers respond to firms' requests for loans like tellers respond to customers' requests for withdrawal of funds. Bankers are nothing but another bunch of tellers.

Bankers as Surfers

In the Schumpeterian view, the heart of the capitalist process is the "perennial gale of creative destruction." Entrepreneurs are competing primarily not in terms of prices but in generating new products, technologies, resources, and modes of organization. Faced with such alluring projects and engulfed in spreading optimism, bankers put aside their natural conservative and cautious attitudes and enable the entrepreneurs to materialize their dreams. "Windfall gains, rising prices, and so on produce waves of optimism" (Schumpeter 1982, 141). Bankers do exercise their skills and judgments in evaluating the project proposals, but ex hypothesi, large enough projects must get funded if the gale (of entrepreneurial discoveries) is to create waves instead of ripples.

Bankers certainly play a significant role in the Schumpeterian schema and they are accurately called ephors or overseers of capitalist economic development (1955, 74). But for Schumpeter, the theory of economic development is but a part of the theory of (capitalist) business cycles; economic growth is the result of cyclical fluctuations.[14]

[I]t is by no means farfetched or paradoxical to say that 'progress' unstabilizes the economic world, or that it is by virtue of its mechanism a cyclical process. . . . [P]ublic opinion [has] persisted in tacitly assuming that "progress" is one thing (and naturally smooth) while fluctuations are another thing, differing from it, perhaps inimical to it. It is, after all, only common sense to realize that, but for the fact that economic life is in a process of incessant *internal* change, the business cycle, as we know it, would not exist. (Schumpeter 1982, 138)

Schumpeter's business cycle theory is based on some composite of various waves of differing amplitudes and frequencies. And since his theory of economic development is an element of the overarching theory of the business cycle, in the ultimate analysis, Schumpeterian bankers are surfers on various Juglar, Kitchin, and Kondratieff waves. They really cannot avoid the temptation of surfing on the waves of discoveries or are unable to hold firm in sight of their surfing comrades.

Bankers as Equilibrists

The modified Austrian view[15] casts bankers in a genuinely entrepreneurial role in both functions of a banking system: in equilibrating the supply of and demand for media of exchange, and in evaluating creative intermediation projects. (Austrians have so far focused largely on the payments function.) It accepts the Schumpeterian vision of bankers as ephors or overseers of capitalist development, especially during the early stages of industrialization and in developing economies. At the same time, it does not accept the other part of the Schumpeterian schema, that capitalist economic development occurs only through cyclical business fluctuations.

If Schumpeter had the benefits of recent historical and theoretical research on free banking (Selgin 1988; White 1984; Greenfield and Yeager 1983), he could easily have separated his theory of economic development from that of the business cycle.[16] Instead of relying on bankers surfing on "waves of optimism" to finance growth, Schumpeter could as well have relied on the profit-motivated entrepreneurial judgments of bankers. Just as it is unprofitable to expand supply of media of exchange beyond the demand for them, it would be unprofitable to expand credit beyond prudential margins of risk. The interest rate by itself does not ration credit; individual bankers' judgments about the viability of projects are at least as important.[17] "Smooth growth" is possible in a capitalist economy with the institutional framework of free banking.

Bankers evaluate projects not only with their technical financial expertise but also with their knowledge and understanding of local, regional, and national/global markets. Active involvement

by bankers results in democratization of the investment process—
the loan applicant must convince at least a few other individuals
of the viability of the project.

Moreover, bankers perform a great balancing act—balancing
the interests of their depositors, creditors, and loan applicants. To
create and maintain their reputation and profits, they learn also
to balance general trends in the economy with their individual
judgments. Neo-Austrian bankers are equilibrists.

Policy Implications

I conclude with the following brief sketch of the nature of reforms
that are necessary in order for banking systems and bankers to
perform their appropriate roles in economic development—in order for them to act as efficient financial intermediaries creating
and converting credit into real capital.

1. *Privatize the banking system.* Nationalized or minutely regulated banking systems leave no room for the equilibrist role of
   bankers. Bureaucratic bankers are a drain on the public treasury, prone to corruption, and risk averse in funding indigenous discoveries, preferring the safe copying of foreign products and technologies. The benefits of financial liberalization
   and the removal of interest rate ceilings that go with privatization are by now well documented (Fry 1988; Kapur 1986; Lau
   1986). Privatization allows prices to reflect true economic realities in the financial markets and perform their allocative, cal-
   culative, and integrating functions. It would turn informal
   credit markets into formal ones and thereby reduce inefficiencies in the process of financial intermediation.
2. *Reforms that encourage bankers to take long-run view and reward
   independence in judgment (as opposed to following the herd).*
   Break artificial barriers between commercial and investment
   banking; allow equity and management participation by banks
   in the companies they finance (Japan and West Germany have
   very successfully used this route for their development and also
   in maintaining their lead in the world);[18] eliminate or severely

restrict government-provided deposit insurance; allow free entry and exit in the banking system.

Notes

1. Despite the fact that Robbins's work was highly influenced by Austrians, for the Austrians the allocation problem commands little attention as it is limited to the realm of "the Pure Logic of Choice" (Hayek [1937] 1980, 47ff.). The main theoretical focus has been on coordination and spontaneously generated order of the social system. In the preface to the first edition, Robbins explicitly recognizes Austrian influence: "I should like, however, once more to acknowledge my especial indebtedness to the works of Professor Ludwig von Mises . . ." ([1932] 1984, xliii).
2. For further elaboration of this link and its ramifications, see Buchanan (1979), chapter 1.
3. Even among the Austrians, various interpretations of Robbins's work exist (Buchanan 1979; Kirzner 1988; Lavoie 1985). The interpretation taken here is more in line with those of Buchanan and Kirzner.
4. Garrison writes on "Time and Money: The Universals of Macroeconomic Theorizing" (1984).
5. Recently Garrison (1991) has urged the profession to "put capital back into macro theory," and create a unified macroeconomics. He provides a history of how capital and money were once main characters in the macro drama and how both have been cast aside in the Keynesian revolution. Monetarist counterrevolution has rehabilitated money and the real business cycle theorists are attempting to bring back capital, albeit very crudely, through their "time to build" hypothesis.
6. For a discussion of these various monetary policies/constitutions and their comparative evaluations, see Dowd (1989). For elaboration of the working of a free banking system based on gold, see Selgin (1988); and for a free banking based on a commodity bundle, see Greenfield and Yeager (1983).
7. But see the references in note 6 above for a mighty effort in persuasion.
8. Kapur (1986, chapter 1) supplies documentary evidence and a formal model of the proposition. He also details the counterarguments from McKinnon and Shaw. See also Fry (1988).
9. In their discussion on the effects of inflation, Kessel and Alchian (1962) early recognized complementarity between money and capital. However, they make a distinction between short-lived and long-lived capital goods, and argue that only the short-lived capital goods are complementary to cash balances.

10. Due to space constraints, I could only provide a rather simplified version of Austrian capital theory and the debates with Clark, Knight, and others. For a detailed account, see Kirzner (1966) and Skousen (1990). The seminal work on complementarity and substitutability of capital goods, and their significance for capital theory and economic policy, is Lachmann (1978).

11. Increased investments would generally add to the size as well as the length of the structure of production. But a falling interest rate (or a falling rate of discount at which future values are discounted) makes it more profitable to invest in higher-order goods.

12. The socialist economies of China and former Soviet Union provide clear examples of banking systems functioning as plan-implementing agencies. Even in countries like India which have nationalized banking systems, a substantial part of credit is allocated according to government directives.

13. Selgin (1989), who has touched upon the issue, has staked out a middle ground between the "Old" and "New" (Tobin's) views of banking. But even here the primary question is regarding the existence of limits to credit expansion by free banks. Bankers' entrepreneurial role is limited to equilibrating supply with the demand for media of exchange.

14. In fact, the subtitle of Schumpeter's celebrated book *The Theory of Economic Development* (1955) is "An Inquiry into Profits, Capital, Credit, Interest, and the Business Cycle."

15. The first choice that came to mind to symbolize the modified Austrian view was "bankers as entrepreneurs." Cameron (1963) wrote an article with a similar title. Even though it captures the spirit of the argument, entrepreneur seems to be too broad a term. I decided to focus on the specific nature of bankers' entrepreneurship—that of balancing payments and intermediation services, and interests of depositors, creditors, and loan applicants.

16. The Scottish free-banking episode provides convincing evidence of economic growth without significant business fluctuations (White 1984). Adam Smith also noted: "That the trade and industry of Scotland . . . have increased very considerably during this period, and that the banks have contributed a good deal to this increase, cannot be doubted" ([1776] 1976, 281).

17. Yes, there is credit rationing as claimed by Stiglitz and Weiss (1981), not because of adverse selection or moral hazard but due to bankers' judgments about the viability of projects.

18. The success of German "universal" or "mixed" banks is well documented by Cameron (1967).

34   Parth J. Shah

References

Bartlett, Bruce R. 1992. "Keynesian Policy and Development Economics." In *Dissent on Keynes*, ed. Mark Skousen, 103–16. New York: Praeger.

Bohm-Bawerk, Eugen von. 1959. *Capital and Interest*. South Holland, Ill.: Libertarian Press.

Buchanan, James M. 1979. *What Should Economists Do?* Indianapolis: Liberty Press.

Cameron, Rondo. 1963. "The Banker as Entrepreneur." *Explorations in Entrepreneurial History* 1(Fall): 50–55.

———. 1967. *Banking in the Early Stages of Industrialization*. New York: Oxford University Press.

———, ed. 1972. *Banking and Economic Development: Some Lessons from History*. New York: Oxford University Press.

Chandavarkar, Anand G. 1987. *Informal Financial Sector in Developing Countries*. Kuala Lumpur: SEACEN Centre.

Dowd, Kevin. 1989. *The State and the monetary System*. New York: St. Martin's Press.

Fry, Maxwell J. 1988. *Money, Interest, and Banking in Economic Development*. Baltimore: Johns Hopkins University Press.

Garrison, Roger W. 1984. "Time and Money: The Universals of Macroeconomic Theorizing." *Journal of Macroeconomics* 6(Spring): 197–213.

———. 1991. "Austrian Capital Theory and the Future of Macroeconomics." In *Austrian Economics*, ed. Richard M. Ebeling, 303–24. Hillsdale, Mich.: Hillsdale College Press.

Goldsmith, Raymond W. 1969. *Financial Structure and Development*. New Haven: Yale University Press.

Greenfield, R. L., and Leland B. Yeager. 1983. "A *Laissez faire* Approach to Monetary Stability." *Journal of Money, Credit and Banking* 15: 302–15.

Hayek, F. A. [1937] 1980. "Economics and Knowledge." In his *Individualism and Economic Order*, 33–56. Chicago: University of Chicago Press.

———. [1945] 1980. "The Use of Knowledge in Society," in his *Individualism and Economic Order*, 77–91.

Kapur, Basant K. 1986. *Studies in Inflationary Dynamics*. Singapore: Singapore University Press.

Kessel, R. A., and A. A. Alchian. 1962. "Effects of Inflation." *Journal of Political Economy* 70: 521–37.

Keynes, J. M. 1930. *A Treatise on Money*. London: Macmillan.

Kirzner, Israel M. 1966. *An Essay on Capital.* New York: Augustus M. Kelley.
—— 1988. "The Economic Calculation Debate: Lessons for Austrians." *Review of Austrian Economics*, 2: 1–18.
Lachmann, Ludwig M. 1978. *Capital and its Structure.* Kansas City: Sheed Andrews and McMeel.
Lal, Deepak. 1985. *The Poverty of "Development Economics."* Cambridge: Harvard University Press.
Lau, Lawrence J. 1986. *Models of Development.* San Francisco: Institute for Contemporary Studies Press.
Laumas, Prem S. 1990. "Monetization, Financial Liberalization, and Economic Development." *Economic Development and Cultural Change* 38(January): 377–90.
Lavoie, Don. 1985. *Rivalry and Central Planning.* Cambridge: Cambridge University Press.
Leijonhufvud, Axel. 1981. "Costs and Consequences of Inflation." Reprinted in his *Information and Coordination*, 227–70. New York: Oxford University Press.
Levin, Peter, 1982. "Perspectives on the Costs of Inflation." *Southern Economic Journal* 48(January): 627–41.
McKinnon, R. I. 1973. *Money and Capital in Economic Development.* Washington, D.C.: Brookings Institution.
Menger, Carl. 1976. *Principles of Economics.* New York: New York University Press.
Mises, Ludwig von. 1976. *Human Action.* 3d revised ed., Chicago: Contemporary Books.
—— 1981. *Socialism.* 2d enlarged ed., Indianapolis: Liberty Press.
Robbins, Lionel. [1932] 1984. *An Essay on the Nature and Significance of Economic Science.* 3d ed., New York: New York University Press.
Rothbard, Murray N. [1962] 1970. *Man, Economy, and State.* Los Angeles: Nash Publishing.
Schumpeter, Joseph A. 1955. *The Theory of Economic Development.* Cambridge: Harvard University Press.
—— 1982. *Business Cycles.* Philadelphia: Porcupine Press.
Selgin, George A. 1988. *The Theory of Free Banking.* Totowa, N.J.: Rowman & Littlefield.
—— 1989. "Commercial Banks as Pure Intermediaries: Between "Old" and "New" Views." *Southern Economic Journal* (July): 80–92.
Shaw, E. S. 1973. *Financial Deepening in Economic Development.* New York: Oxford University Press.
Skousen, Mark. 1990. *The Structure of Production.* New York: New York University Press.

Skousen, Mark. 1991. "Austrian Capital Theory and Economic Development in the Third World." In *Austrian Economics*, ed. Richard M. Ebeling, 355–78. Hillsdale, Mich.: Hillsdale College Press.

Smith, Adam. [1776] 1976. *The Wealth of Nations*. Chicago: University of Chicago Press.

Stiglitz, Joseph E., and Andrew Weiss. 1981. "Credit Rationing in Markets with Imperfect Information." *American Economic Review* 71(June): 393–410.

Todaro, Michael. 1989. *Economic Development in the Third World*. 4th ed. New York: Longman.

White, Lawrence H. 1984. *Free Banking in Britain*. Cambridge: Cambridge University Press.

3

The Theory of Economic Development and the "European Miracle"

Ralph Raico

Introduction

Among writers on economic development, P. T. Bauer is noted both for the depth of his historical knowledge, and for his insistence on the indispensability of historical studies in understanding the phenomenon of growth (Walters 1989, 60; see also Dorn 1987). In canvassing the work of other theorists, Bauer has complained of their manifest "amputation of the time dimension":

> The historical background is essential for a worthwhile discussion of economic development, which is an integral part of the historical progress of society. But many of the most widely publicized writings on development effectively disregard both the historical background and the nature of development as a process. (Bauer 1972, 324–25)

Too many writers in the field have succumbed to professional overspecialization combined with a positivist obsession with data that happen to be amenable to mathematical techniques. The result has been models of development with little connection to reality:

> Abilities and attitudes, mores and institutions, cannot generally be quantified in an illuminating fashion. . . . Yet they are plainly much more

important and relevant to development than such influences as the terms
of trade, foreign exchange reserves, capital output ratios, or external
economies, topics which fill the pages of the consensus literature. (ibid.,
326)

Even when a writer appears to approach the subject historically, concentration on quantifiable data to the neglect of underlying institutional and social-psychological factors tends to fore-
shorten the chronological perspective and thus vitiate the result:

It is misleading to refer to the situation in eighteenth-and nineteenth-
century Europe as representing initial conditions in development. By
then the west was pervaded by the attitudes and institutions appropriate
to an exchange economy and a technical age to a far greater extent than
south Asia today. These attitudes and institutions had emerged gradually
over a period of eight centuries. (Ibid., 219–20)[1]

At the root of the approach criticized by Bauer there appears to
be a methodological holism that prefers to manipulate aggregates
while ignoring individual human actors and the institutions their
actions generate. Yet, "differences in people's capacities and attitudes and in their institutions are far-reaching and deepseated
and *largely explain differences in economic performance and in levels
and rates of material progress*" (ibid., 313–14; emphasis added).

Bauer's critique thus draws attention to the need to study both
the centuries of European history antedating the Industrial Revolution and "the interrelationships between social, political, and
legal institutions" in that period (ibid., 277).[2] Here his assessment
links up with an impressive body of scholarship that has emerged
in recent years emphasizing precisely these points.

The "European Miracle"

While it would be wrong to suggest the existence of any mono-
lithic analysis, a number of scholars concerned with the history of
European growth have tended to converge on an interpretation
highlighting certain distinctive factors. For the sake of convenience, we shall, therefore, speak of them, despite their differences, as forming a school of thought. The viewpoint may be
referred to as the "institutional"—or, to use the title of one of the
best-known works in the field—the "European miracle" approach.[3]

The "miracle" in question consists in a simple but momentous fact: It was in Europe—and the extensions of Europe, above all, America—that human beings first achieved per capita economic growth over a long period of time. In this way, European society eluded the "Malthusian trap," enabling new tens of millions to survive and the population as a whole to escape the hopeless misery that had been the lot of the great mass of the human race in earlier times. The question is: why Europe?

One possible answer, which has long enjoyed powerful support in intellectual circles in the West and among officials in underdeveloped countries, was heavily influenced by socialist and even Marxist tenets.[4] It accounted for Europe's extraordinary growth largely by the more or less spontaneous advance of science, combined with a "primitive accumulation" of capital—through imperialism, slavery and the slave trade, the expropriation of small farmers, and the exploitation of the domestic working class. The conclusion was clear. The extraordinary growth of Europe was at the expense of untold millions of the enslaved and downtrodden, and the European experience should serve decision makers in underdeveloped countries more as a cautionary tale than an exemplar.

The contributors to the newer model, however, reject this venerable legend. Concerned as they are with comparative economic history, they have sought for the origins of European development in what has tended to set Europe apart from other great civilizations, particularly those of China, India, and Islam. To one degree or another, their answer to the question, why Europe? has been: Because Europe enjoyed a relative lack of political constraint. As Jean Baechler, in a pioneering work, pointedly expressed it:

The first condition for the maximization of economic efficiency is the liberation of civil society with respect to the state. . . . *The expansion of capitalism owes its origins and raison d'être to political anarchy.* (Baechler 1975, 77, 113; emphasis in original)

The Uniqueness of Europe

John Hicks partially adumbrated this approach in the late 1960s (Hicks 1969).[5] In *A Theory of Economic History*, Hicks laid out the "chief needs" of the expanding, mercantile phase of economic development—the protection of property and the enforcement of contracts—and stated:

The Mercantile Economy, in its First Phase, was an escape from political authority—except in so far as it made its own political authority. Then, in the Middle Phase, when it came formally back under the traditional political authority, that authority was not strong enough to control it. (Ibid., 33, 100)

Hicks's account, however, proved to be much too schematic, besides limiting itself to economic analysis and deliberately ignoring political, religious, scientific, and other factors (see Bauer 1971).

Around the same time as Hicks, David Landes was sketching the essentials of the newer outlook. In seeking to answer the question why the industrial breakthrough occurred first in western Europe, he highlighted two factors "that set Europe apart . . . from the rest of the world . . . the scope and effectiveness of private enterprise, and the high value placed on the rational manipulation of the human and material environment" (Landes 1970, 14–15). "The role of private enterprise in the West," in Landes's view, "is perhaps unique: more than any other factor, it made the modern world" (ibid., 15).

But what was it that permitted private enterprise to flourish? Landes pinpointed the circumstance that would be vital to the new interpretation—Europe's radical decentralization:

Because of this crucial role as midwife and instrument of power *in a context of multiple, competing polities* (the contrast is with the all-encompassing empires of the Orient or the Ancient World), private enterprise in the West possessed a social and political vitality without precedent or counterpart. (Ibid.; emphasis in original)

Damaging incursions by government did occur, and the situation in some parts of Europe conditioned a social preference for military values; "on balance, however, the place of private enterprise was secure and improving with time; and this is apparent in the institutional arrangements that governed the getting and spending of wealth" (ibid.).

A precondition of economic expansion was the definition and defense of property rights against the political authority. This occurred early on in Europe. Landes contrasts the European method of regular taxation (supervised by assemblies representative of the tax-bearing classes) with the system of "extortion" prevalent in "the great Asian empires and the Muslim states of the Middle East . . . where fines and extortions were not only a source of quick revenue but a means of social control—a device for curbing the pretensions of *nouveaux riches* and foreigners and blunting their challenge to the established power structure" (ibid., 16–17).[6]

Landes's insights, briefly sketched in a few pages of introduction to his *Prometheus Unbound*, have been vastly elaborated upon by the new school. The upshot is an overall interpretation of Western history that may be stated as follows:

Although geographical factors played a role, the key to western development is to be found in the fact that, while Europe constituted a single civilization—Latin Christendom—it was at the same time radically decentralized.[7] In contrast to other cultures—especially China, India, and the Islamic world—Europe comprised a system of divided and, hence, competing powers and jurisdictions.

After the fall of Rome, no universal empire was able to arise on the Continent. This was of the greatest significance. Drawing on Montesquieu's dictum, Jean Baechler points out that "every political power tends to reduce everything that is external to it, and powerful objective obstacles are needed to prevent it from succeeding" (Baechler 1975, 79). In Europe, the "objective obstacles" were provided first of all by the competing political authorities. Instead of experiencing the hegemony of a universal empire, Europe developed into a mosaic of kingdoms, principalities, city-states, ecclesiastical domains, and other political entities.

Within this system, it was highly imprudent for any prince to attempt to infringe property rights in the manner customary elsewhere in the world. In constant rivalry with one another, princes found that outright expropriations, confiscatory taxation, and the blocking of trade did not go unpunished. The punishment was to be compelled to witness the relative economic progress of one's rivals, often through the movement of capital, and capitalists, to neighboring realms. The possibility of "exit," facilitated by geographical compactness and, especially, by cultural affinity, acted to transform the state into a "constrained predator" (Anderson 1991, 58)

Decentralization of power also came to mark the domestic arrangements of the various European polities. Here feudalism— which produced a nobility rooted in feudal right rather than in state-service—is thought by a number of scholars to have played an essential role (see, e.g., Baechler 1975, 78). Through the struggle for power within the realms, representative bodies came into being, and princes often found their hands tied by the charters of rights (Magna Carta, for instance) which they were forced to grant their subjects. In the end, even within the relatively small states of Europe, power was dispersed among estates, orders, chartered towns, religious communities, corps, universities, etc., each with its own guaranteed liberties. The rule of law came to be established throughout much of the Continent.

Thus, there is general agreement that crucial to laying the foundations for the European miracle were, in Jones's words, the "curtailment of predatory government tax behavior" and "the limits to arbitrariness set by a competitive political arena" (Jones 1987, xix, xxi). Over time, property rights—including rights in one's own person—came to be more sharply defined, permitting owners to capture more of the benefits of investment and improvement (North 1981). With the freer disposition of private property came the possibility of ongoing innovations, tested in the market. Here, too, the rivalrous state-system was highly favorable. The nations of Europe functioned "as a set of joint-stock corporations with implicit prospectuses listing resources and freedoms" in such a way as to insure "against the suppression of novelty and unorthodoxy in the system as a whole" (Jones 1987, 119). A new social class arose, consisting of merchants, capitalists, and manufacturers "with immunity from interference by the formidable social forces opposed to change, growth, and innovation" (Rosenberg and Birdzell 1986, 24).

Eventually, the economy achieved a degree of autonomy unknown elsewhere in the world except for brief periods. As Jones puts it:

Economic development in its European form required above all freedom from arbitrary political acts concerning private property. Goods and factors of production had to be free to be traded. Prices had to be set by unconditional exchange if they were to be undistorted signals of what goods and services really were in demand, where and in what quantities. (Jones 1987, 85)

The system protecting the ownership and deployment of private property evolved in Europe by slow degrees—over at least "the eight centuries" mentioned by Bauer. Quite logically, therefore, the economic historians concerned with "how the West grew rich" have directed a great deal of their attention to the medieval period.

The Importance of the Middle Ages

The stereotype of the Middle Ages as "the Dark Ages" fostered by Renaissance humanists and Enlightenment *philosophes* has, of course, long since been abandoned by scholars. Still, the "consensus" writers on economic development whom Bauer faults have by and large ignored the importance of the Middle Ages for European growth—something that makes as much sense as beginning the explanation of the economic and cultural successes of European Jewry with the eighteenth century. Economic historians, however, following in the footsteps of the great Belgian historian Henri Pirenne (Pirenne 1937), have had a quite different estimation of the medieval period. Carlo M. Cipolla asserts that "the origins of the Industrial Revolution go back to that profound change in ideas, social structures, and value systems that accompanied the rise of the urban communes in the eleventh and thirteenth centuries" (Cipolla 1981, 298).

Of Europe from the late tenth to the fourteenth centuries, Robert S. Lopez states:

Here, for the first time in history, an underdeveloped society succeeded in developing itself, mostly by its own efforts . . . it created the indispensable material and moral conditions for a thousand years of virtually uninterrupted growth; and, in more than one way, it is still with us. (Lopez 1971, vii)

Lopez contrasts the European evolution with that of a neighboring civilization, Islam, where political pressures smothered the potential for an economic upsurge:

The early centuries of Islamic expansion opened large vistas to merchants and tradesmen. But they failed to bring to towns the freedom and power that was indispensable for their progress. Under the tightening grip of military and landed aristocracies the revolution that in the tenth century had been just around the corner lost momentum and failed. (Ibid., 57)

In Europe, as trade and industry expanded, people discovered that "commerce thrives on freedom and runs away from constriction; normally the most prosperous cities were those that adopted the most liberal policies" (ibid., 90). The "demonstration effect" that has been a constant element in European progress—and which could exist precisely because Europe was a decentralized system of competing jurisdictions—helped spread the liberal policies that brought prosperity to the towns that first ventured to experiment with them.

Scholars like Cipolla and Lopez, attempting to understand European development in the Middle Ages, make constant reference to *ideas, value systems, moral conditions,* and similar cultural elements.[8] As Bauer has emphasized, this is a part of the distinctive European evolution that cannot be divorced from its institutional history. In regard to the Middle Ages, prime importance, in the view of many writers, attaches to Christianity. Harold J. Berman (Berman 1974)[9] has stressed that with the fall of Rome and the eventual conversion of the Germans, Slavs, Magyars, and so forth, Christian ideas and values suffused the whole blossoming culture of Europe. Christian contributions range from the mitigation of slavery and a greater equality within the family to the concepts of natural law, including the legitimacy of resistance to unjust rulers. The Church's canon law exercised a decisive influence on Western legal systems: "it was the church that first taught Western man what a modern legal system was like" (ibid., 59).

Berman, moreover, focuses attention on a critical development that began in the eleventh century: the creation by Pope Gregory VII and his successors of a powerful "corporate, hierarchical church . . . independent of emperors, kings, and feudal lords," and thus capable of foiling the power-seeking of temporal authority (ibid., 56).[10] In this way, Berman bolsters Lord Acton's analysis of the central role of the Catholic church in generating Western liberty by forestalling any concentration of power such as marked the other great cultures, and thus creating the Europe of divided and conflicting jurisdictions.[11]

In a major synthesis, *Law and Revolution*, Berman has highlighted the legal facets of the development whose economic, political, and ideological aspects other scholars have examined (Berman 1983): "Perhaps the most distinctive characteristic of the Western legal tradition is the coexistence and competition within the same community of diverse legal systems. It is this plurality of jurisdictions and legal systems that makes the supremacy of law both necessary and possible" (ibid., 10).[12]

Berman's work is in the tradition of the great English scholar, A. J. Carlyle, who, at the conclusion of his monumental study of political thought in the Middle Ages, summarized the basic principles of medieval politics: that all—including the king—are bound by law; that a lawless ruler is not a legitimate king, but a tyrant; that where there is no justice there is no commonwealth; that a contract exists between the ruler and his subjects (Carlyle and Carlyle 1950, 503–26).

Other recent scholarship has supported these conclusions. In his last, posthumous work, the distinguished historian of economic thought, Jacob Viner, noted that the references to taxation by St. Thomas Aquinas "treat it as a more or less extraordinary act of a ruler which is as likely as not to be morally illicit" (Viner 1978, 68–69). Viner pointed to the medieval papal bull, *In Coena Domini*—evidently republished each year into the late eighteenth century—which threatened to excommunicate any ruler "who levied new taxes or increased old ones, except for cases supported by law, or by an express permission from the pope" (ibid., 69). Throughout the Western world, the Middle Ages gave rise to parliaments, diets, estates-generals, Cortes, etc., which served to limit the powers of the monarch.[13] A. R. Myers notes:

Almost everywhere in Latin Christendom the principle was, at one time or another, accepted by the rulers that, apart from the normal revenues of the prince, no taxes could be imposed without the consent of parliament. . . . By using their power of the purse [the parliaments] often influenced the ruler's policies, especially restraining him from military adventures. (Myers 1975, 29–30)

In a recent synthesis of modern medievalist scholarship, Norman F. Cantor has summarized the heritage of the European Middle Ages in terms strikingly similar to those employed by the current institutional historians:

In the model of civil society, most good and important things take place below the universal level of the state: the family, the arts, learning, and science; business enterprise and technological process. These are the work of individuals and groups, and the involvement of the state is remote and disengaged. It is the rule of law that screens out the state's insatiable aggressiveness and corruption and gives freedom to civil society below the level of the state. It so happens that the medieval world was one in which men and women worked out their destinies with little or no involvement of the state most of the time. (Cantor 1991, 416)

One highly important factor in the advance of the West, possibly linked to Christianity, has not, however, been dealt with by the newer economic historians. It is the relative lack of institutionalized envy in Western culture. In a work endorsed by Bauer, the sociologist Helmut Schoeck has drawn attention to the omnipresence of envy in human societies (Schoeck [1969] 1987). Perceived as a grave threat by those at whom it is directed, it typically results in elaborate envy-avoidance behavior: the attempt to ward off the dangers of malicious envy by denying, disguising, or suppressing whatever traits provoked it. The antieconomic consequences of socially permitted—or even encouraged—envy and reactive envy-avoidance scarcely lend themselves to quantification. Nonetheless, they may clearly be highly damaging. Drawing on anthropological studies, Schoeck stresses the harm that institutionalized envy can inflict on the process of economic and technical growth (ibid., 73). Western culture, according to Schoeck, has somehow been able to inhibit envy to a remarkable degree. Why this is so is less clear. Schoeck links this fact to the Christian faith: "It must have been one of Christianity's most important, if unintentional, achievements in preparing men for, and rendering them capable of, innovative actions when it provided man for the first time with supernatural beings who, he knew, could neither envy nor ridicule him" (ibid., 79). Yet the evident variation in socially permitted envy in different Christian societies (e.g., Russia as against western Europe) suggests that the presence of Christian faith alone is not an adequate explanation.

Case Studies of Development

Obviously, all of Europe did not progress at the same rate. In particular, in the modern period the Netherlands and then England became the pacesetters of economic growth, while other countries declined. These facts can also be accounted for by the model.

The Low Countries had long benefited from the legal system inherited from the dukes of Burgundy. These rulers, who governed in collaboration with an active estates-general,[14] had promoted an open commercial and industrial system, based on protection of property rights. In the rise of the "northern Netherlands" (the United Provinces, or "Holland") we have a near-perfect example of the European miracle in operation. First, the area had been a major participant in European economic, political, social, and cultural developments for centuries. As Cipolla has observed, "The country that in the second half of the sixteenth century rebelled against Spanish imperialism and then rose to the role of Europe's economically most dynamic nation, was anything but an underdeveloped country from the outset" (Cipolla 1981, 263). Owing its independence to the decentralized state-system of Europe, it emerged itself as a decentralized polity, without a king and court—a "headless commonwealth" that combined secure property rights, the rule of law, religious toleration, and intellectual freedom with a degree of prosperity that amounted to an early modern *Wirtschaftswunder*. It is not surprising that Holland exerted a powerful demonstration effect. As K. W. Swart states:

both foreigners and Dutchmen were apt to believe that the Dutch Republic was unique in permitting an unprecedented degree of freedom in the fields of religion, trade, and politics. . . . In the eyes of contemporaries it was this combination of freedom and economic predominance that constituted the true miracle of the Dutch Republic. (Swart 1969, 20)

The success of the Dutch experiment was noted with great interest, especially in England, whose soil was already well prepared to accept the idea that prosperity is a reward of freedom. The deep roots of economic individualism, and hence of development, in English medieval history have been emphasized by Alan Macfarlane (Macfarlane 1978 and 1987).[15] In the early modern period, the common law, which had evolved over many centuries, acted as a guarantor of the sanctity of property and free entry to industry and trade against the policies of the early Stuart kings. In the face of authoritarian usurpations, Sir Edward Coke and his fellow jurists acted, in the words of North and Thomas, "to place the creation of property rights beyond the royal whim; to embed existing property rights in a body of impersonal law guarded by the courts" (North and Thomas 1973, 148). Crucial in the case of both the Netherlands and England was the preservation, against attempted royal encroachments, of traditional representative assemblies determined to deny the ruler the right to tax at will. Here the antiauthoritarian side exploited—and further developed—the inherited discourse whose key concepts included "liberties," "rights," "the law of nature," and "constitution."

The decline of Spain, on the other hand, is also taken into account in the model. Confiscation of the property of Jews and Moors by the Spanish crown was, according to North and Thomas:

only symptomatic of the insecurity of all property rights . . . seizure, confiscation, or the unilateral alteration of contracts were recurrent phenomena which ultimately affected every group engaged in commerce or industry as well as agriculture. . . . As no property was secure, economic retardation was the inevitable consequence. (Ibid., 131)

The economic decay of Spain, in turn, provided a negative demonstration effect that played a potent role in the policy choices of other countries.

The theme of the autonomy of the market and the inhibition of the predator-state as major factors in economic growth is pursued in the examination of non-European cultures. Baechler, for instance, states that "each time China was politically divided, capitalism flourished," and maintains that Japanese history manifests conditions approximating those of Europe (Baechler 1975, 82–86). Anderson, after surveying economic growth in the history of Sung China and Tokugawa Japan, as well as the Netherlands and England, concludes that the common element is that "they occurred when governmental constraints on economic activity were relaxed" (Anderson 1991, 73–74).[16]

While, needless to say, much more research requires to be done on economic development in the history non-European civilizations, the evidence so far suggests strong support for the basic thrust of the institutional approach.

Contrast of Europe with Russia

The meaning of the European miracle can be better seen if European developments are contrasted with those in Russia. Colin White lists, as the determining factors of Russian backwardness "a poor resource and hostile risk environment . . . an unpropitious political tradition and institutional inheritance, ethnic diversity, and the weakness of such key groups limiting state power as the church and landed oligarchy." (White 1987, 136) After the destruction of Kievan Rus by the Tatars and the rise of Muscovy, Russia was characterized for centuries by the virtual absence of the rule of law, including security for persons and property.

The lawlessness—as well as the poverty—of Muscovite Russia was notorious. When the emissary of Elizabeth I inquired of Ivan the Great the status of his subjects, he was told: "All are slaves" (Besancon, in Baechler, Hall, and Mann 1988, 161). Ivan IV, the Terrible, annihilated the flourishing commercial republics of Novgorod and Pskov, and loosed his *Oprichnina* (Ivan's praetorian guard) on the kingdom for a frenzy of butchery that came to stand for what was permissible in the Muscovite state. Alain Besançon remarks dryly, "Of the three legends (Romanian, German, and Russian) that depict, in the guise of Dracula, the reign of Vlad the Impaler, the Russian alone sings the praises of the prince" (ibid.).

The nobility in Russia was a state-service nobility, lacking any independent base. As White observes: "Russia was never truly feudal in the west European sense of the term" (White 1987, 10). In contrast to Europe and America, the towns, as well, were "sim-

ply another arm of the state" (ibid., 137–38). The differences between Russia and the West can be seen in their respective ideas of
"absolutism." Ivan IV's concept is well known. It may be compared with that of a political writer in the West who is famous as
a defender of royal absolutism, Jean Bodin. Alexander Yanov has
pointed out that, for all his faith in absolutism:

> Bodin regarded the property of the citizens as their inalienable posses-
> sion, in the disposition of which they were no less sovereign than was the
> monarch in ruling his people. To tax citizens of a part of their inalienable
> property without their voluntary consent was, from Bodin's point of view,
> ordinary robbery. (Yanov 1981, 44–45)[17]

In this connection, Yanov reports a telling anecdote. A French
diplomat in a conversation with an English colleague affirmed his
belief in the principle enunciated by Louis XIV, that the king was
ultimate owner of all the property within his kingdom (a principle
which even the Sun-King never dared to act upon). The En-
glishmen retorted: "Did you study public law in Turkey?" (ibid.,
44 n. 17)

The fact that Russia received Christianity from Byzantium
rather than Rome shaped the entire course of Russia's history
(Pipes 1974, 221–43). In the words of Richard Pipes, the Orthodox
church in Russia became, like every other institution, "the servant
of the state." Pipes concludes, regarding the "relations between
state and society in pre-1900 Russia":

> None of the economic or social groups of the old regime was either able
> or willing to stand up to the crown and challenge its monopoly of political
> power. They were not able to do so because, by enforcing the patrimonial
> principle, i.e., by effectively asserting its claim to all the territory of the
> realm as property and all its inhabitants as servants, the crown prevented
> the formation of pockets of independent wealth or power. (Ibid., 249)

What ideas of liberalism came to Russia came perforce from
the West. It was from listening to the lectures on natural law at
the University of Leipzig that Alexander Radishchev first learned
that limits may be put to the power of the tsar (Clardy 1964,
37–38). The beginnings of the shift to a more market-oriented
economic policy before the First World War are traced by Besançon to the fact that the Russian ministers read the liberal economists (Besançon, in Baechler, Hall, and Mann 1988, 166).

The Downfall of Marxist Historiography

The Marxist philosophy of history is filled with manifold, often strategic, contradictions and ambiguities. Yet, if "historical materialism" has any significant content at all it is as a *technological* interpretation of history (Mises 1957, 106–12; Bober 1962, 3–28). Although Nathan Rosenberg has denied that Marx held that "technological factors are, so to speak, the independent variable in generating social change, which constitutes the dependent variable" (Rosenberg 1982, 36; see also 34–51),[18] the weight of evidence is heavily against him (Cohen 1978, 134–50).

According to Marx, Engels, and the theoreticians of the "Golden Age" of the Second International, history proceeds basically via changes in the "material productive forces" (the technological base), which render obsolete the existing "mode of production" (the property system). Because of technological changes, the mode of production is compelled to change; with it, everything else— the whole legal, political, and ideological "superstructure" of society—is transformed, as well (Marx [1859] 1969b, 8–9). As Marx put it aphoristically: "The wind mill yields a society with feudal lords, the steam mill a society with industrial capitalists" (Marx [1847] 1969a, 130).

Marxism has, of course, been subjected for generations to withering rebuttal on many different fronts, not least in regard to its philosophy of history. The newer understanding of European history is particularly destructive of its fundamental claims, however, in that it directs attention to the peculiar *shallowness* of "historical materialism." This newer understanding insists that the colossal growth of technology in the Western world in the past millennium must itself be explained, and the explanation it provides is in terms of *the institutional and moral matrix* that emerged in Europe over many centuries.[19] New and more productive machines did not spring forth mysteriously and spontaneously, nor was the spectacular expansion of technical and scientific knowledge somehow inevitable. As Anderson has summed up the evidence, "the scientific and technical stasis that followed the remarkable achievements of the Song dynasty, or of the flowering of early Islam, indicates that scientific inquiry and technology do

not necessarily possess in themselves the dynamism suggested by
the European experience" (Anderson 1991, 46). On the contrary,
technology and science emerged out of an interrelated set of political, legal, philosophical, religious, and moral elements in what
orthodox Marxism has traditionally disparaged as the "superstructure" of society.

Conclusion

According to the Indian development economist R. M. Sundrum,
if we are to understand how development can be promoted in the
poorer countries today, we must understand the historical process
which transformed developed countries in the past, and why this
process failed to take place elsewhere (cited in Arndt 1987, 177).
This is the position that P. T. Bauer, too, has insisted upon. Re-
jecting the "timeless approach" to economic development, Bauer
has accentuated the many centuries required for economic growth
in the Western world, and the interplay of various cultural factors
that were its precondition. Most important, in Bauer's view, is
that in the Western world institutions and values evolved that
favored private property and the market, set limits to state arbitrariness and predation, and encouraged innovation and the
sense that human beings are capable of improving their lot
through their actions on the market.

Recently, W. W. Rostow, in a summary of Bauer's career, chided
him for failing "to take adequately into account the extremely
large and inescapable role of the state in early phases of development" (Rostow 1990, 386).[20] Such a criticism is not surprising,
coming from one of the leaders of what Bauer has for years assailed
as the "spurious consensus." Yet it finds little support in the work
of the historians dealt with here. (For some reason, Rostow ignores
this whole body of scholarship in his very lengthy history of theories of economic growth; ibid., passim). While some of these authors would stipulate a significant role for the state in certain areas—particularly in defining and enforcing property rights—this
is consistent with Bauer's viewpoint. Moreover, the overall thrust
of their work—which stresses the importance of limits on state action in the development of the West—tends to corroborate Bauer's

position rather than Rostow's. Peter Burke, for instance, writing on one of the earliest examples of European development—the merchant-states of northern Italy and the Netherlands—describes them as "pro-enterprise cultures in which governments did relatively little to frustrate the designs of merchants or hinder economic growth, a negative characteristic which all the same gave those countries an important advantage over their competitors" (Burke in Baechler, Hall, and Mann 1988, 230). William H. McNeill notes that "within Europe itself, those states that gave the most scope to private capital and entrepreneurship prospered the most, whereas better governed societies in which welfare on the one hand or warfare on the other commanded a larger proportion of available resources tended to lag behind." As the growth leaders McNeill cites "such conspicuously undergoverned lands as Holland and England" (McNeill 1980, 65). And E. L. Jones takes as a guiding principle in the explanation of growth a famous passage from Adam Smith: "Little else is requisite to carry a state to the highest degree of opulence from the lowest barbarism, but peace, easy taxes, and a tolerable administration of justice; all the rest being brought about by the natural course of things" (Jones 1987, 234–35, cited in Stewart [1793] 1966, 68).

The new paradigm generated by the work of these and other scholars has already helped produce further major works of research and synthesis.[21] It goes without saying that a great deal more study is required. Yet it is likely that further research will provide additional substantiation of the viewpoint steadfastly represented by Professor Bauer. As Anderson observes: "The emphasis on release from constraints points to a fruitful direction of research into why some societies experienced economic development and others didn't" (Anderson 1991, 73–74) In any case, the subject will continue to be of very great theoretical interest to scholars—and to many millions in the underdeveloped world, a matter of life and death.

Notes

1. Cf. Roberts (1985, 75), who writes of "the general liberation of the economy," which "was well on the way to autonomy everywhere in

western Europe by 1500, if autonomy means regulation by prices providing undistorted signals of demand and a substantial degree of security for property against arbitrary confiscation by king, lord, or robber."

2. Cf. Rosenberg (1976, 286), who raises the question why Western European civilization was able to evolve a uniquely powerful combination of cultural values, incentive systems, and organizational capabilities, and remarks: "Interesting answers to this question are unlikely to come from any single social science discipline."

3. Major works in the field include North and Thomas (1973); Baechler (1975); North (1981); Rosenberg and Birdzell (1986); Jones (1987); Baechler, Hall, and Mann (1988), especially the essays by Michael Mann, John A. Hall, Alain Besançon, Karl Ferdinand Werner, and Peter Burke; and Jones (1988). Summaries of some of the scholar ship are provided by Anderson (1991); and Weede (1988) and (1990, 40–59). See also Osterfeld (1992, 43–46). The essay by McNeill (1980) makes creative use of the fundamental concepts of the approach.

4. F. A. Hayek in the 1950s referred to "a socialist interpretation of history which has governed political thinking for the last two or three generations and which consists mainly of a particular view of economic history." See Hayek (1954, 7).

5. The idea of a strong connection between the relative freedom of European society and its economic success can, of course, be traced back to much earlier authors, including those in the Whig historical tradition. Here it is being considered in the context of recent, mainly economic, historiography.

6. A secondary theme (Landes 1970, 21–22) is the character of the European *Weltanschauung*. Landes points to the emphasis on rationality in European culture, relative to others, fostered by elements in Christianity that ultimately may be traced to Judaism's disparagement of magic and superstition.

7. Cf. Baechler (1975, 74): Europe was "a society based upon the same moral and material civilization that never ended up in political unity, in short, in an Empire."

8. Cf. Douglass C. North, "Ideology and the Free Rider Problem," in North (1981, 45–58).

9. I am grateful to Leonard P. Liggio for calling my attention to this essay.

10. Cf. Roberts (1985, 67–9), on the Hildebrandine reform, and his comment, 68–69: "The preservation of an idea of liberty and its transmission to the future thus owes an incalculable amount to the quarrels of church and state."

11. See Lord Acton's great essay, "The History of Freedom in Christianity" (Acton 1956): "To that conflict of four hundred years [between the Church and the temporal rulers] we owe the rise of civil liberty

... although liberty was not the end for which they strove, it was the means by which the temporal and the spiritual power called the nations to their aid. The towns of Italy and Germany won their franchises, France got her States-General, and England her Parliament out of the alternate phases of the contest; and as long as it lasted it prevented the rise of divine right" (86–87).

12. Cf. Chirot (1986, 23): "The main reason for the legal rationalization of the West, then, was the long, indecisive, multisided political struggle between king, nobles, the church, and the towns."

13. See A. R. Myers (1975, 24), who states of these parliamentary bodies: "they flourished at one time or another in every realm of Latin Christendom. They first emerge clearly towards the end of the twelfth century in the Spanish kingdom of Leon, in the thirteenth century in Castile, Aragon (and also Catalonia and Valencia), Portugal, Sicily, the Empire and some of the constituent states such as Brandenburg and Austria, and in England and Ireland. In the fourteenth century ... in France ... the Netherlands, Scotland, more of the German and Italian states, and Hungary; in the fifteenth century ... in Denmark, Sweden, and Poland."

14. Cf. Chirot (1986, 18): "a Burgundian states-general met 160 times from 1464 to 1567, exercising great fiscal powers and defending the rights of towns and merchants."

15. Cf. Baechler (1975, 79): "If the general political structure of the West was favorable to economic expansion, it would be the most marked in that country where political power was most limited and tolerated the greatest autonomy of civil society." That country, according to Baechler, was England.

16. See also the chapters on Sung China and Japan in Jones 1988.

17. Compare Carlyle and Carlyle (1950, 512): "And most remarkable is it that Budé, who set out the doctrine of the absolute monarchy in France in the most extravagant terms, should have at the same time felt compelled to draw attention to the fact that the French Kings submitted to the judgment of the Parliament of Paris; and that Bodin should have contended that the judges should be permanent and irremovable, except by process of law, because the kingdom should be governed by laws and not by the mere will of the prince."

18. Rosenberg states that the technological interpretation of the Marxist philosophy of history relies upon a few "aphoristic assertions, often tossed out in the heat of debate" (1982, 36). Nowhere in his essay, however, does he allude to the *locus classicus* of the subject, Marx's Preface to *A Contribution to a Critique of Political Economy* (Marx [1859] 1969b).

19. Anderson (1991, 41) rejects technical change as an independent variable explaining economic growth: "Technology is more appropriately seen as dependent on the institutional structure and the availability

of capital, including 'human capital' expressed as an educated, skilled, and healthy workforce. The availability of capital is in turn dependent on a favorable set of institutions."

20. Rostow's dismissive tone in his treatment of Bauer may well have been affected by Bauer's devastating review of Rostow's *magnum opus, The Stages of Economic Growth.* See Bauer (1972: 477–89).

21. See, for instance, Roberts (1985); Chirot (1986); and Kennedy (1987, 19–20), where the author of this celebrated book writes of the "decentralized, largely unsupervised growth of commerce and merchants and ports and markets [in Europe] ... there was no way in which such economic developments could be fully suppressed ... there existed no uniform authority in Europe which could effectively halt this or that commercial development; no central government whose change in priorities could cause the rise or fall of a particular industry; no systematic and universal plundering of businessmen and entrepreneurs by tax gatherers, which so retarded the economy of Moghul India."

References

Acton, John Emerich Edward Dalberg. 1956. "The History of Freedom in Christianity." In *Essays on Freedom and Power*, ed. Gertrude Himmelfarb, 82–112. New York: Meridian.

Anderson, J. L. 1991. *Explaining Long-Term Economic Change.* London: Macmillan.

Arndt, H. W. 1987. *Economic Development: The History of an Idea.* Chicago: University of Chicago Press.

Baechler, Jean. 1975. *The Origins of Capitalism.* Trans. Barry Cooper. Oxford: Basil Blackwell.

Baechler, Jean, John A. Hall, and Michael Mann, eds. 1988. *Europe and the Rise of Capitalism.* Oxford: Basil Blackwell.

Bauer, P. T. 1971. "Economic History as Theory." *Economica*, new series 38, no. 150 (May): 163–79.

——— 1972. *Dissent on Development. Studies and Debates on Development Economics.* Cambridge: Harvard University Press.

Berman, Harold J. 1974. "The Influence of Christianity on the Development of Western Law." In idem, *The Interaction of Law and Religion*, 49–76. Nashville/New York: Abingdon Press.

——— 1983. *Law and Revolution: The Formation of the Western Legal Tradition.* Cambridge: Harvard University Press.

Besançon, Alain. "The Russian Case." In Baechler, Hall, and Mann 1988, 159–68.

Bober, M. M. 1962. *Karl Marx's Interpretation of History.* Cambridge: Harvard University Press.

Burke, Peter. "Republics of Merchants in Early Modern Europe," 220–33. In Baechler, Hall, and Mann 1988.

Cantor, Norman F. 1991. *Inventing the Middle Ages: The Lives, Works, and Ideas of the Great Medievalists of the Twentieth Century.* New York: William Morrow.

Carlyle, R. W., and A. J. Carlyle. 1950. *A History of Medieval Political Theory in the West.* Vol. 6, *Political Theory from 1300 to 1600.* Edinburgh: Blackwood.

Chirot, Daniel. 1986. *Social Change in the Modern Era.* San Diego: Harcourt, Brace, Jovanovich.

Cipolla, Carlo M. 1981. *Before the Industrial Revolution: European Society and Economy, 1000–1700,* 2d ed. London: Methuen.

Clardy, Jesse V. 1964. *The Philosophical Ideas of Alexander Radishchev.* New York: Astra.

Cohen, G. A. 1978. *Karl Marx's Theory of History: A Defence.* Princeton: Princeton University Press.

Dorn, James A. 1987. "Introduction: Development Economics after Forty Years." *Cato Journal* 7, no. 1 (Spring/Summer): 1–19.

Hayek, F. A. 1954. "History and Politics." In idem, ed., *Capitalism and the Historians.* Chicago: University of Chicago Press.

Hicks, John. 1969. *A Theory of Economic History.* Oxford: Oxford University Press.

Jones, E. L. 1987. *The European Miracle: Environments, Economies, and Geopolitics in the History of Europe and Asia.* 2d ed. Cambridge: Cambridge University Press.

———. 1988. *Growth Recurring. Economic Change in World History.* Oxford: Oxford University Press.

Kennedy, Paul. 1987. *The Rise and Fall of the Great Powers: Economic Change and Military Conflict, 1500–2000.* New York: Random House.

Landes, David. 1970. *Unbound Prometheus: Technological Change and Industrial Development in Western Europe from 1750 to the Present.* Cambridge: Cambridge University Press.

Lopez, Robert S. 1971. *The Commercial Revolution of the Middle Ages 950–1350.* Englewood Cliffs, N.J.: Prentice-Hall.

Macfarlane, Alan. 1978. *The Origins of English Individualism: The Family, Property, and Social Transition.* Oxford: Basil Blackwell.

——— 1987. *The Culture of Capitalism.* Oxford: Basil Blackwell.

McNeill, William H. 1980. *The Human Condition: An Ecological and Historical View.* Princeton: Princeton University Press.

Marx, Karl. [1847] 1969a. *Das Elend der Philosophie.* In Karl Marx and Friedrich Engels, *Werke,* 4. Berlin: Dietz.

——— [1859] 1969b. "Vorwort," *Zur Kritik der Politischen Okonomie.* In Karl Marx and Friedrich Engels, *Werke,* 13. Berlin: Dietz.

Mises, Ludwig von. 1957. *Theory and History.* New Haven, Conn.: Yale University Press.

Myers, A. R. 1975. *Parliaments and Estates in Europe to 1789*. New York: Harcourt, Brace, Jovanovich.

North, Douglass C. 1981. *Structure and Change in Economic History*. New York: Norton.

North, Douglass C., and Robert Paul Thomas. 1973. *The Rise of the Western World: A New Economic History*. Cambridge: Cambridge University Press.

Osterfeld, David. 1992. *Prosperity versus Planning: How Government Stifles Economic Growth*. Oxford: Oxford University Press.

Pipes, Richard. 1974. *Russia under the Old Regime*. New York: Scribner's.

Pirenne, Henri. 1937. *Economic and Social History of Medieval Europe*. Trans. I. E. Clegg. New York: Harcourt, Brace.

Roberts, J. M. 1985. *The Triumph of the West: The Origins, Rise, and Legacy of Western Civilization*. Boston: Little, Brown.

Rosenberg, Nathan. 1976. *Perspectives on Development*. Cambridge: Cambridge University Press.

———. 1982. *Inside the Black Box: Technology and Economics*. Cambridge: Cambridge University Press.

Rosenberg, Nathan, and L. E. Birdzell, Jr. 1986. *How the West Grew Rich: The Economic Transformation of the Industrial World*. New York: Basic Books.

Rostow, W. W. 1990. *Theorists of Economic Growth from David Hume to the Present: With a Perspective on the Next Century*. New York: Oxford University Press.

Schoeck, Helmut. [1969] 1987. *Envy: A Theory of Social Behaviour*. Reprint. Indianapolis: Liberty Press.

Stewart, Dugald. [1793] 1966. *Biographical Memoir of Adam Smith*. Reprint. New York: Augustus M. Kelley.

Swart, K. W. 1969. *The Miracle of the Dutch Republic as Seen in the Seventeenth Century*. London: H. K. Lewis.

Viner, Jacob. 1978. *Religious Thought and Economic Society*. Ed. Jacques Melitz and Donald Winch. Durham, N.C.: Duke University Press.

Walters, A. A. 1989. "Bauer, Peter Tamas." In *The New Palgrave: Economic Development*, ed. John Eatwell, Murray Milgate, and Peter Newman. New York: W. W. Norton.

Weede, Erich. 1988. "Der Sonderweg des Westens." *Zeitschrift für Soziologie* 17, no. 3 (June): 172–86.

———. 1990. *Wirtschaft, Staat, und Gesellschaft: Zur Soziologie der kapitalistischen Marktwirtschaft und der Demokratie*. Tübingen: J. C. B. Mohr (Paul Siebeck).

White, Colin. 1987. *Russia and America: The Roots of Economic Divergence*. London: Croom Helm.

Yanov, Alexander. 1981. *The Origins of Autocracy: Ivan the Terrible in Russian History*. Trans. Stephen Dunn. Berkeley: University of California Press.

II

Case Studies of Planning

4

The Political Economy of Development in Communist China: China and the Market

Jan S. Prybyla

1. Argument and Definitions

Outline of Argument

I will argue that

- in order to modernize and prosper, the economic system China adopted from the Soviets in the early 1950s and subsequently modified through spasmodic, often spectacular, but structurally minor policy adjustments, has to be discarded and replaced by the market system. The transformation must be truly intersystemic, that is, total;
- complete transition to the market system, although beset by enormous difficulties and always subject to political hazards, is not only conceivable but likely to happen in the perhaps not too remote future;
- should such transition, spreading as it does from the south, be prevented from materializing in the whole of China, those parts of the country where the process of marketization is presently the most dynamic and advanced—the southern coastal provinces—may try to find alternative ways of bringing about transi-

tion by, for example, establishing some form of economic association with Chinese market areas outside China, such as Hong Kong and Taiwan. Were this to occur (and the attitude of the People's Liberation Army will certainly be critical in this matter), it would have to happen before the takeover of Hong Kong by China in 1997. That is so because within an economically unreformed or half-reformed and politically left-reactionary China, Hong Kong will wither away. Such an event would almost certainly release latent centrifugal political and economic forces in China, and lead to changes in the political makeup of the country as presently constituted;

- transition to a market system in the whole or parts of China requires at some point the removal from monopoly power of the Communist party; the irreversible decay of the plan, combined with emerging but as of now unintegrated or partially linked markets, will have a persuasive but not determining influence on the dissolution of the Chinese communist regime;
- transition to the market system has to fulfill several conditions, which although socially costly in the short run, can be met in China more easily than in some other countries, notably in the formerly socialist republics that once made up the Soviet Union.

Some Definitions

The following are the meanings I attach to terms critical to the understanding of the above argument.

Economic System. An economic system is a mechanism made up of integrated, compatible, internally consistent, interrelated, and interacting institutions (agreed-on and legally protected ways of doing things) and ideas, both positive (analytical theories) and normative (economic ethics). It is a living organism; an evolving, complex, extended social order.

To qualify as an identifiable system, this organism must contain a *critical minimum mass* of such integrated, compatible, and so forth institutions and ideas that define it and clearly indicate what is to be done in society, how that goal is to be accomplished, and for whom. The "things" that the institutions of the system are to do is to continuously apportion the relatively scarce resources of land, labor, capital, and entrepreneurship to the attainment of competing, alternative, changing private and public ends, and to do this with reasonable efficiency, that is, with the least possible resource waste at a point in time and over time.

All this is fairly obvious. But there is more, and as Adam Smith says, it, too, ought to be "so perfectly self-evident, that it would be absurd to attempt to prove it." Yet it has often been ignored, consistently so in socialist practice. This fact is simply that an economic system exists to serve the consumer. "Consumption," says Smith, "is the sole end and purpose of all production; and the interest of the producer ought to be attended to, only so far as it may be necessary for promoting that of the consumer. . . . But in the mercantile [as in the socialist] system, the interest of the consumer is almost constantly sacrificed to that of the producer; and it seems to consider production, and not consumption, as the ultimate end and object of all industry and commerce."[1] In sum, economizing, the "economic" in economic systems, should result in the production of increasing quantities and qualities of goods and services that consumers actually want at prices they are able and willing to pay, this to be accomplished with a minimum expenditure of resources.

A system of resource allocation that fails to fulfill this condition is, strictly speaking, noneconomic. If it fails on a grandiose scale, that is, if at great resource cost it produces increasing quantities of qualitatively inferior goods that consumers do not want or cannot use (value subtraction, production for the warehouse), the system is antieconomic. The Soviet-type system of central administrative command planning, like mercantilism of which it is the highest left-autocratic expression, is normally noneconomic: "it produces more and more of the means of production, that is, machines, equipment, electricity, fuel, materials, and metals in order to again use all this in the next cycle for still more production of nonconsumable goods, that is, things that people can't eat."[2] In times of systemic paroxysms, the essentially noneconomic nature of this system becomes antieconomic. This occurred in China in 1958–60 and again from the mid-1960s through the late 1970s under the regime of the so-called "Third Line" (*san xian*) when, in defiance of rational economic calculation and in deference to Mao's idiosyncratic military doctrine, 117 billion yuan out of a total of 274 billion, or 43 percent of China's fixed capital investments, were put into military-related factories, research institutes, and supporting infrastructures, "dispersed to the mountains and caves" in the most inaccessible and retarded regions, where much of it remains to this day kept alive by subsidies out of the public purse. In Tibet (1965–68), the hinterland crash industrialization program focusing on defense, invested 72.4 million yuan and produced losses of 23 million yuan in three years "on account of inferior products that had to be written off." Over thirty years, 816 small hydroelectric power stations were built in Tibet. By the mid-1980s, two-fifths of them had either been scrapped or were malfunctioning.[3]

Notice that noneconomic or antieconomic systems like bullionism or socialism can be judged successful when measured against internal norms of performance that its handlers set for it (e.g., accumulation of specie, locating defense industries where no one, not even one's own military, can find them, development of the latest techniques of police control, etc.). All we are saying is that such systems institutionally suppress individual preferences and replace them with those of the political power elite, often of one supreme paranoiac; hence that they do not supply the goods that consumers really want ("things that people can eat"), and in the worst cases of antieconomism provide almost no useful goods at all.

Socialism. By socialism is meant the system of central administrative command planning that has actually been applied in this century by ruling Communist parties all over the world: "real, existing socialism." Excluded from the definition are academic constructs of socialism (*Kathedersozialismus*) distilled from Walrasian pure theory, as well as visions of abundant, equal, just, selfless, and communal phalansteries (utopian socialism).

Adjustment and Reform. From its inauspicious War Communism beginnings in Lenin's Russia, the socialist system was given to renovations, repairs, and organ transplants that did not, however, in any substantive way affect its philosophical and institutional foundations. I designate such intrasystemic changes as revisionistic *adjustments,* or adjustments for short. Examples of market system adjustments include the New Deal and, at the theoretical level, Keynesianism. All changes made in the socialist command economies before 1990 (in China before 1978)—including the so-called Kosygin "reforms" of the 1960s, Gorbachev's *perestroika,* and Mao's Great Leap Forward—qualify as intrasystemic adjustments.

By *reform* I mean fundamental changes in the institutions and ideas of the system—a structural intersystemic transformation.

Market System. As a societal phenomenon, the market is a system of communications through step-by-step, voluntary, autonomous, horizontal, competitive, bilateral exchanges of commodities (goods, services, and factors) based on the utilitarian principle, a constant search through comparison and evaluation, which discovers ratios and real interdependencies (scarcity relations) among commodities by reference to coded information that takes the form of money prices. It is an unending, unobstructed movement: "letting people, companies, money, goods, services, and ideas find their right rates of return through free movement."[4] It is a means-connected rather than an ends-oriented order of voluntary mutual exchanges driven by prices. Money both compels and facilitates the process of search and discovery: "the more active the money, the more unequivocal the signal function of prices."[5] Private property—legal rights to the use, transfer, and income from things, vested in individuals, and free associations of individuals created in response to the requirements of exchange—is a necessary condition of communication through money exchange.[6] As Adam Smith puts it: "Give me that which I want, and you shall have this which you want." I can give you this because it is mine, and you can give me that because it is yours, and we shall exchange our property rights according to the regard we each have for our own interest synthesized in money prices.[7] This communication through monetary exchange of private properties presupposes a condition of legality; not just the presence of laws relating to property, tort, contract, and bankruptcy, but of the rule of law, that is, of justice. Within the rule of law, individual choice, responsibility, and personal accountability are given broad freedom of expression.[8] People are left alone as a matter of general principle, not in every detail. *Laissez-faire* does not connote the absence of government. It only requires that the governmental urge to regulate and control be kept in check.

To ensure that laws are not made by criminals and that legal order obtains, the political environment in which the market system operates ought to be one of freedom institutionalized in a secret ballot, unrigged electoral contest of open alternatives on the basis of universal suffrage, and in representative (majority) legislative and executive organs of government as well as an independent judiciary (constitutional democracy). That is the most congenial political environment for the market system, even though the system can accommodate itself to a wide spectrum of authoritarian regimes (but not, by definition, to totalitarianism) and to some quite advanced cultural pathologies.

I shall now argue that market reform in China is necessary (section 2), and feasible (section 3), particularly in such coastal provinces as Guangdong and Fujian.

2. Necessity of Market Reform

Socialist Problems

The problems experienced by China's economy during the Mao era included the following: (1) sluggish progress of real per capita consumption (1.3 percent per year during 1955–77); (2) decline in per capita consumption of a number of key foods during this period (e.g., a 33 percent fall in vegetable oil and 20 percent for poultry and aquatic products); (3) a per capita annual peasant income in 1977 of 134 yuan, 89 yuan of it from collective work in the socialist sector, when the subsistence level in the countryside at that time was officially put at 120 yuan, with one-third of the production teams registering 60 yuan derived from socialist work; (4) a decline of total factor productivity during 1957–78 estimated at 1.5 percent a year and 1.1 percent a year during 1957–82; (5) an industrial labor productivity increase of about 2 percent a year (1957–78); (6) a 33 percent decline in industrial capital productivity during those years; (7) a 53 percent fall of national income (net material product) obtained from a ton of consumed energy between the First Five-Year Plan (1953–57) and 1978; (8) a fall of one-third in the average profit made by industrial enterprises from every one hundred yuan of output value between 1957 and 1980; (9) a doubling of the length of building cycles and construction costs in the same time span; (10) the misemployment in farm work (late 1970s) of between one-third and one-half of total rural labor—some 100 to 150 million people, whereas they could have been more productively employed elsewhere if only the system had had the required sensors to detect opportunity costs and comparative advantages; (11) low educational standards: in Guizhou Province (1983) only 7 percent of primary school teachers of mathematics and 14 percent of junior middle school mathematics teachers passed an examination in their subject, and the results were not much better for other subjects; (12) budgetary deficits at all levels of government caused in large part by a heavy and rising burden of retail food price subsidies and bailouts of inefficient state-sector firms: in the early 1980s food subsidies alone came to one-third of the central government's budgetary expenditures; in 1978 total subsidies averaged 526 yuan per state-sector worker or 82 percent of the nominal wage and 13 percent of national income, whereas total subsidies per peasant were less than 10 yuan; (13) egalitarian pronouncements notwithstanding, the long-term trend (mid-1950s through late 1970s) was for a progressive widening of urban-rural income and welfare differentials, the gap by the late 1970s having probably reached 5:1.

These and many other qualitative problems may be traced to three sources: (1) objective causes ("acts of God") such as a high rate of population increase, a skewed population/land ratio, the climate, availability and distribution of natural resources, cultural heritage; (2) errors of policy, such as erratic policy swings caused, for example, by excessive politicization and factionalism of economic leadership, and sectoral distortions due to dogmatically determined investment priorities; and (3) the system of economic organization. Of these, a defective system of economic organization has been, I think, the most important contributor. Errors of policy can be addressed within a basically unchanged economic structure by either leftward adjustments (increased socialization and command), or rightward adjustments (selective introduction of markets and quasi-markets for individual goods and restricted/truncated private or quasi-private property rights) within a basically unchanged and dominant structure of administrative command planning and state ownership.

This was, in fact, the only way in which economic problems in China had been addressed before December 1978. Left adjustments of the original neo-Stalinist economic model (installed in 1953–57) included the Great Leap Forward (1958–60), which resulted in famine and an absolute decline of population in 1960 and 1961 of 13.5 million (official figures, possibly too low—at the height of the Leap there were only a dozen practicing statisticians in the whole of China, and until recently statistical reporting was regarded as a Leninist political art). A second major left-radical adjustment went by the name of the "Cultural Revolution," (1966–76, but mainly 1966–69) and it, too, claimed millions of victims. Right adjustments toward the market (loosening the reins) were made principally to undo the ravages of left adjustments. The most important of these took place in 1961–65 following the Great Leap, and in 1976–78 in the wake of the Cultural Revolution. There was also a brief rightward adjustment in 1957 (the period of the "Hundred Flowers") following Mao's "little big leap" in rural collectivization (1956). What both left and right adjustments had in common was that they rested on the premise that the socialist, centrally planned system was basically sound. It did exhibit some failures and imperfections, however, and these (most of them due to willful distortions by individual left or right deviationists) could be taken care of by policy changes within a basically unchanged institutional structure. The procedure was known as "perfecting socialism" by either radicalizing it or grafting selective and circumscribed borrowings from the market system onto it. The disagreement in what came to be known as the "two-line struggle" was about the direction of policy, its pace, and instrumentalities, not about principles. The operative phrase in times of rightward adjustments has been *"using* capitalism" to make socialism work better; not replacing socialism with the market system.

The trouble is that the main source of China's economic problems was (as it had been in all other socialist economies) the system of economic organization, and that such systemic problems cannot be solved or even significantly mitigated by ad hoc policy adjustments. What is needed is a change of system, that is, structural reform.

After an initial (1976–78) misdiagnosis and application of largely ineffective rightward remedies during the interregnum of Hua Guofeng, the post Mao leadership in December 1976 reached a fragile consensus, constantly challenged thereafter, regarding the origins of the economy's manifest qualitative failures. The operative causes of the economy's difficulties, it was now (circumspectly and by some leaders quite formalistically) intimated, had to be sought in the foundations and structure of the centrally planned administrative command system: in the system's institutions and in its guiding positive and normative ideas ("emancipating one's thought," "daring to be bold"). From scapegoating the Gang of Four and exorcising ultraleftist work styles, the new dominant leadership faction under Deng Xiaoping shifted to a more reasoned dissection of systemic arrangements with respect to property, mandatory physical allocations (planning), and the price mechanism. The need to find and put in place a new comprehensive theoretical framework that would light the way for and make sense of the changes that were being empirically initiated (e.g., the dismantling of collective agriculture and the emergence of de facto family tenant farming; opening the door to foreign direct private investment) was not seen as compelling for a variety of reasons, most of them having to do with Marxist doctrinal taboos rather than with the difficulty Western mainstream theory has with elucidating problems of systemic transition. For all this dabbling in formerly forbidden thoughts, it is important to keep in mind that from the very onset and to this day, the leadership in general, and Deng Xiaoping in person, insisted repeatedly, emphatically, and consistently that the objective of theoretical debates and institutional changes that were being implemented— cautiously, slowly, and in zigzag fashion ("crossing the river while groping for the stones")—was not to abandon socialism, but to revitalize it; not to replace socialism with capitalism, but to "correctly" select the more promising capitalist methods and procedures, excise from them bourgeois cultural carbuncles and political accretions, and graft them onto the socialist system, to create a "socialist commodity economy" or "socialism with Chinese characteristics." When judged necessary, such disjointed transplants could be insulated from the rest of the economy, as in the case of the four Special Economic Zones in Guangdong and Fujian Provinces that were designed to attract foreign investment and serve as laboratories for innovative economic experiments without contaminating the surrounding landscape of socialist values with capitalist spiritual pollution. To reach such a consensus after the divisiveness of the Cultural Revolution, everyone except the ultraleftist radicals had to be put on board, including the principal architect of China's First Five-Year Plan, Chen Yun. "Stimulating the economy," Chen Yun once said, "is to be done within the framework of the state plan. The relationship between the two is like a bird in a cage. A bird should be allowed to fly, but within the framework of the cage. Otherwise it will fly away."

Chen raises an interesting question, very pertinent to China at the present time. It is whether the capitalist bird can be used to stimulate the socialist economy if confined in the plan cage, or whether its stimulative powers come from its natural condition of being free. The historical record of real socialism clearly suggests that so long as the bars of the state plan are in place, the economy will not be stimulated, or will be stimulated in rather bizarre ways. The cage has to be dismantled. That idea is slowly and surreptitiously insinuating itself into the thinking processes of most scholars, "socialist entrepreneurs," and some officials, particularly it would seem in the more prosperous coastal provinces and the more cosmopolitan cities. But its presence is not officially admitted, certainly not at the center. Despite the existence of

several conceptual "forbidden areas," a lively discussion of technical issues concerning prices, property, and the "commoditization"
(i.e., marketization) of the economy did take place in China after
1978, until it was stopped by the political repression following the
Tienanmen events of June 1989. By early 1992 the discussion
resumed, albeit hesitantly and with decorous circumspection.[9]

Systemic Errors

What is it about the cage that makes it decay and eventually
crumble? The construct of socialist central administrative command planning suffers from three fundamental errors of analysis,
morality, and psychology.

Analytical Error. The system operates on the mistaken idea that
the evolutionary selection process of the market organism working itself out through spontaneous, money price-informed, deper-
sonalized, competitive, utilitarian, search-and-discover, trial-and-
error, bilateral exchanges of private property rights, can not only
be replaced but vastly improved-upon by largely demonetized,
central, administrative (hierarchical), command planning designed by reason, and supported by quasi-total socialization of the
means of production and distribution.

Put another way, the error consists in the assumption (1) that
someone or some elite group (the *nomenklatura*) positioned at the
top or center of a deliberately constructed hierarchical organization can obtain and process diverse information from numerous
dispersed sources concerning degrees of commodity scarcity, in
advance of exchange communication; (2) that this information
is superior to that obtained through the market process of free
exchange; and (3) that it can be used to determine and rank ends
that mandatorily substitute for and are considered superior to
preferences and production functions emerging from individual
buyers' and sellers' utilitarian exchange transactions (exogenous
determination of the structure of the system by the political leadership).

It is theoretically conceivable—on the basis of Western mainstream, friction-free equilibrium models of "substantial rational-

ity"—that, seen simply as computation, that is, central processing of manifold information with the help of computers and mathematical models, the problem is manageable and soluble.[10] However, the communication problem is intrinsically a social process of discovery and learning for which competitive market exchanges of private property rights embedded in commodities are indispensable.[11] In this important sense "the market is the only known method of providing information enabling individuals to judge comparative advantages of different uses of resources of which they have immediate knowledge and through whose use, whether they intend or not, they serve the needs of distant unknown individuals. This dispersed knowledge is *essentially* dispersed and cannot be gathered together and conveyed to an authority charged with the task of deliberately creating order. . . . We are able to bring about an ordering of the known *only by causing it to order itself.*"[12]

The erroneous idea on which socialist economic analysis and hence its institutional structure rest, has had disastrous effects on the quality of information and coordination in the centrally planned system.

Moral Error. The moral error is the arrogant assertion that individual human beings do not and cannot really know what they want and that, therefore, they have to be told what it is that they want by historically chosen vanguards. By virtue of their revolutionary anointment, these latter-day Party high priests have access to the requisite knowledge and superior metaunderstanding of social necessity acquired from immutable laws of history discovered by Marx in German libraries and the British Museum. Of course, this patronizing, self-serving conceit predates Marx's discovery of the secret of history's dialectical progression. Marx merely gave the old elitist fairy tale a purportedly scientific cast that thenceforth enabled any autocrat, if the necessity was upon him, to rationalize in scientological, cryptomodern terms his natural propensity to keep grown-up people in a perpetual condition of infantilism. This insufferable condescension has had the most adverse consequences for socialist incentives to planners, managers, workers, and people as citizens and moral beings and, more than the system's inability to deliver the goods, has contributed to the delegitimation of socialism and the widespread popular contempt in which Communist parties are held.

The moral error is compounded by the almost total suppression of private property and its nationalization, whereby individuals are deprived of "sovereign spheres," their first defense against the encroachment on their liberty by self-appointed state bureaucrats.

Psychological Error. The forced imposition on adult people of someone else's allegedly more insightful preferences, provokes opposition from those many branded as intellectual nullities and moral midgets. There is no mechanism in the system to reconcile opposing ends or settle conflicts of values created by this high-handedness, other than the application of force accompanied by fear (whence the importance attached by socialism to military-police goods and eavesdropping services). In its pure form the system precludes tensions from being resolved by concession, compromise, or retreat of the historically correctly informed class. In fact, doctrinally and from practical necessity, the system regards confrontation (the dialectical clash of opposites, "struggle") as the engine of progress, a virtue that substitutes for what socialist theory decries as the anarchy, greed, and egoistic cruelty of market competition. Unable to directly replace the planners' goals foisted on them, people—as consumers, workers, collective farm chairmen, and managers of state firms—manipulate the means available to them for attaining the planners' mandatory norms, by endless deceptions, prevarications, cynicisms, and imaginative bendings of the rules, to the point where the system becomes a sprawling lie and a bizarre distortion of the advertised intent, and daily life turns into a succession of petty indignities. The exercise of countervailing values by individuals, when not punished by banishment or worse as a counterrevolutionary crime on the lines of Soviet high Stalinism, was seen in China as a symptom of the survival of bourgeois ideas in people's minds, and dealt with by mass campaigns of socialist rectification and intimidating "heart-to-heart chats" conducted with individual offenders by Party cadres. Neither mass movements nor "intimate political solicitation" had the anticipated effect of fundamentally transforming the national psyche and lifting it to a level of superior selfless and collective perfection. The procedure merely debased the already debilitated information, coordination, and incentive systems, and further discredited socialist ethics.

Additionally, the almost total nationalization/collectivization of the means of production and distribution has had a deleterious effect on people's attitudes toward the conservation and preservation of objects that belong to everybody but to no one in particular, resulting in an extraordinary decrepitude of publicly owned assets.

What's to Be Done?

To excise the three errors at the level of ideas and institutions, several reformist measures have to be taken, in China as elsewhere. For several reasons there is, however, a divergence of views among economists on the content, relative importance, pacing, and sequencing of such measures.[13]

One school of thought[14] argues that, at the level of ideas, it is essential that the objective of the changes be clearly defined and explained as the transformation of the socialist system of central administrative command planning and its associated Marxist-Leninist positive and normative theories into a full market system and into market analyses and ethical prescripts, and that the reform commitment be credible, that is, not subject to postponements, retreats, compromises of principle, and surrenders to reform-crippling structural half-way settlements when the going gets tough. This school regards it as perfectly self-evident that such a commitment cannot be made or carried out by any ruling Communist party without that party's denying its philosophical essence, political temper (the will to monopoly power), and organizational structure, that is, without its presiding over its own liquidation. The other school,[15] more given to pure economic speculation, has nothing explicit to say on the subject, but implies that Communist parties (the Chinese, it would seem, in particular) can remold themselves, Zhao Ziyang-like, and gradually bring about a structural transformation of socialism explainable by Lange- or

Vanek-type theories of market socialism or labor-managed market. The first school holds that, at the level of institutions, two critical measures have to be taken, preferably concurrently: (1) property rights have to be truly and fully privatized to the point where they become the dominant ownership form in the system; and (2) physically oriented administrative command planning must be replaced by voluntary, competitive, contractual, money exchange transactions guided by market prices (Chen Yun's cage has to be taken apart so the bird can fly away). True and full privatization means the vesting in individuals and free associations of individuals (firms, partnerships, voluntary cooperatives, households) of the broadest possible rights of use, transfer, and income. Workably competitive (horizontal) money exchange relations and private property rights must constitute the critical minimum mass of the successor system's synchronous institutions.

The second school is more accommodating on both the subject of marketization and privatization. Price reform, the core of marketization, can be piecemeal, carried out gradually and experimentally, leaving room and time for multitier prices and exchange rates. Privatization need not be either true or full; it can be (in fact it is preferable that it be) multitier and often simulated (quasi-private property rights [long-term leases], as in post-1978 Chinese agriculture vested in peasant families; and broader autonomy over assets, investments, and the like, granted to state-owned enterprises under various "responsibility systems," that is no full individualization of property rights). The school does not regard private property either as central to the marketization process, or urgent. What matters is enterprise profitability, the management's profit-orientation and sensitivity to relative prices, not the formal mode of ownership. Price reform, the core of marketization, can on this view be piecemeal, carried out gradually and experimentally; prices need not be fully flexible in the short run, leaving room and socially necessary (from the standpoint of social cost) time for transitional multitier prices and exchange rates.

East European and Soviet experience since 1990 teaches that, contrary to earlier assumptions, capitalism does not just happen when people are left alone. True, a lot of crucial marketization and privatization from below by people freely entering uncoerced exchange transactions will occur, but for a variety of reasons a credible (preferably a democratically elected and democratically removable) government seems to be needed to act as midwife to the birth or rebirth of the market system. On this issue both schools are agreed, although the second is inclined to accept both the possibility and probability of the democratization of Communist parties, and not just in name only, while the first school does not.

Some reasons for intervention by a credible government in the economic reform (marketization/privatization) process include: (1) the need to put in place a system of commercial law favorable to a market economy and private property, and to enforce the laws predictably and impartially; (2) the need to wean accounting and statistical systems away from Marxist concepts and Leninist procedures; (3) difficulties experienced with privatizing very large (internationally uncompetitive) state firms, necessitating the creation by the state of self-liquidating privatization agencies (perhaps on the lines of the German *Treuhand*) to restructure and dispose of state-owned assets to private buyers; (4) the need for structural reform of the monetary and fiscal systems, including the establishment of financial intermediaries (capital markets) and the elimination of budgetary subsidies; (5) the provision of social safety nets (unemployment insurance, income supplements) for those structured out of their jobs and/or inflated out of their incomes by the transition; and (6) the need to reduce and eventually abolish barriers to international commodity and money exchanges, thus importing competition.

3. Feasibility of Market Reform

What Has Been Done since 1978

Let us see what has been done in China since December 1978 when economic changes *combining for the first time policy adjustments and some structural reforms* were initiated. I shall focus on two areas, which appear to me to be central to systemic transition: property and prices.

Property. Chinese privatization has been (1) partial (i.e., devolution of some but not all property rights to individuals, families, workers, managements, local governments, voluntarily constituted groups) and largely simulated (de facto, "as if"); (2) most advanced in agriculture, retail trade, consumer services, and light (consumer- and export-oriented) manufacturing in cooperative and village/township enterprises; and (3) administratively decentralized and most forcefully pursued by regional authorities in the coastal provinces, cities, special economic zones, and other "open" areas. In the state-owned industrial sector, comprised for the most part of large, heavy industry enterprises, "privatization" (if that is the appropriate name for it) has been very modest, limited to governance adjustments, that is, to some expansion of managerial prerogatives and the encouragement of profit-orientation and responsiveness to quasi-market signals by managements.

Take the question of partial de facto privatization in agriculture where property rights changes have been the most advanced. The property rights granted to peasant households are essentially those of tenancy, limited to residual rights of use, that is, (more or less) free use of the product after fulfillment of the tenants' contractual delivery obligations to the state at "negotiated" prices (more or less, because local cadres often restrict that freedom unless paid a gratuity). The contract is in essence compulsory — no contract, no land — and negotiation about prices is not between equals, but between atomistic (but not powerless) households and representatives of a big and powerful state inclined to graft. A birth quota rider is usually attached (or is supposed to be attached) to the produce delivery contract: one child per family or no contract. There is no private right of transfer because the scattered land parcels do not legally belong to the users, except for the availability of use transfer certificates contingent on local government approval. There are restrictions on the hiring of non-family labor and on the size of the household's "responsibility" land holdings, the original distribution and size of which had been determined by socialist criteria of fairness and equality, not by reference to economies of scale, which in any event would have been very difficult to arrive at in the absence of allocatively meaningful prices. The state remains a major supplier of key farm inputs such as chemical fertilizers, pesticides, machinery, fuel, power, and plastics, although inroads into the state's former monopoly position in this regard have been made by proliferating nonstate, cooperative/township and village firms as well as by partially marketizing of state prices for some of the inputs (see below). The state also plays a role (albeit a declining one) in the distribution of farm produce: it purchases a portion of the household's above contract output and polices urban street markets (sometimes and in some places more thoroughly than at other times and in other places) to make sure that prices there do not rise above "exploitative" levels. So even where they are numerically most common and advanced—in agriculture—partial, "as if" private property rights remain encaged by the state. How well encaged is another, largely political and local matter.

Nevertheless, it can be argued—and the argument is made by the second school—that even such partial and simulated rights corrode the cage, particularly in the nonstate, village and township, light, labor-intensive, consumer- and export-oriented industrial sector, particularly when they spread more rapidly than state property, as indeed they have done in China, partly under the impulse of private direct foreign investment (concentrated in certain parts of the country). Beginning in the fall of 1988 and accelerating after the Tienanmen incident of June 1989, there were attempts by the central leadership to resocialize and recentralize parts of the nonstate economy, first on technical grounds as part of an austerity drive intended to check inflation and get runaway provincial and local investment under control, later (after Tienanmen) on doctrinal grounds, that is, expansion of the nonstate sector was seen by the new hard-line leadership as one of the contributory causes of the democracy movement. These attempts were given expression in the so-called 39 Points of the Communist Party's Central Committee promulgated in November 1989, but three years later hardly any of them had been implemented. On the contrary, nonstate, cooperatively owned, private, quasi-private, and foreign joint venture, profit-oriented firms, which buy most of their inputs and sell most of their output on markets (some real, some simulated) at free, somewhat free, and partly controlled prices, and obtain a growing share of their capital on informal credit markets, have expanded quickly, whereas state-owned firms stagnated, 40 percent of them (but probably more) suffering financial losses and surviving on subsidies, and another 30 percent barely breaking even. In 1990 output of state-sector firms grew at roughly 3 percent, whereas the output of cooperative, market-oriented firms rose at three times that rate, private-sector output went up 22 percent, and production of foreign-invested firms 56 percent.[16] In 1991 the centrally planned state-owned sector contributed roughly one-third of China's gross national product, employed 18 percent of the total labor force, and produced 53 percent of total industrial output value compared to 80 percent in 1978 and an average of 70 percent in the 1980s. It was expected that in 1992 the state-owned firms' share of industrial output would for the first time fall below 50 percent.[17] In 1980 nonstate, small and medium, market-oriented, rural/township, industrial consumer and export goods enterprises numbered 1,500; 300,000 ten years later, contributing half of China's total exports and three-quarters of garment exports.

From 1979 through 1991 a total of $48 billion in foreign private investment had been approved by Beijing (41,300 enterprises), $20 billion of which had actually materialized. This was in addition to seventy four joint offshore oil exploration and development projects with a contracted value of $3.4 billion, of which $2.8 billion had actually been used. Altogether, foreign-funded firms accounted in 1991 for 5 percent of the country's industrial output, and 20 percent of export volume.[18] Hong Kong and since 1987 (indirect) Taiwan private investments are the leaders by far.

The southern coastal provinces of Guangdong and Fujian have been the main recipients of direct foreign investment (DFI). In 1987, Guangdong Province alone accounted for 58 percent of DFI and Fujian Province for another 6 percent. The Fujian share has risen between 1987 and the early 1990s. In 1987 there was no (legal) Taiwan investment on the Chinese mainland. The 1990 cumulative total was well in excess of $2 billion, most of it in Fujian, with some three thousand Taiwan-funded firms operating in that province. Hong Kong investments flow mainly to neighboring Guangdong. There are more than sixteen thousand Hong Kong-owned factories in the province, employing three million

Chinese workers, processing materials and producing goods (most of them for export, particularly to the United States) valued (in 1991) at $11 billion, and contributing to Guangdong's per capita GDP of $1,290 (1990), nearly three times the average per capita GDP for China as a whole, and to south China's phenomenal growth rate of around 13 percent a year, about twice the rate of the rest of the country in recent years. Shanghai's share of DFI in 1987 was 7 percent, but has risen since with the establishment in March 1990 of the Pudong investment zone designed principally to attract Taiwan DFI and overseas Chinese capital. The 1987 share of of all the inland provinces was a modest 11 percent, but if the huge (and unsuccessful) Antaibao coal mine cooperative venture with Occidental Petroleum is subtracted, the inland province's share falls to about that of Shanghai (7 percent). The southern coastal provinces, moreover, are not nearly as burdened as the inland regions by stagnant, value-subtracting, state-owned enterprises. In 1991 state-owned firms in Guangdong accounted for 40 percent of the gross value of industrial output, whereas in the rest of the country their share was 53 percent. Shanghai has the highest concentration of state-owned large and medium enterprises in the country. One Chinese author describes their condition in the following terms: "The 'three irons' (the iron rice bowl, iron wages, and iron armchair [guaranteed employment, wages, and managerial positions]) have not been smashed. Neglect of duties and lax discipline are accepted behavior. The great rice pot and equalitarianism are everywhere to be seen. There are no reward/punishment mechanisms for worker incentive and control, or for managing competition and employment."[19]

The second school's argument is that even though the property forms are varied and private property is not full and true, but rather partial and often "as if" (simulated), the changes (1) oblige Chinese entrepreneurs in charge of nonstate-owned firms to broadly conform to the rules of competitive market behavior with respect to most of their sales and purchases, and a rising share of their capital needs; (2) this partial, quasi-private property is not confined to consumer goods and services but exists in a variety of fields: consumer as well as producer goods and services, and exports; and (3) expanding much more rapidly than the state-owned segment of the economy.[20] Conformity with the rules of competitive market behavior may perhaps be questioned. In many instances the commercial success of nonstate ventures depends critically on personal political connections (*guanxi*) and the greasing of bureaucrats' palms. In fact, like the multitier prices (see below), the multitier property arrangement with its truncated and informal private properties, is a major contributor to the pervasive neomercantilistic corruption and rampant special privilege that are characteristic of contemporary China.

Prices. As a result of a combination of administrative price adjustments and partial reforms (price freeing), China today has a two-track price arrangement. Some prices are free. Since the mid-1980s these include prices of industrial capital goods produced and traded outside the plan as well as the prices of most consumer goods. Some prices are loosely controlled by below-province authorities; others are set and more strictly monitored at the provincial level; others still, are fixed by the national government, with a single nationwide price for some commodities and regionally differentiated prices for others.[21] The general trend since 1979 has been toward the expansion of the realm of market-determined prices. The World Bank estimates that at the end of the 1980s one-fourth of all commodity prices in China were fixed by the state, another quarter consisted of prices fluctuating between state-set limits ("floating" prices), and the remaining half were free.[22]

The reasons for the spread of market and quasi-market pricing include the following: (1) The main reason has been the already mentioned rapid growth of the nonstate (collective and private) sector, which as early as 1984 accounted for 95 percent of Chinese industrial firms and 30 percent of the gross value of industrial output (47 percent in 1991).[23] The bulk of transactions among nonstate firms is carried out at almost-market prices (almost because some prices are "negotiated" between buyer and seller, and some, but not all, of these negotiations are not among equals and are, therefore, open to administrative pressures and interventions). (2) A second reason for the gradual marketization of prices has been the phased alignment of many state-set prices (e.g., passenger and freight transport, crude oil, coal, foreign exchange) with market prices, and the periodic withdrawal of controls over the prices of certain commodity groups. For example, wholesale markets replacing in part centrally planned allocation have been opened for wheat, rice, corn, and timber, and gradually expanded for machinery, equipment, intermediate goods, and industrial raw materials. According to the World Bank, 75 percent of all metal-cutting tools were distributed through markets at the end of the 1980s.[24] The marketization of coal, rubber, farm machinery, building materials, chemical products, and nonferrous metals prices is under consideration.[25] (3) The spread of market and marketlike pricing has also been due to the government's allowing its firms to purchase and sell a rising share of their inputs and outputs on the market, that is, outside the state allocation and distribution network. All this leads some observers to conclude that in China "despite problems, market pricing has become well established and appears to be at least reasonably reflective of market equilibrium conditions."[26]

Considerable distortions and rigidities remain in the pricing of labor in the state sector (the "three irons"), as well as of housing space (rent takes less than 1 percent of the average city-resident's income), and this has distorting effects on market pricing elsewhere in the economy. However, in the nonstate "entrepreneurial" sector, as Lardy calls it, wages are largely determined by labor productivity and firm profitability. The government is considering allowing Chinese workers to buy their own homes (in part to defuse widespread dissatisfaction with urban housing conditions that the state is financially unable to improve) but without creating a capitalist housing market.[27] In the absence of such a market, labor mobility, and hence a realistic pricing of labor, are severely hindered.

Informal financial markets have made their appearance. Nonstate-sector firms acquire a not inconsiderable and rising share of the capital they need on such informal (i.e., existing outside the state banking system) credit markets at supply- and demand- determined interest rates. Most of the capital for foreign joint venture firms is supplied at market-determined interest rates by the foreign partner.[28]

Two developments should be noted with respect to external

sector marketization: (1) The number of relatively autonomous (but still state-owned) foreign trade corporations permitted to engage in foreign transactions in specified commodity lines rose from eight hundred in the mid-1980s to five thousand in the late 1980s, consolidated to around four thousand in the early 1990s. At the end of the 1980s, roughly half China's exports consisted of goods outside the trade plans. Competition among the trading corporations, according to Lardy, "meant that by the end of the decade most producers were receiving the international price for their products rather than the state-fixed prices, as they had in the pre-reform foreign trade system."[29] In other words, the competitive influence of the world market was brought to bear on China's domestic economy through better aligned domestic and international trade prices. (2) Steps have been taken to move from planned foreign currency rationing to allocation through market forces. In the mid-1980s foreign exchange markets were set up in major cities and some special economic zones to enable foreign invested-firms to trade foreign currencies among themselves. In 1987–88 this right was extended to domestic firms and the volume of transactions soared, reaching $13 billion in 1990.[30] Because external trade has since 1979 come to represent an increasingly significant share of China's (particularly south China's) national product, the progressive marketization of external trade prices and foreign exchange allocations and pricing cannot but strengthen the drift toward market reforms.

Prognosis

The Chinese like to say that their case is different and that the lessons being learned from the collapse of the centrally planned system and totalitarian polities in the former Soviet Union and Eastern Europe do not necessarily apply to them. In China, they say, what you see is not always what you get; formal structures do not function the way they are described, and there is an infinite number of subtle ways in which rules can be interpreted, so that only natives steeped in ethno-specific millennial cultural traditions can know what these are. Be that as it may, there exist certain systemic regularities and commonalities that equally, perhaps more powerfully, influence final outcomes.

One of them is that for an economic system to function properly, that is, in the interest of the material welfare of the people who live and make their living within it, it must comprise a minimum critical mass of integrated, compatible, internally consistent, interrelated, and interacting ideas and institutions that together constitute an identifiable organism. The integration, compatibility, and so on, need not (perhaps should not) be total—there can be borrowings and transplants from other systems—but there has to be a minimum mass of clearly dominant, related institutions and ideas that give the system structural harmony and internal logic. Two-tier property rights and two-track prices do not seem to fulfill this condition, and are clearly a transitional phenomenon. Sooner or later, one of the two tiers or tracks has to become dominant. At that point an essentially political decision has to be made to pass from using truncated private property in and quasi-markets for individual goods and services as a supplement to the socialist diet to a fully fledged market system. The question in China today is whether the process of informal privatization and simulated marketization has reached the point at which the decision on systemic transition must be made. Indications are that it has done so institutionally in the southern provinces, which are ready for the market system. In much of the rest of the country this has not yet happened. The same seems to be true at the level of ideas. The south is ready to accept the idea of the market system analytically and, with some reservations, ethically as well. This is not the case in some other inland places, notably in the seat of power at Zhongnanghai in Beijing. The market *system*, as distinct from the tactical *use* of markets to keep people busy improving their material condition and thus ensure "social stability" (no more Tienanmens) for the time being at least, is rejected by the central Party leadership, and the rejection is not just rhetorical.

The political nature of economic system transition consists in the fact that however spontaneous the de facto privatization of property rights and marketization of prices may be, the linking-up of scattered and incomplete property rights and individual markets into a market system—of body parts into a functioning body—requires government participation: the establishment of a framework of laws that permit the market system to operate, an even-handed and predictable enforcement of those laws (rule of law), and the removal of the moral opprobrium attached by Marxist moral codes to market behavior. The lesson of Eastern Europe and the former Soviet Union applicable, I think, to communist China despite important cultural differences, is that Communist parties, no matter how revisionistically flexible (e.g., Hungary, Yugoslavia) are philosophically and constitutionally incapable of this crucial act of political will—without, that is, destroying themselves.[31] It is not, as is often asserted, a matter of changing personnel within the Party (e.g., replacing a Li Peng or a Chen Yun with a "moderate" like Zhao Ziyang, or the old guard with a younger generation of communists), but one of replacing the Communist party, peacefully if possible.

The southern coastal provinces of China contain by now the critical minimum mass of property and market arrangements, imperfectly integrated and incomplete though they may be, to make the transition to a market system. The south would benefit from both the spread of its ideas and institutions to the rest of China and from the forging of linkages with other dynamic and more materially (as well as politically) advanced Chinese market areas such as Taiwan and Hong Kong. Both steps require the prior removal of the Communist party from political power at both the regional and central levels. If the transformation is not consummated before Hong Kong returns to the suffocating embrace of an economically half-reformed and politically unreformed motherland, Hong Kong's market economy will suffer possibly irreparable damage and China will have missed a unique chance to leave behind centuries of underdevelopment, an opportunity that is now within its grasp.

Notes

1. Adam Smith, *The Wealth of Nations*, Edwin Cannan edition (1776: reprint, New York: The Modern Library, 1937), 625.
2. Russian economist Vasily Selyunin cited by Bill Keller, "Soviet Econ-

86 Jan S. Prybyla

omy: A Shattered Dream," *New York Times*, 13 May 1990, A12. "For Mao as for Stalin, the rate of growth of national iron and steel output seemed at times the sole criterion by which socialist advance should be judged." Richard Kirby and Terry Cannon, "Introduction," in *China's Regional Development*, ed. David S. Goodman (London and New York: Routledge, 1989), 6. "Over the century the Soviets essentially erased the very notion of economics." "China Globalized," editorial, *Wall Street Journal*, 22 May 1989, 8.

3. Wang Xiaoqiang and Bai Nanfeng, *The Poverty of Plenty* (Basingstoke, England: Macmillan, 1991), 87–88.
4. "The State of the Nation State," *Economist* (London), 22 December 22 1990, 46.
5. Raimund Dietz, *The Reform of Soviet Socialism as a Search for Systemic Rationality: A Systems Theoretical View* (Vienna: The Vienna Institute for Comparative Economic Studies, Reprint Series, No. 130, January 1991), 428. Reprinted from *Communist Economies* 2 (1990).
6. "The crucial point is that the prior development of several [private] property is indispensable for the development of trading, and thereby for the formation of larger coherent and cooperative structures, and for the appearance of those signals we call prices." F. A. Hayek, *The Fatal Conceit: The Errors of Socialism* in *The Collected Works of F. A. Hayek*, ed. W. W. Bartley III (Chicago: University of Chicago Press, 1988), 1: 31.
7. "The ultimate values of [a multiplicity of different ranks of different ends] come to be reflected in a single scale of values of [diverse, mutually substitutable] means—i.e., prices—that depends on their relative scarcity and the possibility of exchange among owners." Hayek, *The Fatal Conceit*, 96.
8. "[T]he justice that political authority must enforce, if it wants to secure the peaceful cooperation among individuals on which prosperity rests, cannot exist without the recognition of private property: 'Where there is no property there is no justice,' is a proposition as certain as any demonstration in Euclid ... (John Locke: 1690)." Hayek, *The Fatal Conceit*, 34. Hayek following F. C. Savigny (*System des heutigen Roemischen Rechts* [1840]) defines private (or as he prefers to call it, "several") property as "an invisible boundary within which the existence and operation of each individual is assured a certain free space." Hayek, *The Fatal Conceit*, 35.
9. Robert C. Hsu, *Economic Theories in China, 1979–1988* (Cambridge: Cambridge University Press, 1992).
10. By "substantial rationality" is meant the assumption of a state of rational affairs from which reality always strays. On this *Harmonielehre* view, the rationality of any system is seen as the system's ability through its coordination mechanism to bring about the posited equilibrium—a problem, by and large, of computational techniques.

Within these confining conceptual parameters, it can be demonstrated that both the market and central planning are equally capable of bringing about substantial rational equilibrium, indeed, any mixture of the two can do it (Oskar Lange). A technical equivalence of market and plan is thus theorized, which is but a step from the moral equivalence of capitalism and socialism with which liberal argument is peppered (or used to be). Dietz, *The Reform of Soviet Socialism*, 422. In his essay on "The Computer and the Market" (in *Socialism, Capitalism, and Economic Growth: Essays Presented to Maurice Dobb*, ed. C. H. Feinstein [Cambridge: Cambridge University Press, 1967]: 158), Lange writes: "Let us put simultaneous equations on an electronic computer and we shall obtain the solution in less than a second. The market process with its cumbersome tâtonnements appears old-fashioned. Indeed, it may be considered as a computing device of the pre-electronic age." Janos Kornai, a practitioner of models of substantial rationality in the 1950s, has this to say after experiencing the Hungarian New Economic Mechanism's attempt to mix market and plan: "The Lange of the 1930s, although a convinced socialist, lived in the sterile world of Walrasian pure theory and did not consider the socio-political underpinnings of his basic assumptions." Janos Kornai, "The Hungarian Reform Process: Visions, Hopes, and Reality," in ed. *Remaking the Economic Institutions of Socialism*, Victor Nee and David Stark (Stanford: Stanford University Press, 1989), 85. Kornai's criticism of the Lange model is on pp. 83–86.

11. Don Lavoie, "Computation, Incentives, and Discovery: The Cognitive Function of Markets in Market Socialism," *The Annals*, American Academy of Political and Social Science, 507 (January 1990): 77–79; idem, *Rivalry and Central Planning: The Socialist Calculation Debate Reconsidered* (Cambridge: Cambridge University Press, 1985); idem, *National Economic Planning: What Is Left?* (Cambridge, Mass.: Ballinger, 1985).

12. Hayek, *The Fatal Conceit*, 77, 83 (emphasis in the original), and idem, "The Use of Knowledge in Society," *American Economic Review* 35 (1945): 519–30.

13. I discuss these reasons at length in my contribution to Franz Michael et al. See also Olivier Blanchard, Rudiger Dornbush, Paul Krugman, Richard Layard, Lawrence Summers, *Reform in Eastern Europe* (Cambridge: MIT Press, 1991).

14. As I read it, with some shifting differences of emphasis among them, the first school includes, Friedrich A. Hayek, Ludwig von Mises, G. Warren Nutter, János Kornai, Jeffrey Sachs, the authors of *Reform in Eastern Europe* mentioned in note 13, Vaclav Klaus, Leszek Balcerowicz, and Yegor Gaidar.

15. In my view the school, again with some changing emphases among

88   Jan S. Prybyla

its members, includes William A. Byrd, Inderjit Singh (both of the World Bank), Nicholas R. Lardy, and Valtr Komarek.

16. Nicholas R. Lardy, *Redefining U.S.—China Economic Relations* (Seattle: The National Bureau of Asian and Soviet Research, NBR Analysis, June 1991, No. 5), 7.

17. *Paishing Semi-Monthly* (Hong Kong), 1 March 1992, 26–27, in *Inside China Mainland* (Taipei) 14 (May 1992): 15.

18. "China Attracts Investment," *Wall Street Journal*, 10 March 1992, A12.

19. Qiu Shi, "Getting the Most Out of State-Owned Large- and Medium-Sized Enterprises," *Finance and Economy Studies*, Shanghai, 1 (1992): 3–7, in *Inside China Mainland* (Taipei) 14 (May 1992): 44; Chuyuan Cheng, *Trade and Investment across the Taiwan Strait: Economic Consequences and Prospects* (Montclair, Calif.: The Claremont Institute, Asian Studies Center, Strategic Study, 1990), Tables 1 and 4. From 1989 through 1990 Fujian Province received 45 percent of Taiwan investment, Guangdong Province 21 percent, Jiangsu Province 16 percent, and Shanghai 7 percent (Table 5). Richard Pomfret, *Investing in China: Ten Years of the Open Door Policy* (Ames: Iowa State University, 1991), 75, 95; "Independent Stance Puts Guangdong at Forefront of Renewed Commitment to Economic Reform," *Asian Wall Street Journal Weekly*, 30 March 1992, 16.

20. William A. Byrd, *The Market Mechanism and Economic Reforms in China* (Armonk, N.Y. and London, England: M. E. Sharpe, 1991), 25–26, sums up the second school's position on the subject: "What is important is that agents producing for and transacting in markets have a considerable degree of autonomy, whether or not they own their enterprises. This requirement is consistent with a variety of different ownership forms, possibly including public ownership." The first school argues that greater autonomy for *nomenklatura* bureaucrats is not enough. What is needed are clear titles of what belongs to whom, so that owners put their money on the line, and discipline those they put in charge of managing that money.

21. Joseph C. H. Chai, and Chi-Keung Leung, "Reform of China's Industrial Prices 1979–1985," in ed. *China's Economic Reforms*, Joseph C. H. Chai, and Chi-Keung Leung (Hong Kong Centre of Asian Studies, University of Hong Kong, 1987), 584–698.

22. World Bank, *China between Plan and Market* (Washington, D.C.: World Bank, 1990), 59.

23. Byrd, *The Market Mechanism and Economic Reforms in China*, 201.

24. World Bank, *China between Plan and Market*, 60.

25. "China to Open Some Markets," *Wall Street Journal*, 15 January 1992: A16.

26. Byrd, *The Market Mechanism and Economic Reforms in China*, 200.

27. Nicholas R. Lardy, "Is China Different?" The Fate of Its Economic

Reform," in *The Crisis of Leninism and the Decline of the Left: The Revolutions of 1989*, ed. Daniel Chirot (Seattle: University of Washington Press, 1991), 147; James McGregor, "China Wants Urban Workers to Purchase Their Homes Abandoning Mao's Vision of Nearly Cost-Free Shelter," *Wall Street Journal*, 23 January 1992, A13.

28. Lardy, *Redefining U.S.-China Relations*, 10; idem, *Foreign Trade and Economic Reform in China, 1970–1990* (Cambridge: Cambridge University Press, 1991), chapter 3.
29. Lardy, *Redefining U.S.-China Relations*, 11.
30. Ibid.
31. Jan Prybyla, "China's Revolution without Borders . . . Will Founder Unless Party Walls Topple," *Asian Wall Street Journal*, 16 March 1992, 6.

5

The Failure of Development Planning in India

Shyam J. Kamath

1. Introduction

Economic policy in India since it gained independence in 1947 has been conducted within a framework of centrally directed development planning combined with intensive government regulation and control of all facets of economic activity. Beginning in 1951–52, a series of Five-Year Plans have provided a comprehensive and complex set of directives and targets for savings, investment, exports, imports, public ownership of the means of production and for regulating private economic activity. Private enterprise and industry have been allowed to function subject to numerous physical, financial, and noneconomic constraints. A bewildering variety of interlinking controls and policy interventions has constrained market forces in a manner quite unlike that experienced in Western developed economies.[1]

The planning and control framework adopted in India grew out of a conviction of the Indian elite in the years preceding independence that economic growth was not possible through the reliance on unfettered market forces because of the "objective" conditions of underdevelopment. According to this view, equitable growth could only be achieved by systematic planning. The establishment of the Indian planning framework followed the recommendations of the officially appointed Advisory Planning Board (1946) and its endorsement by the Economic Programme Committee of the Congress party (1948).[2] The directions for establishing the Indian Planning Commission to develop and coordinate the economywide planning effort were provided by these documents. The subsequent Industrial Policy Resolution of April 1948 outlined the complex of controls that would regulate industrial activity. It was the first of a series of policy resolutions and regulatory interventions that followed. The planning system and control framework, set up in the postindependence era as a result of these initial policy directions, produced unintended but disastrous consequences for the subsequent economic development of the country.

Today, after forty-five years of planned economic development, India's per capita income remains around $300. Almost 40 percent of Indians live below the official poverty line, and the absolute number of Indians in that category increased sharply between the late 1950s and the mid-1980s. India lags behind the majority of nations on most indicators of the quality of life such as literacy, life expectancy, nourishment, access to safe drinking water and sanitation, and so forth. Considering that almost one-sixth of humanity resides in India, the failure of centrally directed development planning has produced an economic and social debacle of much larger proportions than was witnessed by the collapse of socialism in Eastern Europe and the Soviet Union.

This chapter examines the nature and structure of development planning in India in the postindependence period and analyzes the reasons for its failure. It provides a comprehensive critique of the underlying vision, theoretical basis, and actual experience with development planning in India. The lessons that can be drawn from the Indian development planning experience are general and apply to all the developing countries that adopted such planning in the postwar period with essentially similar results.

Section 2 outlines the major characteristics of the underlying "unconstrained" vision of development planning and details the roots and development of this vision in the Indian development experience. The framework of Indian development planning is outlined in section 3. Details of the planning and control regime are provided in section 4. The actual development record of Indian planning is detailed in section 5. A theoretical and epistemological critique of the Indian development planning experience is provided in section 6. Section 7 contains some conclusions.

2. The Unconstrained Vision of Development Planning

Development planning has been shaped and influenced by an underlying vision which is fundamental to its spread and subsequent failure. The principal tenets undergirding this vision are that economic development can be engineered through reason and foresight; that rational economic planning and effective control of an entire economic system are both feasible and desirable; and that centralized knowledge collection and decisionmaking are both feasible and efficacious in human society. This vision may be called the "unconstrained" vision of economic development.[3] It sees no limit to human knowledge or its application through human reason. It attempts to reorganize and rearrange human societies by rational planning and interventionist social and economic policy so as to design the "best of all possible worlds." It believes that centralized governmental decisionmaking and coordination can succeed rather than decentralized, voluntary market-mediated decisions and that quantitative criteria and decisions by "experts" can replace the decentralized price signals of the market.

The unconstrained vision sees the order of human civilization and its institutions as the products of deliberate design by the application of human reason, rather than the spontaneous products of human action in a long-term process of cultural evolution as viewed by the constrained vision.[4] The former vision sees no limits to human knowledge and reason and concentrates on the achievement of *hoped-for results*. The latter vision sees human knowledge as the product of social experience and sees severe limits to the application of human reason, instead focusing on evolved systemic processes and their *systematic effects* and *unintended consequences*.

Since people's views are affected by a variety of beliefs, theories, and thought systems, a clear-cut dichotomy into the two opposing visions cannot be clearly identified in every case. Rather, the two visions can be seen as the ends of a continuum with clearly definable characteristics and we can speak of people with *more* or *less* constrained visions. What is clear is that an individual's or a group of individuals' position along this continuum has a predictive power in terms of the kind of economic and social policies that will be espoused and practiced with a broad pattern of likely outcomes.

Socialism and communism in their many guises conform to the tenets of the unconstrained vision, with a consequent interventionist bent to achieve desired results through social engineering and control. The systematic effects of such a vision are nevertheless predictable and different from the intended consequences, as has been detailed by its critics such as Bohm- Bawerk, Mises, Hayek and Popper.[5] The choice of a particular position along the continuum of visions therefore has predictable and important consequences for the type of society that will evolve as a result of the application of that vision to social and economic policy.

In the case of postindependence India, the particular policy framework adopted and the actual results that emerged can be seen as the product of the *less* constrained or rather unconstrained vision that was adopted by the Indian elites who came to power, especially the vision of India's first prime minister and architect of modern India, Jawaharlal Nehru and his Congress party. While a number of contending factions existed within the Congress party both prior to and immediately after independence, it was Nehru's unconstrained vision that won the day and launched India on its own peculiar version of socialism.[6]

Nehru, who was India's prime minister for the first seventeen years after independence and who was the architect of postindependence India's economic and social policies, was greatly influenced by the ideals of Fabian socialism during his student years at Cambridge and after. His participation in the International Conference Against Oppression and Imperialism in February 1927 left a deep impression on him. A subsequent visit to the Soviet Union in November that year during the tenth anniversary celebrations of the Bolshevik Revolution left him impressed by the achievements of the revolution. On his return to India he intensively studied Marxist thought and the Bolshevik Revolution, and wrote a series of articles on socialism and related topics, which formed the basis of his first book. A famous pamphlet called "Whither India?" which he wrote in the thirties, saw the future of India as an independent socialist state and praised Soviet socialism much as the British Fabian socialists, Sidney and Beatrice Webb (1938) and Nehru's own teacher Harold Laski (1935), had.

Nehru's fascination with and subsequent conversion to the unconstrained socialist vision can be seen from his addresses and writings following his return from the Soviet Union. On September 22, 1928, he told the All Bengal Students' Conference:

I wish to tell you that though personally I do not agree with many of the methods of the communists, and I am by no means sure to what extent communism can suit present conditions in India, I do believe in communism as an ideal for society. For essentially it is socialism, and socialism, I think, is the only way if the world is to escape disaster.[7]

Again, when Nehru became president of the Indian National Congress (the Congress party) at its Lahore session in 1929, he declared his bona fides:

I must frankly confess that I am a socialist and a republican and am no believer in kings and princes, or in the order which produces the modern kings of industry, who have greater power over the lives and fortunes of men than even the kings of old, and whose methods are as predatory as those of the old feudal aristocracy.[8]

In his presidential address to the Congress party in 1936, he spoke of the achievements of the Bolshevik Revolution in the following terms: "Everywhere conflicts grew, and a great depression overwhelmed the world and there was a progressive deterioration, everywhere except in the wideflung territories of the USSR, where, in marked contrast with the rest of the world, astonishing progress was made in every direction."[9] He went on to define the role that he envisaged for socialism in the following manner:

[There is] no way of ending the poverty, the vast unemployment, the degradation, and the subjection of the Indian people except through Socialism. . . . Socialism means the ending of private property, except in a restricted sense, and the replacement of the private profit system by a higher ideal of cooperative service. It means ultimately a change in our instincts and habits and desires. In short, it means a new civilization, radically different from the present capitalist order.[10]

Nehru was instrumental in the setting up of the National Planning Committee of the Congress party in December 1938, which adopted an avowedly socialist and interventionist economic philosophy that had a great impact on the economic regime established after independence. Nehru, as the chairman of the committee, presided over seventy-one meetings between December 1938 and September 1940, missing only one meeting. The committee reaffirmed the party's earlier commitment (in the form of the Karachi Resolution of 1931, also drafted mainly by Nehru) to state ownership of key industries and added services.

As a result of these steps taken by the Congress party spearheaded by Nehru, the National Planning Commission was set up in 1950 under the chairmanship of Nehru and the final version of the First Five-Year Plan in December 1952 contained the following important assertion:

Whether one thinks of the problems of capital formation or the introduction of new techniques or the extension of social services, or the realignment of productive forces and class relationships within society, one comes inevitably to the conclusion that a rapid expansion of the economic and social responsibilities of the State alone be capable of justifying the legitimate expectations of the people. . . . It does . . . mean a progressive widening of the public sector and the reorientation of the private sector to the needs of a planned economy.[11]

Thus, Nehru's unconstrained socialist vision began to increasingly dominate the official documents of the newly formed government. This vision was to now grow to become a more extreme unconstrained credo for both the Congress party and the government. For example, the ruling Congress party's convention in 1955 declared its national objective to be the establishment of "a socialistic pattern of society where the principal means of production are under social ownership and control."[12] Similarly, the government's 1956 Industrial Policy Resolution reiterated that:

The state will progressively assume a predominant and direct responsibility for setting up new industrial undertakings and for developing transport facilities. It will also undertake state trading on an increasing scale. . . . The adoption of the socialist pattern of society as the national objective, as well as the need for planned and rapid development, requires that all industries of a basic or strategic importance, or in the nature of public utility services, be in the public sector.[13]

This vision was implemented with the Second Five-Year Plan, or the "heavy industry" plan which was modeled on the Soviet five-year plans and placed a relative emphasis on the development of state-owned heavy industries and envisaged a dominant role for the public sector in the economy. The reservation of the "commanding heights" of the Indian economy for the public sector involved the exclusive or dominant investment of the state in twenty-five key industrial sectors and a 60:40 split between the public and private sectors in planned investment outlays. A complex and extensive maze of quantitative and price restrictions over every facet of economic activity—such as industrial licensing controls, price and distribution controls, import-export controls, foreign exchange controls, and the like—was introduced to control the private sector and make it conform to the planning system.

Nehru's socialist vision was explicitly incorporated into the Indian constitution by his daughter, Indira Gandhi, India's third prime minister. In 1976, during the "Emergency" period, when major provisions of the 1950 Constitution of India and the Indian Parliament were suspended by Mrs. Gandhi's government, the Congress party effected the infamous 42nd Amendment to the Constitution and changed the political description of the country in the country's preamble from a *Sovereign Democratic Republic* to a *Sovereign, Secular, Socialist Democratic Republic.*

The unconstrained vision of Nehru that has molded India's economic policy since independence can be best illustrated by his comments during an interview with a prominent Indian journalist in 1960:

We have accepted the socialist and cooperative approach. . . . We have adopted also the planned and scientific approach to economic development in preference to the old laissez faire school. We are therefore proceeding scientifically and methodically without leaving things to chance or fate. . . . *But subject to these factors, planning and development have become a sort of mathematical problem which may be worked out scientifically.*[14]

That Nehru's "scientistic" vision was in tune with the academic ethos at that time (at least among even prominent members of the American academy such as Leontief, Samuelson, and others) is borne out by these statements in the same interview: [15]

But, broadly speaking, planning for industrial development is generally accepted as a matter of mathematical formula. It is extraordinary how both Soviet and American experts agree on this. If a Russian planner comes here, studies our projects and advises us, it is really extraordinary how his conclusions are in agreement with those of—say,an American expert . . . the moment the scientist or technologist comes to the scene, be he Russian or American, the conclusions are the same for the simple reason that planning and development today are almost a matter of mathematics.[16]

In spite of this evidence of the depth and durability of Nehru's unconstrained socialist vision, he was also influenced by the liberal values of the West.[17] These liberal values acted as a constraint on his more extreme Fabian socialist views and created a curious ambivalence in him about the nature of political and economic good. This in turn led to the development of India's peculiar brand of socialism, where centrally directed planning of the public sector operated in a mixed economy with a substantial private sector and a democratic polity. To a large extent, this brand of "mixed economy" socialism was also the product of the previous long period of colonial rule which had made the political leaders, intelligentsia, and common citizen suspicious and distrustful of market-mediated institutions (though this was not a factor in other former colonies such as Singapore after they gained independence). The intellectuals and the economic ideas of the time were also greatly influenced by the alleged "failure" of capitalism during the Great Depression and the alleged "success" of the Soviet Union.

But the unconstrained vision of Nehru and the other socialist Congress leaders who ultimately won the battle for leadership of the party was instrumental in shaping the era of socialistic development planning that dominated economic and social policy after independence. Whatever the ultimate source (or sources) of this vision, its limitations were responsible for the poor economic performance, fragmented politics, and social strife that have developed and dominated daily life in the forty-five years since the country gained independence.

3. The Framework of Indian Development Planning

The planning framework that evolved in India, while heavily influenced by the Soviet planning system, differed substantially from the Soviet, Eastern European, or Chinese models. In these latter countries, planning operated in societies under totalitarian political control and in economies where the state owned the means of production without any significant private ownership. Planning was centralized and command-oriented. In India, with a large private sector and a democratic polity, planning could not be only by command and/or through state ownership of the major means of production. Consequently, an elaborate network of controls and regulations had to be set up within the context of a centrally directed planning framework for an enlarging public sector (and to the extent possible for influencing private-sector decisions).

The planning framework that was developed combined such central direction for the public sector with direct, discretionary, quantitative, nonmarket controls and regulations over the private sector, instead of indirect, rule-based, market-mediated transactions operating through the price mechanism as was largely the case in the Western, developed economies at that time. Such a planning framework had predictably disastrous but unintended consequences for efficiency, equity, and political viability, as pointed out by a whole generation of classical economists and by economists of the Austrian School.

The Planning Commission (set up in 1950) at the apex of the planning and control system was given the task of directing and controlling the process of resource generation and allocation. The basic decisions with which the Planning Commission was entrusted were

1. Determine the size of the investment (and savings) outlays.
2. Allocate the investment outlays among alternative uses, down to the product level.

3. Determine the choice of technology, extending to scale, expansion, direct import-export content, and the terms of foreign collaboration and know-how in association with other specialized government departments and agencies.

These formidable tasks were to be achieved within the framework of a mixed economy with a predominant private sector in a country of then 357 million citizens, the majority of whom (85 percent) lived in rural areas without adequate communication and transportation facilities. The main vehicle for the spelling out and transmission of these decisions was five-year plans developed by the Planning Commission and its associated ministries and agencies; short-term targets and implementation guidelines were to be detailed in annual planning documents and budgets.

There were ostensibly three major policy aims of postindependence government economic policy which were achieved through detailed policy interventions and controls. These were

1. To achieve the best possible allocation of investable resources while at the same time reducing the concentration of ownership of productive assets.
2. To raise the maximum of investable resources by way of taxation.
3. To provide essential consumer goods at low prices for the benefit of the poor, while keeping the prices of intermediate and capital goods down in order to stimulate investment and achieve a "low-cost" economy.

These contradictory and inadequately conceived objectives were to be achieved through a poorly paid government bureaucracy in a mixed economy with a dominant private sector and a democratic polity, and could only have led to poor economic performance under conditions of widespread corruption and rentseeking as had been warned by a prior generation of economists. They were implemented through a network of physical and financial controls which very soon became the source of corruption and rent-seeking activity.

In order to finance the planned developmental goals, increasing government efforts were directed at raising the proportion of savings and taxes to GNP. A multitude of policy instruments were designed and implemented to guide economic activity in directions congruent with the planning objectives and targets. The policy instruments were to comprehensively cover both the domestic and foreign sectors of economic activity. The domestic policy instruments mainly consisted of the following:

1. A comprehensive industrial licensing system.
2. Controls over the financial system (the culmination of these controls was the nationalization of the major private-sector banks and general insurance companies).
3. Capital market controls over monopoly houses and restrictive trade practices.
4. Price and distribution controls on agriculture, industry, and tertiary-sector activity.
5. Active encouragement of the public sector (particularly public-sector enterprises or PSEs) to dominate the "commanding heights" (critical sectors) of the economy while providing special preferences for "cottage, village and small" industries.

The successive Industrial Policy Resolutions (IPRs) provided the strategic framework for selectively applying these policy instruments to the industrial sector. Various ministries and governmental agencies at the central and state levels were entrusted with the task of refining, implementing, and monitoring the network of domestic controls.

The foreign-sector policy instruments were designed to support the domestic efforts and included the following:

1. Quantitative restrictions (QRs) for shielding domestic production automatically from foreign competition.
2. An intensive and extensive framework of import licensing policies and controls.
3. Foreign exchange restrictions and rationing.
4. Export control and promotion policies.

Thus, a wide variety of interlinking detailed controls and policy interventions were resorted to as instruments for implementing the strategy of planned development. These controls and interventions can be broadly grouped under domestic and foreign-sector interventions. While the nature of these controls has undergone considerable change in recent years with the programs of liberalization of 1985 and 1991, the major features of the controls and policy interventions that have existed through most of the postindependence period are discussed below.

4. Policy Interventions and Controls—A Detailed Discussion

Domestic controls and interventions in postindependence India have included a variety of controls such as industrial licensing, restrictions on capacity expansion, financial system and interest rate controls, price and distribution controls, labor market and employment controls, and controls on monopoly and restrictive trade practices.[18] Controls on agriculture and the tertiary services sectors constitute other major areas of regulation. Policy interventions include central allocation of major investments, encouragement of and preference for public-sector enterprises, industrial location policy and public-sector control over distribution of major commodities. While the controls have been modified over the years and there has been a move toward economic liberalization in recent years, the majority of the restrictions continue to apply for major sectors of the economy.

The most comprehensive set of capital market controls was related to the industrial licensing system.[19] Under this system, any investment in plant and machinery, structures or other capital equipment above a certain limit had to be approved by the government through various agencies and departments set up for this purpose. The policy aim of these controls was to regulate investment and the allocation of resources and provide preferences for cottage, village, and small industries which did not fall within the ambit of the licensing procedures.

The industrial licensing procedure as originally envisaged was found to be cumbersome and inefficient, sometimes taking years to deliver a decision.[20] Consequently, the government appointed a number of committees to review and streamline the procedures.[21] A number of industries were delicensed in the seventies and eighties (and some were subsequently relicensed) and expansions and diversifications up to 25 percent of existing capacity were permit-

ted following the 1986 liberalization till the most recent liberalization when all except eight "core" industries have been entirely
exempted from licensing. Unlimited expansion of capacity was
also permitted only in certain industries till the most recent liberalization did away with this provision entirely, permitting expansion as dictated by market considerations for the first time since
independence for the majority of industries.

The industrial licensing policy and system has been criticized
for stifling the economic growth of the country and for creating
unemployment, imbalances, and bottlenecks. On the other hand,
academicians and politicians on the left have criticized the policy
for favouring big business and increasing the degree of concentration of economic power. The major criticisms on efficiency and
distributive grounds can be summarized as

1. The licensing policy has been criticized for incorporating too
   many, often contradictory, objectives, for example, promoting
   industrial growth and efficiency but favoring small-scale and
   cottage industries; attempting to check the concentration of
   economic power while allowing the preemption of licensed capacity by large business houses; demanding export promotion
   and growth while progressively requiring (high-cost) import
   substitution, and so forth.
2. Multiplicity of overlapping controls and procedures leading to
   a proliferation of licensing agencies and inordinate time delays
   in clearances.
3. Absence of explicit criteria for evaluating license applications
   in terms of "social," as distinct from private, profitability and
   the consequent ad hoc criteria adopted in licensing approval.
   Bhagwati and Desai (1970, 255) for example, criticize "the absence of explicit economic criteria as also the weighting of
   different objectives, in the grant or rejection of industrial licenses [which] was matched, through the period by the generally poor quality of the "techno-economic" examination of proposed industrial investments which the DGTD was supposed
   to carry out in each case." The impossibility of developing
   "rational" criteria was evidenced throughout the postindepen-

dence period by the large number of committees that were set up to examine issues of industrial and import licensing.[22]

4. An overemphasis on "targeted" capacity and the sanctioning of such capacity without regard to technoeconomic or market viability. This had simultaneously resulted in the setting up of noneconomic units, the preemption or "foreclosure" of licensed capacity, and the nonrealization of large volumes of licensed capacities in certain areas. According to the Hazari Committee (1967) and the Dutt Committee (1969) this led to the perpetuation of monopolies in certain key sectors and the chronic shortage of "essential" commodities like fertilizer, aluminum, cement, mineral oils, and so forth. The deliberate preemption of capacity by the practice of making multiple applications in different names for the same item had been viewed by these committees as being helped and abetted by the lending policies of the public financial institutions, thus leveling the accusation of large business houses building private empires with public money.

5. The administrative exemptions and restrictions were without economic rationale. For example, the arbitrary exemption limits established (e.g., units under Rs 30 million investment being exempt) often interfered with the objectives and efficiency of the planning process itself as conceived by the authorities. This made the whole planning process self-contradictory. With regard to restrictions, the position was even worse. The severe restrictions on the manufacture of "new articles" effectively prevented innovation and efficiency and protected existing products excessively. The emphasis on administrative rules of allocation had a built-in bias against efficiency.

Under the rubric of capital market and interest rate controls, a number of specialized governmental development finance and other institutions were set up to provide concessional loans and other kinds of financial services to "priority" sectors. The most important institutions are the Industrial Finance Corporation of India (IFCI) set up in 1948, the National Industries Development Corporation of India (NIDCI) founded in 1954, the Industrial

Credit and Investment Corporation of India (ICICI) set up in 1956, and the Industrial Development Bank of India (IDBI) and Unit Trust of India (UTI), both set up in 1964. In addition, there are corporations for financing individual industries (small-scale industries, tea plantations, etc.). Beginning in 1951, each state has also set up its own industrial and investment corporations. In 1969, the largest twenty private-sector banks were nationalized and have since been regarded as a major instrument of state financial development effort and policy. These financial system interventions and controls have been used to target funds to chosen sectors. These interventions have made India's financial sector grossly inefficient and antiquated, and created a bureaucratic maze unresponsive to market needs.

Interest rate controls were implemented through the regulation of deposit and lending rates of the commercial banks. In addition, the rates of cooperative banks, public-sector financial institutions, and other types of financial institutions were also regulated. Interest rate ceilings applied selectively to certain classes of borrowers such as agriculture, small sector units, export units, and so on. Lending rates of commercial banks were controlled to certain maximums through most of the period, while ceilings on deposit rates were announced from time to time. Similarly, ceilings were imposed on company deposit rates depending on the period of deposit and public limited companies' rates of deposit. Besides this there were lending rate ceilings on export, small-scale industry, food procurement, and interbank loans.[23]

Price and distribution controls in India have been pervasive and are so even today after two major periods of liberalization. The Essential Commodities Act (1965) empowered the central government to control, regulate, or prohibit the production, distribution, transport, trade, consumption, or storage of a large number of commodities. All foodstuffs, principal raw materials, iron and steel products, consumer goods like paper, sugar, vegetable and mineral oils, textiles, and so forth, inputs like fertilizer, cement, and so on, and the import of industrial components have been under some kind of distribution controls throughout most of the postindependence period. The Act also empowered (but not necessarily enabled) the government to set prices and to take over stocks on conditions set by itself. A total of eighty-three control orders and enactments have been put on the statute-books by Parliament since 1947. There is a good deal of overlap between the provisions of the Essential Commodities Act and Section 18(g) of the Industrial Development and Regulation (IDR) Act (1951) which empowers the central government to regulate supply and distribution of trade and commerce in any article relating to a "scheduled" industry. Other goods such as cars, trucks, scooters, drugs and pharmaceuticals, have also been price controlled but have been distributed through nongovernmental channels. Prices were set by the Indian Tariff Commission so as to limit profits to 8–12 percent of invested capital for the representative firm for most of the period.

Distribution controls for consumer goods have been primarily applied by the establishment of a public distribution system for foodgrains and "essential" commodities such as kerosene, cooking oil, sugar. The system consists of government procurement agencies, storage and distribution agencies, and a vast urban network of Fair Price Shops (FPRs) operated by the private trade but with government control and monitoring. The distribution controls vary from product to product and include restrictions on interregional movements, purchase and processing restrictions, and a ban on certain kinds of trading such as (till recently) forward markets in a number of commodities. The distribution controls have been most often combined with a system of formal statutory rationing for all the urban centres (in the latter sixties, for example) and a system of informal rationing in rural areas. Unproductive rent-seeking activity and corruption have been the rule rather than the exception. Capture of the regulators by the regulated and black-market activity has been widely prevalent.[24] A common practice is to secure allocations of the controlled commodity on some pretext and to resell the item on the open (or black) market at a substantial premium.

No comprehensive formal system of controls exists in the labor market. However, minimum wage laws have been enacted in urban areas though these are largely inoperative due to the over-abundant supply of labor and the impossibility of effectively policing the large rural and informal labor market. The only major area of labor market intervention is in the public sector. Government employees on the average receive significantly higher wages than those in comparable jobs in the private sector. The discrepancy in wages is the source of considerable rent-seeking behavior aimed at obtaining government jobs through investment in human capital and other unproductive means.[25] Another area of policy intervention in labor markets is the area reservation of a certain percentage (often, a majority) of jobs for identified groups in Indian society.

In addition, Indian labor law has been patterned on post-depression era British labor law and is extremely pro worker. It is virtually impossible to close down a failing business and the majority of court decisions go against the employer. As a result, industrywide unions in banking, finance, and the industrial and service sectors can paralyze whole sectors of the economy, with no recourse for employers.

An important area of labor market control is in regard to the appointment and remuneration of managerial personnel under the Companies Act (1956) amended from time to time. Restrictions cover the nature of appointments that can be made and their approval, the number of directorships an individual may hold, and limits on managerial remuneration. These provisions have led to some very creative ways of remunerating and appointing top company personnel. The provisions have also been alleged to have caused the departure of quality managers abroad to more remunerative and less restrictive environments.

Social policies and controls have included the active legislation and implementation of preferential policies for targeted local majorities and national "backward" minorities, much more comprehensive and detailed than similar "affirmative action" policies in the United States Dirigiste labor-market and employment policies, and government control over the broadcast media and educational and social policy, have gone hand-in-hand with the unrestrained growth of a bureaucratic, redistributive state and a national policy focused on "the uplift and social betterment of the weaker sections of society." These policies have been the source of considerable social strife, communal and caste unrest, and political protests and violence.

Controls on monopolies, large business, and "restrictive trade practices" are exercised under the Monopolies and Restrictive Trade Practices (MRTP) Act (1969), under the aegis of the Monopolies Commission.[26] The major thrust of these controls is to limit the "concentration of economic power" and prevent monopolistic and restrictive practices as functions of such concentration. The controls have been implemented through the regulation of investment by large industrial houses. The intent of these controls has been the denial of new licenses to large firms and the setting up of public-sector capacity or uneconomic small capacity in areas where economies of scale and large economic size are technoeconomic prerequisites (e.g., cement, fertilizers, paper, heavy engineering). The provisions of the Act have paradoxically often provided a preemptive barrier for large industrial houses to monopolize certain industries by setting up capacity in key areas while simultaneously being the source of considerable rent-seeking activity. (As already mentioned, the restrictions have been circumvented by other means, like preemption of capacity by "shell" corporations.)

On the other hand, the MRTP Act has been claimed to have not stood in the way of investment and industrial progress because its provisions apply to only about 10 percent of the industrial license cases.[27] However, since the majority of these cases are in key sectors of the economy and involve large investments and capacities, the effect has been considerably greater than envisaged. Even though the government has in recent years granted licenses to large firms in selective areas and has revised the list of industries covered, the deterrence and inefficiency effects of the provisions of the MRTP Act have been considerable.

Controls on the external sector of the economy include quantitative restrictions (QRs) mainly in the form of an elaborate import-licensing system and the use of prohibitive tariffs.[28] A number of restrictions on foreign investment have also shielded domestic production for a major part of the postindependence period. Throughout this period an elaborate exchange policy regime has been in place which, along with the import controls, has been aimed at comprehensive, direct control over foreign exchange utilization. Export policy, on the other hand, has grown from a position of almost complete neglect in the early fifties to one of escalating subsidization, proliferating incentive schemes, and increasing direct government promotion and involvement.

The most important and deleterious of the external-sector controls is the system of import licensing. These controls are both comprehensive and complex, and have the following harmful general objectives:

1. To allocate "scarce" foreign exchange to various users in order to meet the input requirements of priority sectors.
2. To enable progressive import substitution in order to reduce the deficits on the balance of payments over a few years.
3. To enable domestic industry to grow to the exclusion of competition from foreign industries.

Items for which licenses were issued have been subject to different degrees of restrictions and different forms of licensing. The variety of categories have included Open General Licenses (OGLs), Actual User (AU) licences, Replenishment licences (REPs), restricted items, banned items, items subject to quota for "established importers" and even "free licensed" items. Till recently, there were sixteen main types of licences, with various subcategories to cater to the specific requirements of each type of importer. Each type of licence was governed by a different set of procedures and carried its own list of items, each subject to different forms of restrictions.

The form and degree of these quite extraordinary restrictions also changed frequently over time. Categories were changed without any clear economic rationale and often created conflicts with other license categories and items. Economists, administrators, and committees appointed by the government have pointed out the following adverse effects of the import-licensing system:[29]

1. Inordinate procedural delays.
2. Multiplicity of agencies and lack of coordination.
3. High administrative and other costs.
4. Inflexibility in policies and procedures.
5. Discrimination against small entrepreneurs.
6. Inherent bias in favor of industries based on imported rather than domestic inputs.

7. Pervasive rent-seeking activity and corruption.
8. Absence of market competition for protected industries.
9. Anticipatory and automatic protection given to certain industries regardless of costs.
10. Discrimination against exports vis-à-vis domestic sales and consequent loss of revenue and foreign exchange.
11. Encouragement of the indiscriminate growth of noneconomic industries on the basis of import substitution.
12. Adverse distributional effects of administrative allocation.
13. Loss of government revenues.

Two prominent economists, Bhagwati and Srinivasan (1975), have pointed out the kinds of economic costs and inefficiencies involved as follows:

> The elaborate bureaucratic machinery for operating the licensing mechanisms involved direct costs as also the costs resulting from the necessity for actual and potential entrepreneurs to maintain elaborate and frequent "contacts" with the licensing authorities. Admittedly, alternative allocation mechanisms also must necessitate "administrative" and information gathering costs. But the specific type of "command" mechanism involved in the Indian QR and industrial licensing regimes added to these costs by making necessary expenditures to ensure "file-pushing" by bribe-seeking bureaucrats at lower levels, for example. . . . And if we could only disentangle (as we cannot) the job expansion in the bureaucracy which has resulted from the licensing machinery, much of the enormous expansion on current governmental expenditures during 1956–71 may turn out to be a net cost of the regime.[30]

A number of state trading or "canalization" agencies have also been set up as an important element of the external trading system. There were until recently close to twenty-five canalization agencies which together handled over two hundred products. The products handled by these agencies included steel, petroleum products, fertilizer, cement, metals and minerals, pharmaceuticals, chemicals, electronics, film, newsprint and silk and cotton. The major canalization agencies included the State Trading Corporation, the Mines and Minerals Trading Corporation and the Handlooms and Handicrafts Corporation. A considerable amount of rent-seeking activity in the area of external trade involved private- and public-sector agencies seeking the rents allocated by other government agencies.

A protective tariff system operated concurrently with the import-licensing system. Tariff rates range up to 450 percent, with around 40 percent of imports having tariffs imposed on them of between 75 and 120 percent. The Alexander Committee (1978) analyzed 626 restricted items and found that 252 of them received a "high" degree of protection, both through the licensing system and the tariff system assuming that tariff rates above 100 percent implied a high degree of tariff protection; 230 items were subject to less rigorous licensing controls and tariff levels below 100 percent; while 39 items had either rigorous import controls or "high" tariff levels above 100 percent.

In recent years, a number of relaxations in the import control policies and procedures have been attempted with the improvement in India's foreign exchange reserve position. A number of items have been delicensed up to a certain limit, irrespective of indigenous availability. Export-oriented industries have been given special import clearance exemptions and incentives. Procedures have been simplified and even eliminated in a few cases. However, an extensive framework of controls continues to exist, considerably hampering the efficient operation of economic activity and providing scope for extensive rent-seeking activity and corruption. The extent of rent-seeking activity in the area of import policies and procedures has been on a massive scale. In spite of the high duties and quantitative restrictions, it is more profitable to import commodities and market them in India on the black market than to produce and sell the same good in the country. A number of governmental committees have analyzed and detailed the types of malpractices resorted to in the import-export trade.[31] These include smuggling, imports of prohibited items, imports through bogus firms' licenses, underinvoicing and overinvoicing practices, and trafficking in licenses. The most widespread illegal practice has been the profiteering on import licenses. Data obtained by the author from trade sources indicate that premiums on import licenses varied from 20 percent to 500 percent of the value of goods during the period 1958 to 1982.[32] It has been estimated that in the sixties approximately Rs 5,500 million ($550 million) worth of import licenses were annually available in the black market.[33] Krueger (1974) estimated the value of rents for imports to be around Rs 10,271 million (about $1,000 million) in 1964.

Till the recent policy change making the Indian rupee partially convertible, the exchange rate policy regime in India was, along with the QR and tariff regimes, explicitly directed at control over the utilization of foreign exchange and its "conservation." The Foreign Exchange Regulation Act (FERA) of 1947 stated that "it is expedient in the economic and financial interests of India to provide for the regulation of certain payments, dealings in foreign exchange and the import and export of currency and bullion." The Act empowered the Reserve Bank of India (RBI) to secure foreign exchange transactions by recording, controlling, and channeling all such transactions. The central government was empowered to set and change the rules for the RBI to act upon.

The permission of the RBI was till very recently required for all investment made abroad by Indian residents as well as for investment in India by nonresidents. Recent regulations with regard to Non-Resident Indians (NRIs) and relaxed rules for foreign ownership of stocks listed on the stock exchange have however considerably relaxed a number of restrictions, resulting in a flood of such investment by NRIs and foreigners. The Foreign Investment Board (FIB) was the single agency within the government to deal with all matters relating to foreign investment and collaboration. Foreign participation in certain consumer goods industries was completely banned till recently. There were policies controlling the list of industries where foreign collaboration was permitted and where no foreign participation was permitted. Transfer of some kinds of securities or creating any interest in a security in favor of a nonresident, as well as issuing an Indian security to a nonresident required Reserve Bank approval.

Other general provisions of the Act included

1. No person resident in India, other than an "authorized dealer," can buy or otherwise acquire any foreign exchange except with the permission of the RBI. This provision however does not apply to NRIs and their foreign exchange accounts.
2. An Indian company cannot, except with the permission of the RBI, open an account in foreign countries.

3. A company resident in India cannot make any payment to a nonresident out of the money held by it abroad excepting in a case where the account was in existence prior to 1947.
4. All business and vacation travel outside India requires approval of the RBI on release of foreign exchange for such travel. In addition, there are ceilings to the amounts that can be taken abroad.

All these provisions of FERA resulted in a thriving black market for foreign exchange.[34] Foreign exchange could be easily purchased or sold on the black market in any major city or town. The scale of illegal practices involving foreign exchange can be judged by the Finance Ministry's finding that during 1964–65 14,300 violations of the foreign exchange rules were detected, as against 5,192 in 1959–60.[35] Considering that only a small percentage of the actual violations is actually detected, the practice must have been rife.

Policy intervention on the export side of the external sector involved controls and bans on the export of certain items, along with export incentives for other products. Both types of intervention generated rent-seeking activity and have been attributed by various economists and committees as being the source of illegal activity.[36]

The executive authority for export control was vested in the Office of the Chief Controller of Imports and Exports (CCI&E). The list of items subject to export control consisted of those considered "essential" for domestic consumption, many of which were in short supply due to price and other domestic controls. Items completely banned included certain oil seeds, paraffin wax, poultry, and sugarcane. However, the restrictions on other items such as gold, silver, minerals, have been quite onerous and the continual changes can make export planning difficult.

Starting from the years of neglect of export promotion in the First and Second Plan Periods (1951–61), the government embarked on a policy of escalating subsidization and export encouragement and participation.[37] Export subsidization policies essentially took two major forms, (1) fiscal measures and (2) import entitlement schemes which entitled exporters to premium-carrying import licenses. Other promotional activities adopted included the setting up of various trade development agencies and bodies as well as budgetary appropriations for market development, with the intent of indirectly raising the profitability of foreign sales to domestic traders and producers.

Among the major fiscal measures adopted for export promotion were cash subsidies, excise and customs duty drawbacks on inputs, sales tax exemptions on final sales, direct tax concessions, other outright subsidies, and rail freight concessions.[38] Other indirect incentives included cheap export-credit facilities through the Export Credit Guarantee Corporation, the supply of raw materials at international prices, and tax holidays and investment rebates to export-oriented units. The scope and coverage of these export incentive schemes continued to expand, and in 1982–83 and 1983–84 new incentives were awarded to both export houses and to what were called "100 percent export-oriented-units." A five-year tax holiday was also granted to such units.

Import replenishment schemes through REP licenses were the principal instruments of export promotion. These licenses attracted high import premiums pro-rata to the value of exports effected.[39] The import entitlement schemes, unlike the simpler exchange retention schemes of countries like Pakistan, were complicated by the wide variety of entitlement rates, the segmentation of the market to prevent the transfer of REP licenses, the differences in premiums on entitlements and their fluctuations over time, the widespread overinvoicing of exports, and frequent changes in coverage of the entitlement schemes.

The government has set up a number of agencies and entities for export promotion such as the Market Development Fund (1963) for grants-in-aid to the various Export Promotion Councils; the Market Development Assistance Committee; the Export Credit Guarantee Corporation (ECGC); the RBI's Standing Committee on Export Finance and the Export Credit Cell; the Export Houses Scheme for providing incentives to registered Export Houses; the Trade Development Authority (TDA); and various Commodity Boards like the Tea Board, the Coffee Board, and the Tobacco

Board. The public-sector corporations were also directed to export a certain percentage of their output under various promotion schemes.

5. Economic Performance

India's system of centrally directed five-year planning and regime of comprehensive controls generated a growth rate of per capita income of only around 1.7 percent over the 1950–85 period when the planning and control framework was operative (see table 1). This "Hindu rate of growth" (as the well-known Indian economist Raj Krishna called it) is to be compared with annual per capita real income growth rates of 5.5–6.5 percent that were achieved in the market-oriented economies of Hong Kong, South Korea, Singapore, and Taiwan over the same period. The three Southeast Asian nations of Indonesia, Malaysia, and Thailand also averaged per capita annual growth rates in real income of 3–4 percent over this period. Thus, India's economic performance over most of the postindependence era has been dismal, both relatively and absolutely.

With almost 40 percent of Indians living below the official poverty line and per capita income around $300 after almost forty-five years of centrally planned economic development, India remains one of the poorest nations in the world. In 1987, life expectancy at birth was 59 years, the literacy rate was 43 percent, and it was estimated that less than 60 percent and 10 percent of the population had access to safe drinking water and sanitation facilities, respectively.[40]

Over twenty million Indians are on the public payroll, with around 70 percent of all organized sector employment in the public sector. The government's wage bill in 1990 was estimated to account for two-thirds of its annual revenue budget. Over the last forty years, the public sector has accounted for around 60 percent of total investment. India's jungle of red tape is said to be one of the largest and most complex in the world. For example, permission to open a hotel involves around forty-five applications which are reviewed by over twenty-five different governmental agencies. Till very recently, it took anywhere from twenty-seven to sixty-

Table 1. Annual Growth Rates of GNP and Per Capita
NNP—India (1951–1990)

Period	Real GNP (percentage)	Real NNP per capita (percentage)
First Plan	3.6	(−)1.7
(1951–55)		
Second Plan	4.0	1.9
(1956–61)		
Third Plan	2.5	0
(1961–66)		
Annual Plans	4.1	1.8
(1966–69)		
Fourth Plan	3.5	1.1
(1969–74)		
Fifth Plan		
(1974–79)	5.2	2.9
1974–75	1.2	(−)0.7
1975–76	9.6	7.3
1976–77	0.9	(−)1.5
1977–78	8.7	6.5
1978–79	5.9	3.2
Annual Plan		
(1979–80)	(−)5.1	(−)7.7
Sixth Plan		
(1980–1985)		
1980–81	7.7	5.4
1981–82	4.6	2.2
1982–83	1.7	(−)0.5
1983–84	7.4	5.2
1984–85	3.9	1.5
Seventh Plan		
(1985–1990)		
1985–86	5.1	2.8
1986–87	3.9	1.6
1987–88	3.6	1.4
1988–89	9.0	6.8
1989–90	5.3	3.3

Source: Government of India, *Economic Survey* (various years).

three months to obtain government clearance for any medium- or large-sized private-sector industrial project.[41]

Confiscatory tax rates, combined with ever-escalating controls in the 1960s, led to the growth of one of the largest and most thriving underground economies in the world, with around 50 percent of economic activity estimated to be generated in this sector.[42] Corruption and rent-seeking activity pervade every facet of daily life.

The result of India's statist development policies has been the neglect and systematic suppression of voluntary exchange and market activity. Even though the law formally upholds private property and India is the world's largest functioning democracy, private property rights and private voluntary activity are severely attenuated and circumscribed.[43]

India's agricultural sector, which is the least regulated and has been characterized by predominantly private property rights, has grown by about 3 percent per year in the 1950–85 period. This represents a substantial improvement over the preindependence period and is largely responsible for the improvement in the over-all growth rate as compared to that period since the growth rate of industry has remained unchanged over the two periods. Even in agriculture however, the per capita increase has been a mere 1 percent per year and may be attributed to the one-sided forced focus on planned (mainly public-sector) industrialization and the regime of price, procurement, and distribution controls imposed on agriculture by the government.

Yet, and perhaps as a consequence, agriculture dominates the economy, accounting for about one-third of the gross domestic product and about 70 percent of the total labor force, with over half the people living in the rural areas falling below the official poverty line. However, improvements in agriculture have made the country self-sufficient in food, though the distribution of this food supply has most often been quite unequal.[44]

The system of controls in agriculture has nevertheless led to substantial distortions and the coalescence of powerful interest groups. Price and distribution controls have led to the widespread diversion of controlled supplies to the black market, with the consequent generation of "black" incomes and corruption. Agencies like the Coffee Board, the Rubber Board, and the Tea Board. have been set up ostensibly to promote exports and the development of these commodities, but instead act as production and marketing boards to control and regulate their activities. Regulation has been captured by the regulated groups in commodities like wheat, sugar, rice, and milk, and black-market activity is still widely prevalent in many commodities. Vested rural interests in the form of "sugar baron" or "milk baron" politicians have garnered political control and economic benefits out of proportion with their participation in the real economic activity of the country.[45]

The result of India's centrally directed industrialization policy has been the growth of a highly protected and inefficient industrial base which has made India a high-cost economy unable to grow fast domestically and in the international economy. Indian exports as a percentage of gross domestic product decreased from around 8 percent in 1947 to 7 percent in 1985, while India's share of world exports fell from around 2.5 percent to 0.4 percent over the same period. They grew at a rate considerably below the rate of expansion of world trade and much below that of other countries in Asia such as Japan, Korea, Taiwan, Thailand, Indonesia, Singapore, and Hong Kong.

Centrally planned industrialization also led to the growth of a large and inefficient public sector, which absorbed the major share of capital investment in the postindependence period but produced an abysmally low and sometimes negative rate of return. By 1979, the gross fixed assets of the central government public sector excluding the joint public-private sector—public-sector companies owned by the individual states comprising the union and the assets of the central and state-owned railways and public utilities—exceeded that of the private sector in industry by over 16 percent. The inefficiency of these public-sector industries can be seen by the fact that they accounted for 66 percent of total capital and 27 percent of total employment, but only 25 percent of industrial output and total value-added.[46] This situation existed despite the fact that the public sector had a near monopoly in production in industries like oil production and distribution, power generation, rail and air transport, coal mining, certain minerals and metals, life and general insurance and banking. In 1980–81, the top 157 out of India's 215 public-sector companies (including the always profitable oil companies, but excluding companies which by virtue of large cumulative losses had negative total capital employed) made an overall loss of around $160 million on a total capital employed of over $20 billion.[47] In 1984–85, India's public sector (except for the oil companies) still made an overall loss of over $160 million, with the most disastrously unprofitable areas being coal and textiles. The National Textile Corporation (with some 145 'sick' textile mills taken over from the private sector) had accumulated losses of $576 million in 1985. Worse, in many areas such as power generation, chronic shortages coexist with massive investment because of a woeful underutilization of capacity.

Economic liberalization in the mid-eighties under Prime Minister Rajiv Gandhi (Nehru's grandson) resulted in a spurt in per capita economic growth to around 3.5–5 percent per annum over the 1986–90 period. India's Seventh Five-Year Plan, which ended in March 1990, achieved an annual average growth rate in real GNP of 5.25 percent, in spite of farming suffering the consequences of three consecutive years of drought in 1985–87. The annual growth of industrial output averaged around 8.5 percent during this period.

This unprecedented economic performance was made possible by the relaxation of controls on the private sector and the considerable liberalization that took place in industry, foreign trade, and the financial sector. Private investment flows were allowed largely unimpeded into previously tightly controlled consumer goods industries and licensing controls were significantly altered to allow greater competition in these sectors. A large amount of investment went into automobiles, motorcycles, television sets, other consumer electronics industries, home appliances, an improved telephone system, processed foods, and a number of other consumer goods that were previously in short supply, unavailable, or had to be smuggled into the country.

But, in spite of the liberalization by the Gandhi government, the majority of controls and the centralized framework of planning were allowed to remain. Intervention in markets, the continued growth of the public sector, and the restriction of private property rights and voluntary exchange in a number of areas continued to limit the potential for economic growth. The statist economic policies of the previous forty-five years finally came to a head during the Gulf War. Despite the 'Gandhi' liberalization of the mid-eighties, the mounting budget deficits of successive spendthrift Indian governments, the maintenance of the framework of 'socialist' planning and onerous controls, and the continuing abysmal performance of the dominant public sector led to a situation where the foreign exchange reserves of the impoverished nation had dwindled to less than a couple of months' requirements by mid-1990 and to about one billion dollars by May 1991, just enough to cover about two weeks' imports. The foreign debt of the nation rose to over $75 billion and the robust economic growth of the late eighties seemed to skid back to the old 'Hindu rate of growth' in the early nineties.

The new government that was elected in June 1991, after securing emergency international assistance, set in motion a rapid and hitherto unprecedented package of economic reforms. Given the critical domestic and international situation of the country's finances, a stabilization program was embarked upon to reduce the central government's ballooning budget deficit and the current account deficit which had reached unfinanceable levels of around eight to nine billion dollars. With regard to the domestic fiscal crisis, policy and spending changes were made to reduce the budget deficit, a major factor in the long-term worsening of the balance of payments, from 8.5 percent of GDP in 1990–91 to 6.5 percent in 1991–92. With regard to the external sector, the adjustment package consisted of a steep devaluation of the rupee and the squeezing of imports through stringent import-financing requirements (except for imports used in export production). These elements of the reform program were conventional in that they did not involve any change in the institutional structure of the economy.

The more important elements of the reform package consisted of a set of institutional changes which marked a fundamental shift toward a market-driven and open economy. The industrial licensing system that had long shackled private Indian industry was all but scrapped, except for eighteen "critical" industries, including absurdly sugar, automobiles, and drugs and pharmaceuticals. Constraints on capacity expansion that were introduced in the sixties to check concentration in Indian industry and to slow the growth of the "monopoly" large Indian industrial houses were also all but scrapped. In addition, as compared to the scores of business areas that were previously reserved exclusively for government-owned enterprises, only eight such sectors are reserved for the public sector now. Even this amounts to eight too many, but constitutes some progress. Also, price controls on a number of items such as steel have been removed.

Most encouraging of all, the government has announced its intention to make the rupee fully convertible within three to five years (most observers of Indian economic affairs expect this to happen much sooner). As a first step, 60 percent of any deal involving foreign exchange can be made at a market rate, the remaining 40 percent being consummated at the official fixed rate. In addition, rules on foreign investment, hitherto some of the most discouraging anywhere, have been relaxed. Majority foreign equity participation is now permitted, albeit only for companies whose export growth exceeds future profit remittances expected. Foreign companies are also permitted to purchase property, use their own brand names, open branch offices, and accept deposits with minimal extradomestic requirements—things hitherto not possible. Even more recently, foreign institutional investors were permitted to purchase up to 25 percent of the shares of a company, as long as no single foreign investor held more than 5 percent of a company's outstanding shares.

With regard to the foreign trade sector, the quantitative import controls that excluded most goods unless large bribes were paid, have been almost completely done away with—except for consumer goods. But the import tariff system still exists, though tariff rates have been lowered. For example, the top tariff rate for consumer goods has come down from 150 percent to 110 percent, while that for capital goods has come down from 80 percent to 60 percent.

In addition, the government has in principle announced its intent to sell 49 percent of its share in government-owned companies to the public, though the implementation of this intent is yet to materialize. Privatization of the huge public sector, so essential if the economic reforms are to succeed, is likely to represent the biggest problem in the economic reform program since it will pose a big threat to the entrenched special-interest groups that dominate the politico-economic arena.

The limited economic reform program that has been acted upon has had some encouraging short-term results. The trade deficit in 1991–92 shrank to one-third its 1990–91 level, mainly due to a sharply reduced import bill. The lower trade deficit, combined with quick disbursing loans from the IMF and the World Bank and a turnaround on the capital account due to the return of the private money deposits of overseas Indians (estimated at $50 million every day) which had drained out of the country in 1990–91, have led to a large improvement in foreign exchange reserves to the healthy amount of $6.5 billion by the end of April. Most importantly, the fear of a major debt rescheduling, which seemed inevitable in 1991, has faded. Encouraged by the improved external financial situation, the import financing controls introduced last year have been relaxed.

The limited but radical economic reforms that have been introduced have, however, created some short-term problems and are likely to face some major problems in the longer term. The slow pace of reforms, especially in their implementation, are likely to create a situation similar to that faced by Gorbachev's Soviet Union and the countries of Eastern Europe.

The problem with the current reforms is that, even though they are radical as compared to the policies of the last forty-five years, they are neither comprehensive nor complete. While they represent a significant overthrow of the ideology of central planning and Nehruvian socialism, they still fail to effect the radical institutional surgery that is necessary for them to succeed.

The reforms that have been implemented till now have been politically easy since they have not posed a real threat to the special-interest groups that have been the legacy of the statist ethos that has dominated the country since it became independent. The accumulated rents that have accrued and continue to accrue to the most powerful interest groups have not yet been seriously threatened. While major elements of the "permit-licence raj" have been jettisoned, the privileges and protections of the major interest groups in society—politicians, bureaucrats, union leaders and members, public-sector employees, selected business groups, farmers and agriculturists, and so forth—remain intact.

Most fundamentally, while various dimensions of property rights have been taken out of the political commons because of the dimantling of some of the domestic and external-sector controls mentioned above, private property rights are still not guaranteed or protected from government encroachment. The heavy hand of government is still present in the regulation of the sale of private homes and commercial property; purchase and sale of land; the ownership of many kinds of private property; price and distribution controls for commodities such as sugar, oil, kerosene, gasoline, certain categories of cereals; and the distribution of "critical" commodities like steel, fertilizers, and foodgrains.

A major area where private property rights are still in the political (and state) domain is in the massive and inefficient public sector. Despite the talk of privatization, not a single major public-sector or state-sector undertaking has been privatized. Only "partial privatization" of selected public-sector undertakings is envisaged, with no fundamental privatization in terms of complete sale to private-sector companies interested in purchasing the companies or outright purchase of all the shares by the public. This is so despite the fact that a recent survey of 233 of the better run central public-sector undertakings found that their return on equity in 1989–90 averaged just 0.9 percent.[48]

Although the licensing and foreign trade controls as well as a whole ministry have been abolished, not a single bureaucrat or public-sector employee has lost his or her job. The most inefficient government enterprises and departments continue to hold steady or grow in employment. And the stronger the union in a state industry, the greater the government subsidy to prop up the industry without any attempt to reduce its size.

Another major area in which state ownership and the old controls and regulations continue to maintain their stranglehold is in the area of the country's banking and financial system. The state-owned banks and insurance companies, which were nationalized in the late sixties and early seventies, account for over 90 percent of the debt finance and insurance coverage in the organized sector and no attempt has been made to return them to the private sector. State-owned banks employ just under a million people, who are represented by militant bank unions which push up wages and resist any measures to improve productivity. A gamut of central government and state government specialized financial institutions own the major share of private companies and act to retard the entrepreneurial policies of these companies.

The government's tax policies, despite a drastic reduction in marginal tax rates under previous Prime Minister Rajiv Gandhi, still remain onerous and a drag on industrial efficiency because the excise and import tax regime and machinery still remain in place. These taxes account for almost 80 percent of the government's revenue and have been very resilient to attempts to reduce or rationalize them, reflecting politicians' and bureaucrats' desires for revenues.

Last but not least, the onerous and nihilistic Nehruvian planning system and the five-year plans remain in place. The Planning Commission in New Delhi continues to set targets for public investment and plan allocations for various sectors, based on an impossible mandate. This is being done despite the fact that planned economic development has failed in every country where it has been tried and has proven unable to raise the standard of living of Indian citizens.

6. A Theoretical Critique of Indian Development Planning

The discussion above has detailed the failure of Indian development planning in the postindependence era. Yet, this dismal development record has been defended by a number of wellknown economists on a variety of grounds.[49] Consequently, it is necessary to show why Indian development planning was doomed to fail on epistemological and theoretical grounds, and the experience of forty-five years was not needed to manifest its failure.

The major contention made by both the critics and supporters of Indian development planning is that its failures can be attributed to either the selection of the wrong instruments and policies for planning and control (such as the licensing system or the foreign trade policy regime) or to administrative or political failure in ensuring proper implementation.[50] The more enlightened critics, such as Shenoy (1971), Roy (1984), and Lal (1988a, 1988b), have focused on the role of dirigisme and statism, correctly arguing that it was the eschewal of market mechanisms in favor of nonmarket policies and instruments, and the consequent distortions of incentives, that led to the failure of Indian development planning. They have not attempted to adequately detail the fundamental epistemological and theoretical considerations that have resulted in this failure. This section briefly sketches out these considerations.

Indian development planning has failed for fundamental reasons that have to do with what Hayek (1937, 1945) has called the knowledge problem, the attempt to do away with the complex of legal and economic institutions (such as the institution of private property and the price mechanism) that enable the achievement of a solution to this fundamental problem and the stifling of the role of entrepreneurship in the context of market processes that is the source of wealth and prosperity. Only secondarily is the failure due to government failure and public choice considerations, which, though important, are found to crucially depend on the first three considerations.

An Information and Knowledge Critique of Indian Planning

The fundamental economic problem of any society is what Hayek (1945) has characterized as the problem of knowledge. The major portion of human knowledge, especially economic knowledge, consists of knowledge of a particular time and place known to the myriad individual economic actors in society. Such knowledge is widely dispersed in society and unknowable to a single mind or group of minds (even, and especially so, in the age of high-speed microcomputers). Consequently, any attempt to comprehensively plan or micro-manage a complex, modern economy (or for that matter a backward, as-yet-underdeveloped economy) is doomed to fail since the coordination of plans and actions of individual economic actors, each possessed with dispersed knowledge of time and place that cannot be communicated to any centralized or decentralized authority, by such a centralized or decentralized planning agency is theoretically and practically impossible. The knowledge problem is the contention that a central or decentralized planning agency, even with the best of intentions, would lack the knowledge to coordinate and combine resources in a manner economic enough to sustain a functioning economy.[51]

It is only through the price system in a private property, free-market economy that information relevant to their own decisions is communicated to the individuals in a large society. Only prices in freely functioning markets can play the role of coordinating the plans and actions of individuals in any economy, since prices provide an adaptive mechanism by which changing wants and conditions are communicated to these individuals in an economizing manner. Thus, it is the market and the price mechanism that provide the discovery procedure which makes possible the utilization of the dispersed knowledge of time and place better than any other mechanism or system known to man. It is the price mechanism in a market economy that provides the incentives for individuals in a society to constantly strive to discover new information necessary for adaptation, survival, and growth in the face of ever-changing circumstances facing that society.

Nehru and the other architects of India's development planning system never cared to educate themselves or understand the knowledge problem. In actual fact, most of them were ignorant of the literature on the problem, as were most economists in the developed market economies at that time.[52] By opting for comprehensive development planning, they in fact attempted to overcome the problem of knowledge through government direction and control, and by replacing market prices and incentives with government-formulated plans and directives. This was entirely consistent with their unconstrained vision of economic and social processes. By so doing, they eliminated or attenuated the very means of communication and coordination which made the functioning and growth of an economy possible. In any case, the knowledge necessary to make the millions of economic decisions that are made individually by the Indian population was impossible to collect or act upon, especially since most of this knowledge was tacit or inarticulate.[53] The Planning Commission of India embarked on an impossible task and its plans were doomed to fail from the start, just as planning in the Soviet Union, China, Eastern Europe, Africa, Latin America, and even in ostensibly capitalist countries such as South Korea, France, and Japan did.

The impossibility of centralized economic planning and market socialism had earlier also been clearly pointed out by its opponents during the celebrated socialist calculation debate of the 1930s.[54] The major focus of these earlier criticisms of socialist planning had been that by doing away with the rivalrous competitive process for which private property and free-market prices were essential, such planning would lose the very anchor which made economic life sustainable and growing. The situation was analogous for development planning even in the presence of partial private property, since the rivalrous process would be severely attenuated.

The conceptual, administrative, and implementational failures of Indian development planning lamented by both proponents and opponents of such planning identified above can be traced to the existence of the knowledge problem. No Indian planner or bureaucrat could either theoretically or in practice ever have been able to collect, collate, analyze, and act upon the dispersed knowledge of time and place possessed by the millions of economic actors then living in Indian society. Even if some magical mechanism had been made available (clearly a fiction) for such information to be made available, the tacit and inarticulate knowledge possessed by individuals could never have been so conveyed.

Further, by setting up the elaborate planning and control system of postindependence India, Indian planners did away with any rivalrous competitive process that might have flourished had an alternative market-based voluntary exchange system been adopted. By constraining and severly restricting voluntary exchange, Indian development planning undermined the very mechanism that was the basis for wealth-generation and doomed India to the "Hindu rate of growth."

A Property Rights Critique of Indian Planning

By encouraging and effecting the growth of government and public property ownership, Indian development planning contributed to the erosion of private property rights so indispensable for economic development. As has been shown by legions of economists since Adam Smith, private property is essential for a functioning economy.[55] The most important link is with the knowledge problem outlined above. There can be no coordination of the dispersed knowledge of time and place without the existence of a free-market price system based on private property.

Private property rights emerged as a consequence of trying to cope with the ignorance and uncertainty caused by the need to constantly adapt to changing circumstances and their harmful and beneficial effects. Specialization in private property ownership allows people to specialize in knowledge about the best use of the property that they own and allows them to expect certain kinds of predictable behavior with respect to theirs' and others' property. Individuals specialize their ownership in areas where they have a comparative advantage, thus leading to greater productivity and utilization of specialized knowledge. If their rights to property did not exist or were attenuated, individuals would not make the necessary investments in specialized knowledge which contribute to greater productivity, since they would not obtain the fruits of their activity.

Private property rights also permit owners to measure, monitor, control, and react to changes in circumstances and knowledge. Changes in their prices signal owners about changes in economic circumstances and allow owners to take advantage of their dispersed knowledge of time and place by changing the composition of their bundle of property rights. Such changes in property bundles facilitate the decentralized coordination of dispersed knowledge and hence provide a solution-mechanism for the knowledge problem. Under public ownership, on the other hand, even though employee specialization can still exist, the specialization of ownership inherent in private property and hence the facilitation of the solution to the knowledge problem is excluded because of compulsory ownership.

A major feature of public property is that ownership is vested in all members of the public and no member can divest him- or herself of that ownership. This lack of transferability of ownership implies a lack of specialization in ownership and the loss of the gains of specialized knowledge, specific riskbearing, foresight, and judgment. Also lost are the concentration of the rewards and costs of decisions on the persons most directly responsible for them and the comparative advantage effects of the specialized applications of knowledge in control and risktaking. The loss of these important dimensions of private property ownership results in the prevention of a solution to the knowledge problem.

It is a central proposition of property rights economics that under public ownership, the costs of any decision or action are less fully thrust upon the decisionmaker than under private property rights. The cost-benefit calculus is changed toward lower costs, even though the true costs are most often raised. This leads to fraud, corruption, and misuse of public property by managers. Since the gains to any owner resulting from any cost-saving actions are less fully effective, costly devices have to be used to prevent such fraud, corruption, and misuse. The development process consequently becomes prone to high costs, failure, and lack of accountability.

The Indian development planning framework, with its heavy emphasis on public ownership and control, systematically reduced the scope and coverage of private property rights in the Indian economy with predictable effects. This had disastrous consequences for the coordination of knowledge, entrepreneurship, and riskbearing, and the fostering of innovation. It gave rise to the fraud, corruption, and misuse of property that became so prevalent in the seventies and eighties. It led to uncertainty, arbitrariness, and capriciousness in economic affairs. The problems identified in the conventional literature on Indian planning (discussed above) originated in the Indian planners' decision to opt for public ownership leading to the poor economic performance of the post-independence era.

The consequences of seriously attenuating the regime of private property rights that existed at the time of independence were to be seen in the decline in private sector agricultural and industrial growth over time, the rise of widespread corruption and rent-seeking activity, and the politicization of everyday life. For example, the consequences of all the controls on the private sector, coupled with the drastically increased uncertainty of control over one's private property, caused a large-scale distortion of incentives away from encouraging firms to improve technology and/or quality and/or lower prices to attract more customers toward encouraging them to concentrate on rent seeking and other nonproductive activity.

Similarly, the policy of banning futures markets and forward trading in commodity and other markets forced both buyers and sellers to carry more risk than they would have normally been prepared to carry and caused the economy to lose out on trades that were beneficial for its growth and development. It also led to the use of quantitative and alternative underground credit market systems for financing and conducting business, with the consequent higher costs and inefficiency.

The growth of one of the largest public sectors in the noncommunist world as a result of the Indian government's progressive socialist-oriented industrial policy further created a huge problem of inefficiency, corruption and rent seeking. Private-sector activity, was systematically reduced as a proportion of total industrial activity with disastrous consequences for the Indian consumer and tax-payer. Large-scale political interference in and legislation affecting the legal process further compromised the ability of Indians to own, use, and transfer their own property, leading to the growth of one of the democratic world's largest underground economies and a high-cost economy. Confiscatory tax rates through the sixties and early seventies (which can be viewed as a severe reduction of the right to collect the fruits of private property ownership) further exacerbated the situation.

Thus, the problems that arose as a result of the statist planning policies of the Indian government in the post independence period can be seen as the result of the wholescale attenuation of private property rights that occurred as a result of these policies.

An Entrepreneurship Critique of Indian Planning

A third important but often neglected ingredient of the economic development process, inextricably linked to the two aspects discussed above, is the crucial role of entrepreneurship. As Frank Knight (1921), Joseph Schumpeter (1934, 1942), George Shackle (1972), Israel Kirzner (1973, 1979, 1985), and a number of other economists have pointed out, long-run economic development is instigated, stimulated, and nourished by the process of entrepreneurial discovery, invention, and innovation. It is the very open-endedness of market-based price systems that allows for the process of entrepreneurial discovery and innovation so necessary for economic development.

Economic development is a process of changing old ways of doing things, of venturing into the unknown, and of maximizing opportunities for flexibility, experimentation, and innovation. Entrepreneurship plays a critical role in taking advantage of these opportunities and making development happen.

By viewing the process of economic development as fundamentally dependent on the market process as a facilitator of the coordination of the plans of individual decision makers with dispersed knowledge, the role of entrepreneurship and private property as essential to such individual plan coordination becomes clear. Entrepreneurship implies the focusing of the benefits and costs of entrepreneurial action on specific individuals. Profits (and losses) are the result of unpredictable ex ante value changes. Such value changes signal the direction in which entrepreneurial activity should be directed. Exclusive title to the ownership, use, and transfer of property enables the profits and losses to be focused on the decision maker who is responsible for their measurement, monitoring, and control. This facilitates the entrepreneurial discovery process.

Public ownership of property, on the other hand, blunts this process and makes value changes difficult to measure, monitor, and control. The lack of transferability implicit in public ownership removes the disciplining mechanism of owners divesting when negative value changes occur. Other mechanisms of administrative control are poor substitutes because of the knowledge problem.

Buchanan and Faith (1981) have analyzed the role of entrepreneurship and the internalization of externalities under alternative property rules. After pointing out the asymmetric impact of the "property rule" versus the "liability rule" in encouraging entrepreneurship, they show how governmental rule- setting regulation and/or ownership is worse than either of these legally evolved rules in encouraging entrepreneurship. Their argument is predicated on the view that potential spillover or external costs or benefits of economic activity are not fully predictable in advance and on "the elementary fact that new ventures will necessarily be unpredictable, both with respect to their internal profitability and to their spill-over effects." Since political decision makers would typically not have the dispersed knowledge regarding the potential market opportunity/activity, they will necessarily tend to be relatively more pessimistic than the entrepreneur and inhibit the entrepreneurship so essential for development and growth. Consequently, they argue that the entrepreneurial discovery process should be unimpeded by government regulation and rules (and by extension, government ownership) and the liability process of tort law, where those who generate physical damage to others stand liable, should be allowed to be the only (naturally evolved) restraint on this process.[56]

Development planning and centralized coordination introduce rigidity and inflexibility into the economic development process and stifle entrepreneurship. They redirect entrepreneurial skills toward rent seeking, corruption, and political influence peddling. It presupposes that government officials can determine, select, and operate projects better than private entrepreneurs can, even though the latter risk their own funds and therefore are less likely to make mistakes and mismanage specific endeavors. Development planning, by restricting the freedom of entrepreneurial free-entry into economic activity, prevents entrepreneurial discovery and dynamic competition, thus stifling the process of economic growth and development.

India's experience with development planning bears out the

correctness of the entrepreneurial critique of such planning. The growth of entrepreneurship in India was effectively strangled in the postindependence period by the government's planning and policy regime.[57] This phenomenon is evident in the declining share of private investment over the 1951–85 period and the control of the "commanding heights" of the Indian economy by the public sector. Entrepreneurial activity was redirected to rent seeking, corruption, and influence peddling, as has been documented by study after study.[58] Even as entrepreneurship was stifled, the relative efficiency of Indian industry vis-a-vis other countries declined rapidly.[59] Meanwhile, as noted above, the share of India's exports in world exports also declined rapidly to less than one-third the level that had existed at the time of independence, as government control replaced private enterprise.

As has been pointed out by others, the Indian development planning process produced the following consequences that had important impacts on the quality and quantity of entrepreneurship in India:[60]

1. India's heavy industry-based import substitution strategy of planned development displaced private entrepreneurship with government direction and decisionmaking by bureaucrats. Despite preferential policies toward the cottage and small industries sectors, the controls and regulations placed on private entrepreneurs in order to get them to conform to plan targets severely constrained and inhibited private entrepreneurship. Resources were increasingly directed by decree to industries that were to either become uneconomical or fail because of the lack of private entrepreneurship or the distortion of the incentives for successful entrepreneurship through price, distribution, licensing, or other controls.
2. Since agriculture with its geographical dispersion and plethora of producers was not amenable to planning, the industrial sector bore the brunt of the planning and control system that was set up. This had a consequent large negative impact on entrepreneurship in the one sector where India could have developed tremendous comparative advantages and which could

have bootstrapped the country out of its poverty, as had happened in the case of the developed Western economies and the Southeast Asian "miracle" economies including Japan.

3. The expansion of the public sector to occupy the "commanding heights" of the Indian economy in producing "basic goods" and infrastructure automatically militated against the expansion of private entrepreneurial activity.

4. The nature of the instruments used to legislate the plan targets and the complex system of controls created systematic incentives for diverting entrepreneurial activity toward rent seeking and other directly unproductive activity.

These consequences of Indian planning dealt wealth-creating entrepreneurship a major blow despite a substantial private sector, leading to a retardation of growth and the failure of Indian planning.

Recent analyses of the Indian development planning experience (e.g., Chakravarti 1987; Jalan 1991) misunderstand the nature of national development planning and the import of the epistemological and theoretical criticisms of such planning detailed above. Consequently, they tend to be unsound *apologia* for a fundamentally flawed process which has the seeds of its own failure embedded in it from the start. Much grief to the Indian population and the development process could have been avoided if they and the originators of the Indian development strategy had properly understood the nature of the development process and the inherent contradictions of planning.

7. Conclusion

The detailed review of the underlying vision, policy framework, outcomes, and epistemological and theoretical weaknesses of the Indian development planning process in this chapter demonstrates the disastrous consequences of faulty economic analysis and inappropriate policies for the wealth of nations. The Indian development planning debacle has many lessons to offer for those who are still espousing a third way of "market socialism," although the carcass of that "hybrid" system has been effectively laid to rest during the socialist calculation debate.[61] What is required in India today are fundamental changes in the planning and policy framework, rather than the half-hearted attempts at liberalization that have been initiated in the middle eighties and again in 1991.

In India's case, such fundamental changes would involve an across-the-board scrapping of all remaining domestic and external-sector controls and regulations, the dismantling of the overbearing and nihilistic planning system, a drastic and complete reduction in the centralized bureaucratic edifice, comprehensive privatization of the central and state public-sector undertakings, a restoration of absolute rights to private property and voluntary exchange, and a comprehensive reliance on market forces in every facet of daily life. A completely free-trade regime, combined with a freely convertible currency, needs to be established as an immediate step toward achieving the objective of economic and political freedom.

Social policy needs to be drastically altered by a scrapping of all discriminatory policies, such as India's caste-based "affirmative action" policies, and the removal of all state controls on mobility, hiring, and appointments. A credible system of rule of law, based on equal access to justice but not equality of outcomes, needs to be established. A constitutional convention to limit the powers of government and guarantee a decentralized, truly federal system of government is also urgently needed.

The focus of such a radical liberal agenda for change should be on *processes* rather than redistributive *outcomes*, the latter policies having failed miserably in India and in every country where they have been tried. The attempt should be to make economics dominant and politics subservient. It should involve a complete abandonment of the planning and control system for a private property market system that encourages private entrepreneurship. Otherwise India will remain poor and its economy will continue to unravel. Only the failure of India's dirigiste development planning path and its brand of socialism will be left to burden future generations.

Notes

1. Bhagwati and Desai (1970) provides an excellent review and analysis of Indian economic planning and performance for the first three plan periods (1951–66) and remains the locus classicus on the subject of industrial policy, control, and plan implementation difficulties and failures. Shenoy (1971) and Roy (1984) provide excellent critiques of the role of the planning process and politics in India's economic development. Roy and James (1992) contains recent analyses of Indian planning, governance, development, and social progress.

2. Officials from the British colonial administration for postwar economic planning and industrial development was provided by the constitution of the Reconstruction Committee of the Viceroy's Council in 1943 and the setting up of a Department of Planning and Development in 1944. By 1945, a number of official and unofficial planning documents and plans had been formulated, including those of the Congress National Planning Committee and the "Bombay Plan," a planning memorandum prepared by a group of leading Indian industrialists (Thakurdas et al., 1944). See Tomlinson (1992) for a recent, but flawed, treatment of the historical roots of postindependence Indian economic policy.

3. The seminal discussion of the "unconstrained" vision of human nature and society is to be found in Sowell (1987). He contrasts this vision with the "constrained" vision of man where human society and development are seen as the product of human action and adaptation through trial and error, rather than rational design, and where the power of unarticulated and unplanned social processes to mobilize and coordinate knowledge is such as to render centralized knowledge collection and decision making impossible.

4. Hayek (1973) has characterized the former view as that of "constructivist rationalism" which sees human institutions as "made" orders or "taxis," while the latter view is characterized as the "evolutionary approach" which views many important human institutions as spontaneous prders or "cosmos" (while recognizing that there are "made" orders which are also important). These two views fall into the classification of the unconstrained and constrained visions respectively as identified by Sowell (1987).

5. See Bohm-Bawerk (1949), Mises ([1922] 1981), Hayek (1944, 1948, 1988) and Popper ([1945] 1966, 1957). Hayek (1988) contains a recent systematic treatment of the fallacies of what he calls the "fatal conceit" of socialism—the idea that "man is able to shape the world around him according to his wishes." Sowell (1985) contains a systematic critique of the philosophy and economics of Marxism, which underlies most modern attempts at establishing a socialist system.

6. The major opposing visions to Nehru's were that of India's acknowledged leader of the independence movement, Mahatma Gandhi and his other protégé, Vallabhbhai Patel. These visions can only be characterized as *less* unconstrained than Nehru's, since they too had elements of socialism amd statism built into them. See Rudolph and Rudolph (1987), Akbar (1988), and Tomlinson (1992) for discussions of the struggle of the three separate relatively unconstrained visions espoused by these men, albeit from a different perspective. It is also necessary to note that the *more* constrained vision in the preindependence period was that of the members of the British colonial government till the late thirties, who espoused *laissez-faire* in matters of economic policy. But the Great Depression and wartime shortages and controls changed this vision to a *more* unconstrained one. In both the pre- and postindependence era, the constrained vision was espoused by C. Rajagopalachari, independent India's first governor-general. Rajagopalachari founded the Swatantra (Independence) party, which espoused a liberal, market-oriented economic policy. India's first president, Dr. Rajendra Prasad, also espoused a more constrained vision, but was considered "a man of inferior intellect" and was ineffective in changing the dominant policy ethos through his largely ceremonial office.
7. Quoted in Singh (1977).
8. Quoted in Akbar (1988, 466).
9. Quoted in Singh (1977, 87).
10. Ibid.
11. See Government of India (1951, 6).
12. Quoted in Roy (1984, 34).
13. Government of India (1956b, 3).
14. Quoted in Karanjia (1960, 49–50).
15. The term "scientism" was coined by Hayek ([1952] 1979) to describe the "slavish imitation of the method and language of Science" (or the natural sciences) by the social sciences. See Hayek ([1952] 1979) for a brilliant critique of scientism.
16. Quoted in Karanjia (1960, 50–51).
17. See Gopal (1976) and Rudolph and Rudolph (1987) for discussions of this aspect of Nehru. He was a firm believer in the parliamentary version of the liberal state, including its concern for a government of laws and civil rights.
18. The sources for the discussion that follows include Hazari (1966), Hazari Committee Report (1967), Bhagwati and Desai (1970), Dasgupta and Sengupta (1978), and the Government of India, Ministry of Industry, *Guidelines for Industries* (1983).
19. The various Industry Policy Resolutions and other industrial controls are documented and detailed in the Government of India, Ministry of Industry, *Guidelines for Industries* (1983).

20. See the Hazari Committee report (1967) and the Dutt Committee report (1969).
21. The important committees include the Committee on Industries Development Procedures (Swaminathan Committee 1965), the Committee on Industrial Planning and Licensing Policy (Hazari Committee 1967), the Industrial Licensing Policy Inquiry Committee (The Dutt Committee 1969), and the Committee on Import-Export Policies and Procedures (The Alexander Committee 1978).
22. See particularly chapter 5 of the Dagli Committee report (1979) for the confusion in this area.
23. For a discussion on money market controls, see Kamath (1985a, 1985b).
24. Estimates of the size of the black market in India vary from 15 percent to over 50 percent of GNP. For a recent survey, see Gupta and Gupta in Monga and Sanctis (1984). Official reports on the black market and rent-seeking activity are the Wanchoo Committee report (1971) and the Dagli Committee report (1979). The Raj Committee on steel control documents cases of graft and gross misuse of the control mechanism for steel (Raj Committee, 1963). See Kamath (1992).
25. For a discussion, see Blaug, Layard, and Woodhall (1969).
26. A number of committees have reviewed and modified the monopoly provisions of the IDR Act of 1951. These include the reports of the Committee on Distribution of Incomes and Levels of Living (Mahalonobis Committee 1960), the Committee on Industrial Planning and Licensing Policy (Hazari Committee, 1967), the Monopolies Inquiry Commission (Government of India, 1965b), and the Industrial Licensing Policy Inquiry Committee (The Dutt Committee 1969).
27. For a clear statement of this view, see Dasgupta and Sengupta (1978).
28. The major sources for this discussion include Bhagwati and Desai (1970), Bhagwati and Srinivasan (1975), Dasgupta and Sengupta (1978), Foreign Exchange Regulation Act (1947 and amendments), *Report of the Committee on Import-Export Policies and Procedures* (Alexander Committee 1978), *Report of the Committee on Export Strategy—1980s* (Tandon Committee 1980), and *Report of the Import Substitution Committee* (Agarwal Committee 1980).
29. See Bhagwati and Desai (1970) for a detailed discussion. Shourie (1966) contains a detailed description and criticism of the allocation procedures adopted by the Indian authorities.
30. Bhagwati and Srinivasan (1975, 42–43).
31. See especially the reports of the Estimates Committee of the Lok Sabha (Parliament) (Government of India, 1963–64, 1967–68), the Santhanam Committee on the Prevention of Corruption (1964), the Kaul Committee (1971) on leakage of foreign exchange through invoice manipulation, the Wanchoo Committee on direct taxes (1971), and the Dagli Committee (1979) on controls and subsidies.

32. Data were obtained from the vernacular newspaper *Vyaapar* (Business), published daily in Bombay. The paper fairly regularly publishes data on import license and commodity "black-market" premiums by polling traders in the market as well as by occasionally bidding in the market through other business concerns. The Santhanam Committee report (1964) stated that import licenses were worth 100 to 500 percent of their face value.
33. See Shenoy (1968, 1971), and Roy (1984, part 3) for a further discussion of the abuses of trading and corruption in India during the postindependence period.
34. Regular series for black-market exchange rates are to be found in various issues of the *Far Eastern Economic Review* and *Pick's Currency Year Book*. For an excellent, detailed study of black-market exchange rates in India and other countries, see Gupta (1980).
35. See *Report of the Estimates Committee of the Lok Sabha* for 1967–68 (Government of India 1963–64, 1967–68).
36. See Bhagwati and Desai (1970), Bhagwati and Srinivasan (1975) and the reports cited in note 28.
37. Possible factors for the neglect of exports during the first planning decade (1951–61) are discussed in chapter 18 of Bhagwati and Desai (1970). It is interesting to note that they attribute this neglect to the investment strategy adopted by the Indian planners. The emphasis in the Second Plan toward investments in capital goods industries and the implicit export pessimism entailed therein may have been due to the most influential planner at that time, Prof. Mahalonobis, being a physicist and not an economist and hence not seeing the foreign trade transformation possibilities as a way of procuring capital goods. Bhagwati and Desai point out that the adoption of a material balances-oriented Soviet-type planning model ("the Mahalonobis Model") seems to have been due to the influence of Soviet thinking on Prof. Mahalonobis.
38. See Bhagwati and Desai (1970), chapter 19, for a detailed discussion of the characteristics and deficiencies of these schemes in the 1960s.
39. Bhagwati and Desai (1970) calculated the implied effective subsidization at premiums of about 70–80 percent in 1963–64 to be around Rs 500 million, which significantly exceeded the subsidy from any or all of the other measures of export promotion. As already mentioned in note 32, data collected by the author showed the existence of higher premiums on import licenses.
40. United Nations Development Programme (1990, 130).
41. Jagannathan and Guha Thakurta (1991, 53).
42. Gupta and Gupta (1982).
43. Bhagwati and Desai (1970) and Lal (1988a, 1988b).
44. Dandekar and Rath (1971) and Chaudhuri (1978).

45. For detailed analyses of the politician-cooperative nexus, see Bavish-kar (1968, 1980). See also Kamath (1992).
46. Bardhan (1984, 102).
47. These figures are calculated from Ezekiel (1984, 149–67).
48. *Economist* (1992, 57).
49. For example, see Patel (1985), Chakravarti (1987), and Jalan (1991).
50. The supporters and advocates of planning in India, such as Bardhan (1984), Patel (1985), Chakravarti (1987), and Jalan (1991), argue that it was the selection of inappropriate policy instruments rather than any inherent weakness of the planning process that led to the failures of Indian planning. Bardhan (1984) also argues that it was the "lack of political insulation from conflicting interests, coupled with the strong power base of the white-collar workers in the public bureau-cracy that keeps the Indian state, in spite of its pervasive economic presence, largely confined to regulatory functions, avoiding the hard choices and politically unpleasant decisions involved in more active development functions" (74). Critics of Indian development planning such as Bhagwati and Desai (1970) and Bhagwati and Srinivasan (1975), on the other hand, have stressed the choice of inappropriate policy frameworks and instruments, but in addition have also stressed the role of administrative and political failures in implemen-tation. More cogent and comprehensive critiques have been provided by Shenoy (1971) and Roy (1984), but even they, like the others, have ignored more fundamental epistemological and theoretical consider-ations.
51. See Sowell (1980) for a book-length discussion of the theoretical un-derpinnings and consequences of the knowledge problem. Lavoie (1985a) focuses on the knowledge problem as the centerpiece of his critique of national economic planning.
52. There is certainly no mention of the knowledge problem in any of Nehru's or Mahalonobis's writings. Another prominent architect and proponent of Indian planning, Chakravarti (1973, 1987) mentions Hayek and the knowledge problem (and that too obliquely) but dis-poses of the issues raised by the recognition of such a problem as being too efficiency oriented and therefore not of much value in understanding real-world planning in the context of underdevelop-ment and the major structural changes that occur in such economies!
53. See Polanyi (1958) for a discussion of tacit knowledge. Also see Lavoie (1985a), especially chapter 2.
54. The major critics of socialist calculation were Mises ([1920] 1935, [1922] 1981), Robbins (1934), and Hayek (1935). For an excellent revisionist account of this debate, see Lavoie (1985b).
55. The modern property rights literature is summarized in Furubotn and Pejovich (1972), Alchian (1965, 1969), and Demsetz (1964, 1966,

1967, 1969) which contain the major contributions to the modern economics literature on property rights.

56. For a full-blown analysis of the inhibiting and detrimental effects of taxes and regulations on the entrepreneurial discovery process, see Kirzner (1985, chapters 5 and 6).

57. Buchanan (1966) contains an excellent account of the development of entrepreneurship and capitalistic enterprise in India.

58. See, for example, Bhagwati and Desai (1970), Krueger (1974), Bhagwati and Srinivasan (1975), Jha (1980), Gupta and Gupta (1982), Mohammed and Whalley (1984), Monga and Sanctis (1984), Acharya and Associates (1985), Kamath (1992), and a host of government committee reports (e.g., Santhanam Committee 1964, Kaul Committee 1971, Dagli Committee 1979, etc.).

59. Lal (1988a).

60. For example, see Lal (1988b, 24).

61. For a recent exhumation of this discredited and buried idea, see Bardhan and Roemer (1992).

References

Acharya, S., and Associates. 1985. *Aspects of Black Economy in India*. New Delhi: National Institute of Public Finance and Policy.

Agarwal Committee. 1989. *Report of the Import Substitution Committee*. Delhi: Govt. of India Press.

Akbar, M. J. 1988. *Nehru: The Making of India*. London: Penguin.

Alchian, A. A. 1965. "Some Economics of Property Rights." *Il Politico* 30, no. 4: 816–29.

————. 1969. "Corporate Management and Property Rights." In *Economic Policy and the Regulation of Corporate Securities*, ed. Henry Manne, 337–60. Washington, D.C.: American Enterprise Institute.

Alexander Committee. 1978. *Report of the Committee on Import-Export Policies and Procedures*. Delhi: Govt. of India Press.

Bardhan, P. K. 1984. *The Political Economy of Development in India*. Delhi: Oxford University Press.

Bardhan, P. K., and J. E. Roemer. 1992. "Market Socialism: A Case for Rejuvenation." *Journal of Economic Perspectives* 6, no. 3 (Summer), 101–16.

Bavishkar, B. S. 1968. "Cooperatives and Politics." *Economic and Political Weekly* 3, no. 12, March 23, 1968, 490–95.

————. *The Politics of Development: Sugar Co-operatives in Rural Maharashtra*. Delhi: Oxford University Press. 1980.

Bhagwati, J., and P. Desai. 1970. *India-Planning for Industrialisation:*

Industrialisation and Trade Policies since 1951. Delhi: Oxford University Press.
Bhagwati, J., and T. N. Srinivasan. 1975. Foreign Trade Regimes and Economic Development: India. New York: National Bureau of Economic Research and Columbia University Press.
Blaug, M., R. Layard, and J. M. Woodhall. 1969. Causes of Graduate Unemployment in India. Harmondsworth: Allen Lane.
Bohm-Bawerk, E. V. 1949. Karl Marx and the Close of His System. Clifton, N.J.: Augustus M. Kelley.
Buchanan, D.H. 1966. The Development of Capitalist Enterprise in India. London: Frank Cass.
Buchanan, J. M., and R. L. Faith. 1981. "Entrepreneurship and the Internalization of Externalities." Journal of Law and Economics (April): 95–111.
Chakravarti, S. 1973. "Theory of Development Planning: An Appraisal." In Economic Structure and Development: Essays in Honor of Jan Tinbergen, ed. H. C. Bos, H. Linnemann, and P. de Wolff. Amsterdam: Elsevier.
———. 1987. Development Planning: The Indian Experience. Oxford: Clarendon Press.
Chaudhuri, P. 1978. The Indian Economy: Poverty and Development. New Delhi: Vikas Publishing House.
Dagli Committee. 1979. Report of the Committee on Controls and Subsidies. New Delhi: Govt. of India Press.
Dandekar, V. M., and N. Rath. 1971. Poverty in India. Pune: Indian School of Political Economy.
Dasgupta, A., and N. K. Sengupta. 1978. Government and Business in India. Calcutta: Allied Book Agency.
Demsetz, H. 1964. "The Exchange and Enforcement of Property Rights." Journal of Law and Economics 7 (October): 11–26.
———. 1966. "Some Aspects of Property Rights." Journal of Law and Economics 9 (October): 61–70.
———. 1967. "Toward a Theory of Property Rights." American Economic Review 57, no. 2 (May): 347–73.
———. 1969. "Information and Efficiency: Another Viewpoint." Journal of Law and Economics 12 (April): 1–22.
Dutt Committee. 1969. Report of the Industrial Licensing Policy Inquiry Committee. Delhi: Govt. of India Press.
Economist. 1992. May 23–29, 21–23, 57.
Ezekiel, Hannan, ed. 1984. Corporate Sector in India. New Delhi: Vikas Publishing House.
Furubotn, E. I. and S. Pejovich. 1972. "Property Rights and Economic Theory: A Survey of Recent Literature." Journal of Economic Literature: 1137–62.

Gopal, S. 1976. *Jawaharlal Nehru: A Biography.* 3 vols. Delhi: Oxford University Press.

Government of India. Various years. *Economic Survey.* Delhi: Govt. of India Press.

———. 1947. *Imports and Exports (Control) Act.* Delhi: Govt. of India Press.

———. 1951. *Industries (Development and Regulation)* Act. Delhi: Govt. of India Press.

———. 1955a. *Essential Commodities Act.* Delhi, Govt. of India Press.

———. 1955b. *Imports (Control) Order.* Delhi: Govt. of India Press.

———. 1956a. *Companies Act.* Delhi: Govt. of India Press.

———. 1956b. *Industrial Policy Resolution.* Delhi: Govt. of India Press.

———. *1963–64, 1967–68. Report of the Estimates Committee of the Lok Sabha.* Delhi: Govt. of India Press.

———. 1965a. *Essential Commodities Act.* Delhi: Govt. of India Press.

———. 1965b. Report of the Monopolies Inquiry Commission. *Delhi: Govt. of India Press.*

———. 1969. *Monopoly and Restrictive Trade Practices Act.* Delhi: Govt. of India Press.

———. 1970. *Industrial Licensing Policy.* Delhi: Govt. of India Press.

———. 1973. *Industrial Policy Government Decisions.* Delhi: Govt. of India Press.

———. 1977. *Exports (Control) Order.* Delhi: Govt. of India Press.

———. 1977, 1980 & 1981. *Industrial Policy Statement.* Delhi: Govt. of India Press.

———. Ministry of Industry. 1983. *Guidelines for Industries.* Delhi: Govt. of India Press.

Gupta, S. 1980. "An Application of the Monetary Approach to Black Market Exchange Rates." *Weltwirtschaftliches Archiv* 116, no. 2: 235–52.

Gupta, P., and S. Gupta. 1982. "Estimates of the Unreported Economy in India." *Economic and Political Weekly*, January 16, 69–75.

Hayek, F. A. 1937. "Economics and Knowledge." *Economica* 4(NS): 33–54.

———. 1944. *The Road to Serfdom.* Chicago: University of Chicago Press.

———. 1945. "The Use of Knowledge in Society." *American Economic Review* 25, no. 4: 519–30.

———. 1948. *Individualism and Economic Order.* Chicago: University of Chicago Press.

———. [1952] 1979. *The Counter-Revolution of Science: Studies on the Abuse of Reason.* Indianapolis: Liberty Press.

———. 1973. *Law, Legislation and Liberty.* Vol. 1, *Rules and Order.* Chicago: University of Chicago Press.

———. 1988. *The Fatal Conceit: The Errors of Socialism.* Chicago: University of Chicago Press.

Hayek, F. A. ed. 1935. *Collectivist Economic Planning: Critical Studies on the Possibilities of Socialism.* London: Routledge.

Hazari, R. K. 1966. *The Structure of the Corporate Private Sector.* Bombay: Asia Publishing House.

Hazari Committee. 1967. *Report of the Committee on Industrial Planning and Licensing Policy.* Delhi: Govt. of India Press.

Jagannathan, R., and P. Guha Thakurta. 1991. "The Government: Wanton Ways." *India Today,* April 30, 52–59.

Jalan, B. 1991. *India's Economic Crisis: The Way Ahead.* New Delhi: Oxford University Press.

Jha, P. S. 1980. *India—A Political Economy of Stagnation.* Bombay: Oxford University Press.

Kamath, S. J. 1985a. "The Demand for and Supply of Money in India—1951–76." *Weltwirtschaftliches Archiv* 121 no. 2: 501–23.

———. 1985b. "Money, Income and Causality in a Developing Economy." *Journal of Economic Studies* 12, no. 3 (October): 36–53.

———. 1992. *The Political Economy of Suppressed Markets: Controls, Rent Seeking and Interest Group Behaviour in the Indian Sugar and Cement Industries.* Delhi: Oxford University Press.

Karanjia, R. K. 1960. *The Mind of Mr. Nehru.* London: Allen & Unwin.

Kaul Committee. 1971. *Report of the Committee on Leakage of Foreign Exchange through Invoice Manipulation.* Delhi: Govt. of India Press.

Kirzner, I. 1973. *Competition and Entrepreneurship.* Chicago: University of Chicago Press.

———. 1973. *Perception, Opportunity and Profit: Studies in the Theory of Entrepreneurship.* Chicago: University of Chicago Press.

———. 1985. *Discovery and the Capitalist Process.* Chicago: University of Chicago Press, 1985.

Knight, F. H. 1921. *Risk, Uncertainty and Profit.* New York: Houghton Mifflin.

Krueger, A. O. 1974. "The Political Economy of the Rent-Seeking Society." *American Economic Review* 64 (June): 291–303.

Lal, D. 1988a. *Hindu Equilibrium.* Vol. 1. Oxford: Clarendon Press.

———. 1988b. *India—Country Study No. 5.* Panama and San Francisco: International Center for Economic Growth.

Laski, H. 1935. *Law and Justice in Soviet Russia.* London: Allen & Unwin.

Lavoie, D. 1985a. *Rivalry and Central Planning: A Reexamination of the Socialist Calculation Debate.* Cambridge: Cambridge University Press.

———. 1985b. *National Economic Planning: What Is Left?* Cambridge: Cambridge University Press.

Mahalonobis Committee. 1960. *Report of the Committee on Distribution of Income and Levels of Living.* Delhi: Govt. of India Press.

Mises, L. von. [1920] 1935. "Economic Calculation and the Socialist Commonwealth." Trans. S. Adler. In *Collectivist Economic Planning,* ed. F. A. Hayek (originally published in 1920 in German).

Mises, L. von. [1922] 1981. *Socialism: An Economic and Sociological Analysis.* Trans. J. Kahane. Indianapolis: Liberty Press (originally published in German).

Mohammed, S., and J. Whalley. 1984. "Rent Seeking in India: Its Costs and Policy Significance." *Kyklos* 37 (December): 817–31.

Monga, G. S., and V. J. Sanctis. 1984. *The Unsanctioned Economy in India.* Bombay: Himalaya Publishing House.

National Council of Applied Economic Research. 1978. *A Study of Price Control and the Impact of Excise Duties on Selected Industries.* New Delhi: NCAER.

Patel, I. G. 1985. *On the Economics of Development: Towards a Consensus.* Stemp Memorial Lecture, London: University of London.

Pick's Currency Year Book. Various years. New York.

Polanyi, M. 1958. *Personal Knowledge: Towards a Post-Critical Philosophy.* Chicago: University of Chicago Press.

Popper, K. R. [1945] 1966. *The Open Society and Its Enemies.* London: Routledge.

———. 1957. *The Poverty of Historicism.* London: Routledge.

Raj Committee. 1963. *Report of the Committee on Steel Control.* Delhi: Govt. of India Press.

Robbins, L. 1934. *The Great Depression.* New York: MacMillan.

Roy, S. 1984. *Pricing, Planning and Politics: A Study of Economic Distortions in India.* London: Institute of Economic Affairs.

Roy, S., and W. E. James, eds. 1992. *Foundations of India's Political Economy: Towards an Agenda for the 1980s.* New Delhi: Sage Publications.

Rudolph, L. I., and S. H. Rudolph. 1987. *In Pursuit of Lakshmi: The Political Economy of the Indian State.* Chicago: University of Chicago Press.

Santhanam Committee. 1964. *Report of the Committee on the Prevention of Corruption.* Delhi: Govt. of India Press.

Schumpeter, J. A. 1934. *The Theory of Economic Development.* Cambridge: Harvard University Press.

———. 1942. *Capitalism, Socialism and Democracy.* New York: Harper & Row.

Shackle, G. L. S. 1972. *Epistemics and Economics: A Critique of Economic Doctrines.* Cambridge: Cambridge University Press.

Shenoy, B. R. 1968. *Indian Economic Policy.* Bombay: Popular Prakashan.

———. 1971. *India: Progress or Poverty? A Review of the Outcome of Central Planning in India, 1951–69.* London: Institute of Economic Affairs.

Shourie, A. 1966. "Allocation of Foreign Exchange in India." Unpublished Ph.D. diss., Syracuse University.

Singh, V. B., ed. 1977. *Nehru on Socialism.* New Delhi: Govt. of India Press.

Sowell, T. 1980. *Knowledge and Decisions.* New York: Basic Books.
———. 1985. *Marxism: Philosophy and Economics.* New York: William Morrow.
———. 1987. *A Conflict of Visions: Ideological Origins of Political Struggles.* New York: Quill/William Morrow.
Swaminathan Committee. 1965. *Report of the Committee on Industries Development Procedures.* Delhi: Govt. of India Press.
Thakurdas, Sir P., et al. 1944. *Memorandum Outlining A Plan of Economic Development for India* (Bombay Plan). Harmondsworth: Penguin.
Tomlinson, B. R. 1992. "Historical Roots of Economic Policy." In Roy and James 1992.
United Nations Development Programme (UNDP). 1990. *Human Development Report 1990.* New York: Oxford University Press.
Vyaapar. Various issues. Bombay.
Wanchoo Committee. 1971. *Report of the Direct Taxes Enquiry Committee.* Delhi: Govt. of India Press.
Webb, Sidney, and Beatrice Webb. 1938. *Soviet Communism: A New Civilization?* New York: Scribner's.

6

The Failure of Development Planning in Africa

George B. N. Ayittey

Introduction

"Development planning" is a beguiling and innocuous term which should not be confused with the daily necessity of planning one's life activities. Most people have "some plan" designed to achieve a certain objective, which may be financial, political, or career-related. For example, an individual may plan to save say five thousand dollars at the end of the year. Such a plan or goal may entail an adjustment—most likely a reduction—in current consumption expenditures. Another individual may aspire to become an astronaut in the future. With this goal in mind, she may plan on securing the necessary type of training and preparation.

Corporations also plan their production and investment activities. For example, a company that cans tomatoes would not plan on starting production when farmers have not harvested their produce. Nor would a fish-processing company plan on opening a new plant in the middle of a desert.

Similarly, the government plans its activities. Its budget is really a statement of its fiscal plans for the coming year. It provides statements of *planned* expenditures on the basis of anticipated revenue. More generally, however, the government, like in-

146

dividuals, also "thinks ahead." For example, if a city's population is growing, an increase in demand for infrastructural services (electricity, water, schools, and roads) must be anticipated and additional provisions planned for.

These processes—thinking ahead, planning a career, and corporate investment plans—are all normal features of human existence. Not all plans are realized however. The person who plans on saving $5,000 at the end of the year may rather find himself in debt (negative savings). And the government may discover that the actual deficit at the end of the fiscal year is larger than anticipated or planned. When plans fall short of expectations, each individual or unit must make painful corrections and adjustments.

Development planning, on the other hand, is a pretentious attempt by the state to plan, not only its activities, but those of its citizens as well. Therein lies the fundamental problem. It is difficult enough for an individual to formulate a plan and achieve its objectives, let alone to do so for others.

Killick (1976) distinguished six characteristics of development planning:

1. A definition of *policy objectives*. These may be specified as achieving a "target rate" of economic growth of say 6 percent, reducing the rate of illiteracy to say 30 percent, and increasing the rate of employment.
2. A formulation of a *strategy* by means of which the objectives are to be achieved. The strategy may take the form of raising the rate of investment, from say 5 percent to 20 percent of GNP, and such an increase in investment may be concentrated in industry, as opposed to agriculture.
3. For implementation of the strategy, a *centrally coordinated, internally consistent set of principles and policies* is chosen as the optimal means of achieving the plan's objectives.
4. The intended area of impact may be the entire economy in which case the plan is *comprehensive*, or a limited area (sector) of the economy, in which case the plan is *partial*.
5. A *formalized macroeconomic model* provides the basis of the plan. The model is used to assure internal consistency and

optimality, as well as to project the intended future performance of the economy.
6. A time frame. A development plan typically covers a period of *five* years and finds physical expression as a *medium-term plan document*. A ten-year plan is not unusual and it may be supplemented by *annual plans*.

Most African governments, *both* socialist and capitalist, have adopted a development plan of one type or another during their postcolonial history. Among them may be mentioned Ghana (The Seven-Year Development Plan 1963/64–1969/70), Zambia (The First Development Plan 1965–69), Zimbabwe (The Transitional National Development Plan 1982/83–1984/85), Kenya (The Fifth Development Plan 1984–1988), Nigeria (The Third Development Plan 1975–1980), and Zaire (The Five-Year Development Plan 1986–1990).

The African Rationale for Development Planning

In the 1950s and 1960s, development planning was very much in vogue across the Third World. The case for planning rested on four economic arguments. The first was the familiar "market failure" argument: that markets in developing countries are characterized by imperfections in structure and operation. Commodity and factor markets are often poorly organized and the existence of "distorted prices" often means that producers and consumers are not responding to economic signals and incentives which truly reflect "real" costs to society. This failure of the market to price factors of production correctly often leads to a divergence between social and private valuations of alternative investment projects and ultimately to misallocation of present and future resources.

Externalities formed the basis of the second argument. Financial and skilled manpower resources are limited in the Third World and must therefore be utilized where their effects would be most widely felt; that is, with the greatest linkages or external economies. Private investors may be unable or unwilling to undertake investment large enough to exploit these externalities. Further, competitive markets may not only generate less investment but may also direct this investment into socially unproductive, speculative ventures (hoarding or consumption goods for the rich) and ignore the extra benefits that would accrue from a planned and coordinated long-term investment program.

The third argument was national cohesion. A developing country is often composed of a fractiously diverse and fragmented population. The adoption of a development plan may help rally the people behind the government in a national campaign to eradicate poverty, ignorance, and disease. By mobilizing popular suport across class, caste, racial, religious, and ethnic divisions, a government may be able to "unite" the people in a collective effort to build the nation.

Foreign aid provided the fourth argument. The formulation of detailed development plans with specific sectoral output targets and carefully designed investment projects was often a necessary condition for the receipt of bilateral and multilateral foreign aid. The existence of such a plan "convinced" foreign donors of the commitment and seriousness of the recipient government's intentions about development. Indeed, it was deemed an unpardonable travesty for an LDC government not to possess a development plan.

In Africa, these arguments were reinforced by the continent's especial circumstances and historical expcrience. Markets were simply assumed to be nonexistent or severely underdeveloped. Even where they existed, they were rejected as an allocative mechanism since Africa's peasants were assumed to be unresponsive to market or price incentives. Bound by the chains of tradition, these peasants produced only the bare minimum to feed themselves (subsistence agriculture).

Perhaps the most compelling need for development planning, in the eyes of African leaders, was Africa's colonial legacy Colonial objectives were not to develop Africa but to undertake only such forms of development as were compatible with the interests of European metropolitan powers. Since they were mostly industrialized, the colonies were envisaged to function as nonindustrial appendages to the metropolitan economy: consumers of European manufactured goods and providers of minerals, agricultural, and wood commodities. As a result, the development of the colonial economies was perniciously "skewed": overspecialized in one or two main cash crops (mono-export culture), making African economies highly vulnerable to oscillations in commodity prices on the world market.

Specialization in cash crops, it was argued, also destroyed Africa's ability to feed its people and supply their other needs internally. Most domestic industries collapsed from competition: from cheaper and probably better imported manufactures. Because of collusion among foreign firms and discrimination from colonial banks, the modern sector was completely in foreign hands. Thus, most of the surplus profit generated by the economy flowed overseas and was not invested in the colony. Local industrialization was flatly discouraged.

The prime motivating force behind colonialism was exploitation, not social development. Infrastructural facilities provided by the colonialists were pitiful. Only a few roads, schools, and hospitals were built. As Nkrumah (1973, 39s) scolded:

Under colonial rule, foreign monopoly interest had tied up our whole economy to suit themselves. We had not a single industry. Our economy depended on one cash crop, cocoa. Although our output of cocoa is the largest in the world, there was not a single cocoa processing factory. There was no direct rail link between Accra and Takoradi. There were few hospitals, schools and clinics. Most of the villages lacked a piped water supply. In fact the nakedness of the land when my government began in 1951 has to have been experienced to be believed.

Kwame Nkrumah of Ghana, Julius Nyerere of Tanzania, and other African leaders vowed to demolish that miserably distorted colonial economic structure Africa had inherited and erect in its place alternatives that would serve the needs and interests of Africa, not those of Europe. To accomplish this, Africa could not rely on markets, which in any case were introduced by the colonialists and as such constituted decaying relics of the old colonial order. Nor could Africa rely on its peasants for an agricultural revolution because, according to Nkrumah, these peasants were "too slow to adapt or change their practices to modern, mechanized scientific methods" (Uphoff 1970, 602).

True African development required a carefully planned and massive transformation of African economies. Such an investment could only be undertaken by the state. Furthermore, transformation of African societies required state control of the economy. This set the stage for massive state interventionism in the 1950s and 1960s in Africa. Rather interestingly, the World Bank, US AID, the State Department, and even development experts from Harvard University supported these arguments and channeled considerable aid resources to African governments (Bandow 1986).

To initiate development, it was widely held that the African state needed wide-ranging powers to marshal the resources from the rural area and channel them into national development. Extensive powers were conferred upon African heads of state by rubber-stamp parliaments. Other heads of state simply arrogated unto themselves these powers. If a piece of land was needed for highway construction, it was simply appropriated by the state and if an enterprise was needed, it was established by the government without any consultation with the people it was intended to benefit. In this way, *all* African governments, regardless of their ideological predilections, came to assume immense powers. Most of these powers were ultimately vested in the hands of the head of state. As President Felix Houphouet-Boigny of Ivory Coast put it succinctly: "Here in Ivory Coast, there is no Number 1, 2, or 3. I am Number 1 and I don't share my decisions" (*West Africa*, Aug. 8, 1988, 1428).

The drift toward state interventionism and development planning, however, was accentuated by the socialist ideology. After independence, many African elites and intellectuals argued for an ideology to guide the government on the road to development. The choice almost everywhere was socialism. The dalliance and fascination with socialism emerged during the struggle for political independence and freedom from colonial rule in the 1950s. Many African nationalists harbored a deep distrust of and distaste for capitalism. In fact, capitalism and colonialism were adjudged to be identical and since the latter was evil and exploitative so too was the former—a monumental syllogistic error. Socialism, the antithesis of capitalism, was advocated as the only road to Africa's prosperity.

A wave of socialism swept across the continent as almost all the new African leaders succumbed to the contagious ideology, copied from the East. The proliferation of socialist ideologies that emerged in Africa, ranged from the "Ujamaa" (familyhood or socialism in Swahili) of Julius Nyerere of Tanzania; the vague amalgam of Marxism, Christian socialism, humanitarianism, and "Negritude" of Leopold Senghor of Senegal; the humanism of Kenneth Kaunda of Zambia; the scientific socialism of Marien N'Gouabi of Congo (Brazzaville); the Arab-Islamic socialism of Ghaddafi of Libya; the "Nkrumaism" (consciencism) of Kwame Nkrumah of Ghana; and the "Mobutuism" of Mobutu Sese Seko of Zaire. Only a few African countries such as Ivory Coast, Nigeria, and Kenya were pragmatic enough to eschew doctrinaire socialism.

Although there was a general disposition among African leaders to erase the "exploitative, capitalistic tendencies of colonial structures," there were sharp individual differences between them on the need for the ideology. Kwame Nkrumah of Ghana, generally regarded as the "father of African socialism," was convinced that "only the socialist form of society can assure Ghana of a rapid rate of economic progress without destroying that social justice, that freedom and equality, which are a central feature of our traditional way of life" (*Seven-Year Development Plan*. Accra: Government of Ghana, 1963, 1).

Nyerere of Tanzania, on the other hand, misread the communalism of African traditional life as readiness for socialism, which he was first exposed to during his schooling in Scotland. He castigated capitalism or the money economy, which in his view, "encourages individual acquisitiveness and economic competition," as if there is anything wrong with economic competition. The money economy was, in his purview, foreign to Africa and it "can be catastrophic as regards the African family social unit." As an alternative to "the relentless pursuit of individual advancement", Nyerere insisted that Tanzania be transformed into a nation of small-scale communalists ("Ujamaa") (Nyerere 1962).

Accordingly, in 1973 Tanzania undertook massive resettlement programs under "Operation Dodoma," "Operation Sogeza," "Operation Kigoma," and many others. Peasants were loaded into trucks, often forcibly, and moved to new locations. Many lost their lives in the process and to prevent a return to their old habitats, abandoned buildings were destroyed by bulldozers. By 1976, some thirteen million peasants had been forced into eight thousand cooperative villages and by the end of the 1970s, about 91 percent of the entire rural population had been moved into government villages (Zinsmeister 1987). All crops were to be bought and distributed by the government. It was illegal for the peasants to sell their own produce.

In the rest of Africa, planned socialist transformation of Africa meant the institution of a plethora of legislative instruments and controls. All unoccupied land was appropriated by the government. Roadblocks and passbook systems were employed to control the movement of Africans. Marketing Boards and export regulations were tightened to fleece the cash-crop producers. Price controls were imposed on peasant farmers and traders to render food cheap for the urban elites. Under Sekou Toure of Guinea's program of "Marxism in African Clothes,"

Unauthorized trading became a crime. Police roadblocks were set up around the country to control internal trade. The state set up a monopoly on foreign trade and smuggling became punishable by death. Currency trafficking was punishable by 15 to 20 years in prison. Many farms were collectivized.

Food prices were fixed at low levels. Private farmers were forced to deliver annual harvest quotas to "Local Revolutionary Powers." State Companies monopolized industrial production. (*New York Times*, Dec. 28, 1987, 28)

Under Nkrumah, socialism as a domestic policy in his Seven-Year Development Plan was to be pursued toward "a complete ownership of the economy by the state." A bewildering array of legislative controls and regulations was imposed on imports, capital transfers, industry, minimum wages, the rights and powers of trade unions, prices, rents, and interest rates. Some of the controls were introduced by the colonialists, but they were retained and expanded by Nkrumah. Private businesses were taken over by the Nkrumah government and nationalized. Numerous state enterprises were acquired.

Even in avowedly capitalist countries like Ivory Coast and

Kenya, the result became the same: government ownership of most enterprises, and a distrust of private-sector initiative and foreign investment.

The Results of Development Planning

Almost everywhere, statism and development planning failed miserably to engineer development. In their wake, economic atrophy, repression, and dictatorship followed with morbid staccato. As Mabogunje (1988, 25) asserted, "It is generally agreed that the false start in all African countries has been due largely to the high level of governmental and bureaucratic domination of the economy with its consequences of inefficiency, profligacy and inappropriate control."

Ghana's Seven-Year Development Plan achieved little if any by way of development. The indictment of Killick (1978, 143) was more scathing:

The 7–Year Plan, then, was a piece of paper, with an operational impact close to zero. Why? It could be argued that this was due to defects in the plan itself, to shortages of staff to monitor and implement it, and to the intervention of factors beyond Ghana's control, especially the falling world cocoa prices of the early and mid-sixties. [But] in retrospect, we see an almost total gap between the theoretical advantages of planning and the record of the 7-Year Plan. Far from providing a superior set of signals, it was seriously flawed as a technical document and, in any case, subsequent actions of government bore little relation to it. Far from counteracting the alleged myopia of private decision-takers, government decisions tended to be be dominated by short-term expediency and were rarely based upon careful appraisals of their economic consequences. The plan was subverted, as most plans are, by insufficient political determination to make it work.

Similarly in Tanzania, Nyerere's social transformation was also a crushing fiasco. According to Japheth M. M. Ndaro, director of the Institute of Development Planning at Dodoma, during the period 1961–70, the inhabitants of Dodoma devised and adopted strategies that did not conform with the political slogan of nation building which was dominant in the early 1960s. In some parts of the district, the concept of *Ujamaa* actually stifled local initiative. "All in all, the Arusha Declaration of 1967 and the *Ujamaa* Policy of 1968, which marked an important milestone in the development of the country as a whole, did not inspire the people of Dodoma to engage in development initiatives that were alien to their sociocultural environment" (cited in Taylor and Mackenzie 1992, 178).

Elsewhere in Africa, the experience with development planning proved to be an unmitigated disaster. From 1965 to 1986, Africa's annual rate of growth of gross national product (GNP) averaged a deplorable 0.9 percent. With a population growth rate of 3 percent, that meant declining levels of economic welfare for the average African. Real income per capita dropped by 14.6 percent for all of black Africa from its level in 1965. Unadjusted for inflation, GNP per capita grew by a mere 1.4 percent in the 1960s and 0.5 percent in the 1970s. The 1980s began with declines in income per capita.

Agricultural growth was negligible, with output growing at less than 1.5 percent since 1970. Food production did not keep pace with the population explosion. Food production *per person* fell by 7 percent in the 1960s, 15 percent in the 1970s, and continued to deteriorate in the 1980s. Cereal production, for example, fell by 9.2 per cent in 1987 according to the Food and Agricultural Organization (FAO), necessitating food aid to stave off starvation.

Industrial output across Africa has also been declining, with some regions experiencing *deindustrialization*. The state enterprises established under Africa's various development plans were hopelessly inefficient:

There are countless examples of badly chosen and poorly designed public investments, including some in which the World Bank has participated. A 1987 evaluation revealed that half of the completed rural development projects financed by the World Bank in Africa had failed. A cement plant serving Côte d'Ivoire, Ghana and Togo was closed in 1984 after only four years of operation. A state-run shoe factory in Tanzania has been operating at no more than 25 percent capacity and has remained open only thanks to a large government subsidy. (World Bank 1989, 27).

More dramatic has been the decline in foreign investment in Africa. Net foreign direct investment in Africa in 1985 was $2482 million but dropped to $1,505 in 1987 (World Bank/UNDP 1989, 43).

Table 1. Comparative Performance

| Group | Population, 1989, millions | Growth of real GDP per capita, 1965–2000 (Average annual percentage change) | | | Projection |
		1965–73	1973–80	1980–1989	1990s
Industrial Countries	773	3.7	2.3	2.3	1.8–2.5
Developing Countries	4053	3.9	2.5	1.6	2.2–2.9
Sub-Saharan Africa	480	2.1	0.4	−1.2	0.3–0.5
East Asia	1552	5.3	4.9	6.2	4.2–5.3
South Asia	1131	1.2	1.7	3.0	2.1–2.6
Europe, Mid. East, North Africa	433	5.8	1.9	0.4	1.4–1.8
Latin America and Caribbean	421	3.8	2.5	−0.4	1.3–2.0

Source: World Bank, *World Development Report* (1991, 3).

To maintain income and investment, African governments borrowed heavily in the 1970s. Total African foreign debt has risen nineteen-fold since 1970 to a staggering $270 billion in 1990 which was equal to its gross national product (GNP), making the region the most heavily indebted of all (Latin America's debt amounted to around 60 percent of GNP). Debt service obligations absorbed 47 percent of export revenue in 1988, but only half were actually paid. The arrears were constantly being rescheduled.

With scarce foreign exchange increasingly being devoted to service debt obligations, less became available for imports of spare parts, drugs, textbooks, and other essential supplies. Infrastructure began to crumble for lack of maintenance. Roads started to deteriorate and telephones refused to work. Even the World Bank, the font of perpetual optimism, grew uncharacteristically brusque and alarmed:

The decline in Africa's per capita output during the 1980s, together with the decline in the 1970s, will wipe out all its rise in per capita output since 1960. As a result, low-income Africa is poorer today than in 1960. Improvements over those years in health, education, and in infrastructure are increasingly at risk. For the first time since World War II, a whole region has suffered retrogression over a generation. (World Bank 1989, 9).

The 1980s offered no economic revival for Africa. In fact, its economic performance so deteriorated that the eighties were written off as "a lost decade." "Africa's deepening crisis is characterized by weak agricultural growth, a decline in industrial output, poor export performance, climbing debt, and deteriorating social indicators, institutions, and environment" (World Bank 1989, 2).

The overall picture was even more distressing when compared to the performance of other regions of the Third World. Social and economic indicators of development, such as output growth, health, and literacy, have shown even weaker performance in black Africa. Consider, for example, the rates of growth of gross domestic product (GDP) per capita, as shown in table 1.

In sub-Saharan or black Africa, the crisis has been particularly trenchant. In 1990 black Africa, with a population of four hundred and fifty million, had a gross domestic product (GDP) of $135 billion, which was about the same as that of Belgium, with a population of only ten million. Worse, black Africa's income per

Table 2. GNP per capita: Average Annual Rates of Growth

	1965–73	1973–80	1980–1987
Black Africa	2.9	0.1	−2.8
Excluding Nigeria	1.2	−0.7	−1.2
Exceptions:			
Botswana	9.3	7.3	8.0
Mauritius	0.8	3.9	4.4
Cameroon	−0.4	5.7	4.5
Senegal	−0.8	0.5	0.1

Source: World Bank (1989).

capita fell consistently, from $621 in 1981 to $352 in 1987. The decline has been calamitous in Nigeria, which could not translate its oil bonanza into sustainable economic prosperity.

In 1991, twenty-four of the world's thirty-four poorest nations were in black Africa (*World Development Report* 1991, 204). In the 1960–80 period, fourteen black African countries had growth rates of less than 1 percent per annum. In the 1965–84 period, this number had grown to eighteen. The exceptions to the general economic atrophy in black Africa have been few: Botswana, Mauritania, Cameroon, and Senegal, as table 2 shows.

In the early 1980s, Ivory Coast and Kenya used to be members of this select club but now suffer from serious economic crises. The worst performers have been Ethiopia, Ghana, Liberia, Mozambique, Niger, Nigeria, Sao Tome and Principe, Sudan, Uganda, Zaire, and Zambia—all of which are ruled by civilian/ military dictatorships.

Africans themselves have realized how their state has failed them. Nigerian scholar Claude Ake noted:

Most African regimes have been so alienated and so violently repressive that their citizens see *the state* and its development agents as enemies to be evaded, cheated and defeated if possible, but never as partners. The leaders have been so engrossed in coping with the hostilities which their misrule and repression has unleashed that they are unable to take much interest in anything else including the pursuit of development. These conditions were not conducive to development and none has occurred. What has occurred is regression, as we know only too well. (*Africa Forum* 1, no. 2, 1991, 14).

Indeed, to solve Zaire's economic crisis, Amina Ramadou, a peasant housewife, suggested: "We send three sacks of angry bees to the governor and the president. And some ants which bite. Maybe they eat the government and solve our problems" (*Wall Street Journal*, Sept 26, 1991, A14).

Why Statism and Planning Failed in Africa

Development planning, generally, may fail to achieve its objectives on account of a variety of problems: technical, financial, political, and administrative. A development plan is a technical document and as such can be flawed: the document may not be internally consistent; target growth rates may be overambitious; and the underlying assumptions may be unrealistic. Financing of the plan may encounter severe constraints. Availability of foreign exchange may be reduced by a reduction in export earnings (due to a fall in the price of an export cash crop or the physical volume of exports) and/or by a rise in the import bill (occasioned by say an oil price shock).

Most African development plans were predicated on substantial inflow of foreign capital or aid. The actual inflow of private foreign capital into Africa has been less than expected. Private foreign investors increasingly found Africa unattractive. Low return on investment was the main reason. "Africa's investment and operating costs are typically 50 to 100 percent above those in South Asia—the most comparable region" (World Bank 1989, 3). Unreliable and decaying infrastructure as well as price distortions (especially overvalued exchange rates, price controls, and subsidized credit) were another. More fundamental perhaps was the deteriorating quality of government, epitomized by bureaucratic obstruction, corruption, pervasive rent-seeking, weak judicial system, and arbitrary decision making. Not surprisingly, net private investment declined sharply by about 50 percent between 1970 and 1982 (World Bank 1984, 13).

This decline in foreign investment in Africa, however, was more than made up for by increases in official development assistance:

Even in 1965 almost 20 percent of the Western countries' development assistance went to Africa. In the 1980s, Africans, who are about 12 percent of the developing world's population, were receiving about 22 percent of the total, and the share per person was higher than anywhere else in the Third World—amounting to about $20, versus about $7 for Latin America, and $5 for Asia. (Whitaker 1988, 61)

This was corroborated by the World Bank:

In 1982, Official Development Assistance (ODA) per capita was $19 for all sub-Sahara African countries and $46 per capita for the low-income semiarid countries—compared, for instance, with $4.80 per capita for South Asia. Aid finances 10 percent of gross domestic investment in Africa as a whole, but up to 80 percent for the low-income semiarid countries and over 15 percent for other low-income countries. For some [African] countries, ODA finances not only all investment, but also some consumption. (World Bank 1984, 13)

This substantial provision of ODA however did not make much difference to successful development planning, suggesting the operation of other factors. Absence of political will, the reluctance of ministers to submit to the discipline of planning, and political interference by the head of state impeded the achievement of planning objectives. In addition, there were serious implementation problems in Africa. African governments lacked the administrative capability or expertise to implement development plans successfully. In most cases, implementation was executed by a small cadre of incompetent and corrupt bureaucrats, overwhelmed by the dictates of comprehensive planning for the entire economy.

Perhaps it would be useful to discuss the failure of one African development plan in some detail. Killick (1978), in a detailed study of Ghana's Seven-Year Development plan offered the following reasons for lack of success:

• "Ghana's is not a very 'plannable' economy, not least because its export sector is peculiarly sensitive to the behavior of one of the world's most volatile commodity markets" (136).
• "A grave shortage of qualified Ghanaian economists was equally serious; when the 7YP was being formulated the Office of Planning Commission included only 4 qualified Ghanaians, reinforced by 16 foreign advisers of varying expertise and command

of the English language, but having in common limited knowledge of the national economy" (136).

- "One [weakness] was the attempt a plan covering as long as seven years, which was too long in view of the uncertainties of the [future]. It seems that this was Nkrumah's [the head of state's] decision, resulting from a visit to Russia which launched its own first seven-year plan in 1959" (136).
- "The 7YP was overly preoccupied with macro-economic variables and paid insufficient attention to sector programs and projects. One manifestation of this was the use made of an aggregate gross incremental capital: output ratio to derive overall investment requirements for the plan period. A ratio of 3.5:1 was used, which together with a target annual growth rate of 5.5 percent, implied gross investments of slightly over 2 billion *cedis*" (137).
- "Doubts were also expressed about the realism of some aspects of the plan. For example, its treatment of private investment was unsatisfactory, being derived simply as the difference between aggregate and government investment. Aside from the aluminium smelter, foreign private capital inflows were projected to rise substantially, despite the emergence by 1963 of a distinctly frosty investment climate" (138).
- "The manpower and educational aspects of the plan were similarly open to complaints of unrealism. The plan was unrealistic in its projected output of trained teachers, with actual graduations from teachers' training colleges numbering less than half the planned number" (138).
- "Despite the plan's recognition of the critical importance of agriculture, the chapter dealing with it was among the least satisfactory. The targets were ambitious . . . being handicapped by an absence of statistics on private food production. The plan made no specific provision for cocoa at all. This industry, the most important of Ghana's exports, claimed just two paragraphs of the whole chapter" (138).
- "Although the 7YP provided detailed fiscal projections, it was conspicuously silent on the coordination of it, and its annual plans, with the annual budgets, and in practice Ministers of Finance paid little heed to it. The budget speech of 1963/64 made

only one passing reference to the 7YP and, in direct opposition
to its strategy, proposed an increase in government consumption
relative to capital expenditure" (139).

• "The reluctance of individual Ministers to submit to the disci-
plines of a plan was even more serious for implementation. A
struggle for control over the capital budget quickly developed
between the Planning Commision and the Ministry of Finance. . . . The absence of Ministers from membership of the
Planning Commission probably contributed to the estrangement
between the planners and politicians but Nkrumah, who was
chairman, was no better at keeping within the limitations of the
plan" (143).

Even if these technical, financial, and political problems had
been resolved, it was highly unlikely Africa's experience with development planning would have been successful. The whole approach embodied by development planning was flawed and objec-
tionable on both practical and philosophical grounds. A contrite
World Bank expressed this rather neatly:

The postindependence development efforts in Africa failed because the
strategy was misconceived. Governments made a dash for "modernization," copying, but not adapting, Western models. The result was poorly
designed public investment in industry; too little attention to peasant
agriculture; too much intervention in areas in which the state lacked
managerial, technical, and entrepreneurial skills; and too little effort
to foster grass-roots development. The top-down approach demotivated
ordinary people, whose energies most needed to be mobilized in the
development effort. (World Bank 1989, 3).

Exploitation of the Peasantry

Under statism and development planning, African governments
envisioned huge surpluses in the rural sector to be tapped for
development. Large resources could be transferred to the state by
extracting wealth from peasant producers. The milking devices
used included the following: poll taxes, low producer prices, export marketing boards, hidden export taxes, price controls, development levies, and forcing peasant farmers to sell annual quotas
to government organs. The assumption was that, when such re-

sources were ceded to the state, they would be used by develop-ment planners for the benefit of all.

The prices peasants received for their produce were dictated by many African governments, not as determined by market forces in accordance with African traditions. Under a system of price con-trols, Africa's peasants came to pay the world's most confiscatory taxes.[1] They faced stiff penalties and outright confiscation of their produce if they sold above the government-controlled prices.

Markets were burned down and destroyed at Accra, Kumasi, Koforidua and other cities when traders refused to sell at government-dictated prices. In February 1982, the Tamale Central Market was set ablaze, causing the destruction of large quantities of foodstuffs, drugs and im-ported spare parts. Then John Ndeburge, the Northern Regional Secre-tary, set up a 5–member Committee of Inquiry to investigate the circum-stances leading to the incineration of the market. (*West Africa*, March 8, 1982, 684)

Unbelievable brutalities were heaped upon peasant farmers and traders under Ghana's inane price controls (1982–83). Fur-thermore, Ghanaian cocoa farmers in 1983 were paid less than 10 percent of the world market price for their produce.

In Gambia, peanut producers received about 20 percent for their produce in the same year. According to *West Africa* (Feb. 15, 1989, 250):

On the average, between 1964/65 and 1984/85, the peasants of Gambia were robbed of 60 percent of the international price of their groundnuts! For 20 years, the Jawara Government 'officially' took, free of charge, 3 out of every 5 bags, leaving the peasant with a gross of 2. With deductions for subsistence credit fertiliser, seeds, etc., the peasant would end up with a net one bag out of five. . . . With these facts, it is simply wrong to say that the poverty of the peasant derives from the defects of nature—drought, over-population, laziness, and so on.

In 1981, the government of Tanzania paid peasant maize farm-ers only 20 percent of the free-market price for their produce. "Studies by the International Labor Organization have indicated that taxation levels in the agricultural sector in Sierra Leone averaged between 30 and 60 percent of gross income" (*West Africa*, Feb. 15, 1982, 446).

In Zambia, when traders refused to sell their produce at government-dictated prices, authorities raided markets in May 1988. They arrested hundreds of people, took their money, and tore down market stalls, seizing sugar, detergents, salt, maize meal, soft drinks, candles, flour, and clothing. Back in 1984 in Ghana, Mr. Kwame Forson, the Agona Swedru District Secretary, "called on some unidentified soldiers who make brief stopovers at Swedru to check prices, and instead threaten and rob innocent traders, to desist from such acts" (*West Africa*, July 23, 1984, 1511).

In this way, the peasantry was systematically robbed of considerable resources. For example, in a January 1989 New Year's address, President Houphouet-Boigny of Ivory Coast admitted that peasant cash-crop producers "have over the years parted with four-fifths of the value of what they produced to enable the government to finance development" (*West Africa*, May 1–7, 1989, 677). But development for whom?

The resources extracted from the peasants were seldom used to improve their lot, but instead used by the elite minority to develop the urban areas for themselves. For example, over 80 percent of the "development" of the Ivory Coast was concentrated in Abidjan for the benefit of the urban elites, not the rural peasants.

The standard of living enjoyed by the elites far outstripped those of the peasants. Contrast the plush and subsidized amenities of the ruling class in the urban areas with the dingy and wretched lives of the rural peasants. In Mauritania, for example, while the elites, the Arabs, had access to subsidized tap-water supplies, the peasants, often black, paid seven to forty times more for their water from sellers with donkey carts. In 1982, while the leadership in Zaire was making between $5,000 and $9,000 a month, a peasant was lucky to make $50 a month (*Africa Now*, March 1982, 17). In 1985, Cameroon, with a per capita income of less than $1,000 a year, was the world's ninth-largest importer of champagne. The elites were living high: "The governor of the Dakar-based African central bank can reach his 13th floor office without having to step out of his car. One of the many perks that go with the region's highest-paying job is a private lift (elevator) to hoist him and his Mercedes to work" (*South*, May 1988, 34).

"Only socialism will save Africa!!" African leaders and nationalists chanted. But the socialism practiced in Africa was a peculiar type—"Swiss bank socialism"—which allowed the head of state and a phalanx of kleptocrats (armed government looters) to rape and plunder African treasuries for deposit in Switzerland. As African economies deteriorated, Africa's tyrants and elite cohorts furiously developed pot-bellies and chins at a rate commensurate with the economic decline. While Africa's peasants were being exhorted to tighten their belts, vampire elites were loosening theirs with fat bank balances overseas. Even the Paris newspaper, *Le Monde,* complained bitterly in March 1990: "Every franc we give impoverished Africa, comes back to France or is smuggled into Switzerland and even Japan" (cited in *Washington Post,* March 26, 1990, A17).

The manager of the failed *Banque Commerciale de Benin* put it rather tersely:

The basic problem here, beside a lack of competence, is total corruption. The top people line their pockets through political influence. The president's (Mathieu Kerekou's) adviser, Cisse, called *le Marabout*—"the priest"—stole 5 billion CFA (about $14 million) from this bank. We've traced it to Switzerland, London and Monte Carlo. . . .
The chief bandit is the president, along with his associates in the politburo. The chief prosecutor is the next biggest bandit. Another is the minister of justice: all court decisions are determined by bribes. I went to the presidential palace along with a representative of the World Bank. We were asked when the stolen money would be recovered. It was a rather difficult to answer, 'Mr. President, *you* have the money" . . .
The top men will have 10 or 15 mistresses who used to run up big debit accounts here, and then go to the *Palais* and say, "You've got to straighten me out with the bank."
The rulers now admit that they never understood Marxism, and as a sop to opinion a few people have been jailed. But new *marabouts* have been brought in, and are still at the center of the decision-making. (*American Spectator*, May 1990, 31)

In Angola, the socialist system operated as a kind of reverse Robin Hood, funneling the richest benefits to the least needy:

Angolans who own cars can fill their tanks for less than a dollar, and international telephone calls cost only pennies. One local boasts of getting a round-trip ticket to Paris on Air France for the equivalent of two cases of beer. Luanda does not even pick up its own garbage; the job is contracted out to a foreign company using Filipino workers lured to Angola with fat paychecks, special housing and First World garbage trucks.

Of course, the chief beneficiaries of all this are the city's westernized elite and their foreign business bedfellows. Many of life's necessities, on the other hand, are not available at subsidized prices. For the poorest residents, survival is impossible without resort to *candonga*, or illegal trading. (*Insight*, Oct. 1, 1990, 13)

But peasants, despite their lack of formal education, proved that they were no fools or pushovers. They rebelled against naked state exploitation by withholding their produce, switching to other crops, producing enough to feed only themselves, or simply by smuggling their produce to places where it fetched higher prices. One Ghanaian peasant, Amoafo Yaw, said exactly that:

In this country, much noise is being made about the exploitation of the people. . . . But as far as I am concerned, it is the STATE, as the Chief Vanguard, and her so-called Public Servants, Civil Servants which actually exploit others in the country. . . .

The money used in buying the cars for Government officials, the cement for building estates, and other Government bungalows which workers obtain loans to buy, the rice workers eat in their staff canteens, the soap, toothpaste, textiles cloth which workers buy under the present distribution system all come from the farmers' cocoa [cash crop] and coffee money. . . .

This STATE-MONOPOLY CAPITALISM has been going on since the days of the colonial masters and even our own Government after independence have continued the system. . . .

The farmers realising this naked exploitation decided that they would no longer increase cocoa and coffee production, they would not increase food production and any other items which the State depends on for foreign exchange. In effect, there will be no surplus for the state to exploit. (*Daily Graphic*, Accra, Feb. 17, 1982, 3)

The results elsewhere in Africa were falling agricultural and export production. For example, in 1988, diamond dealers and miners in Sierra Leone told Mr. A. R. Turray, the governor of the Central Bank, that, "The government's gold and diamond marketing board (GGDO) was being sidestepped because it does not offer attractive enough prices. . . . Mr. Turray admitted that smuggling could be minimised if the GGDO paid better prices" (*West Africa*, January 23–29, 1989, 125). GGDO did not and consequently between April and December 1988, its purchases were nil. In Tanzania, the amount of maize and rice sold through official channels in 1984 was less than one-third the level in 1979.

In 1983, the government of Ghana complained that cocoa smuggling was depriving the nation of at least one hundred million dollars in foreign exchange annually. Diamond smuggling cost Angola and Sierra Leone at least two hundred million and 60 million dollars respectively, yearly. In Sierra Leone, in just one year, "the diamond output of 731,000 carats in 1975 was reduced to 481,000 in 1976 (34 percent decline) mainly by the activities of smugglers" (*West Africa*, July 18, 1977, 1501). Uganda coffee was regularly smuggled to Kenya. Guinea-Bissau diamonds and coffee ended up in Ivory Coast. Nigeria's consumer goods and petrol were regularly smuggled to Cameroon.

Denouncing smuggling as an economic felony, African governments responded by closing their borders and issued threats: "Convicted cocoa smugglers in Ghana will be shot by firing squad in future, the Chairman of a Public Tribunal, Mr. Agyekum, has said in Accra" (*West Africa*, December 6, 1982, 3179). In February 1989, Nigeria's justice minister, Prince Bola Ajibola, declared that, "Henceforth, anyone caught smuggling or in possession of smuggled items will be sentenced to life in prison" (*Insight*, Feb 6, 1989, 38). For almost a decade, 1975–84, Tanzania closed its border with Kenya to prevent smuggling, but to no avail. Economic barbarism was running amok.

In the 1980s Zimbabwe used to be a net food exporter, but by 1992 it was importing food. It is true the 1991–92 drought devastated agricultural production in southern Africa. But in the case of many countries in southern Africa, the drought merely exacerbated an already precarious food supply situation. In Zimbabwe, the culprit was low government-dictated prices. As John Robertson, the chief economist of the First Merchant Bank in Harare, observed, "The Government [of Robert Mugabe] could have avoided half the total food import with better policies. . . . In the last several years, the Government decided to pay a low price to farmers who grew corn, the staple crop. This meant that the farmers switched to other crops" (*New York Times*, July 10, 1992, A11).

Development by Imitation

The resources siphoned off from the rural sector were to be used for "national development." But development was misinterpreted by African leaders and elites to mean "change" rather than an "improvement" upon existing ways of doing things. Traditional ways of doing things were denigrated as "unmodern," "backward and primitive." To develop, they thought, Africans must adopt new ways, values, and systems. This mentality reached a low level of depravity when in 1975, the government of Ghana declared twelve *imported* items as "essential commodities." These were tinned corned beef, sardines, rice, sugar, tinned milk, and flour. The implication was that the native foodstuffs, upon which their forebears had subsisted for centuries, were not "essential." Therefore, Africans have to foreswear their culture or diet in order to develop—as if the Japanese, Koreans, and Singaporeans did so.

The propensity to copy foreign paraphernalia became pervasive in Africa. Cuba had People's Defense Committees; so too must Ghana. France once had an emperor. So in 1976, Bokassa of the Central African Republic spent 20 million dollars to crown himself "emperor" just to prove that Africa too has come of age. At his trial in Bangui, in December 1986,

Bokassa berated the court for stripping him of his self-imposed title of field marshal and demoting his to private first class. "You can sentence me to death," he said indignantly, 'but you have no power to reduce me to the ranks!' At another point Bokassa raised his arms in a salute reminiscent of his hero, the late French President Charles de Gaulle. "I was always a faithful soldier of General de Gaulle," he said, "and I have always done my duty." (*Time*, December 29, 1986, 27)

France also had a revolution. In June 1989, when it held its bicentennial for its 1789 Revolution, several African despots showed up in Paris. Even the *West Africa* magazine, which is 60 percent owned by the Nigerian government, noticed something odd. According to an editorial in its June 24–30, 1990, issue:

Some of the African guests, such as President Mobutu of Zaire, whose human rights record is grim, looked out of place at such a ceremony, although Zaire is one of the African countries which, ironically, has the word "revolution" in the name of its ruling party. . . .

Most of the African leaders present barely related to the anniversary in any case, and would have been on the wrong side in 1789. For the challenges it still embodies are far from being met in Africa, and the spectre of chaos and bloodshed that haunted it, still lurk in the background.

The former Soviet Union was a Marxist-Leninist state. So Robert Mugabe vowed to establish a one-party Marxist-Leninist state in Zimbabwe! Even a fool could see clearly that Marx and Lenin were not black Africans. Said Enos Nkala, the former defence minister: "Marxist-Leninist policies were useless to black people" (*New African*, July 1992, 21).

Rome has a basilica; so too must Ivory Coast. The United States has only two political parties. So the Babangida military government of Nigeria created exactly two political parties for the people: the National Republican Convention and the Social Democratic Party.

The same unimaginative aping was also taken to the field of development. American farmers use tractors; so too must the peasant farmers of Africa. British farmers use chemical fertilizers; so too must Africa. New York has skyscrapers; so too must Africa in the middle of nowhere. The former Soviet Union had state enterprises; so too must Africa. China has state farms; so too must Africa. California grows apples; so too must Africa.

Even the supposedly "backward and illiterate" peasants know that what grows well in one part of the world may wither in another because soil conditions, rainfall, and topography may be different. Common sense suggest planting what is suited to Africa's own environment. By "environment" is meant the whole gamut of indigenous institutions and systems of the people of Africa—the peasants who are the majority.

The scurrilous imitation by African elites is even drawing attention in the foreign press. Elaborating on the problem of Africa's black elite to a *Washington Post* reporter, a diplomat from the Embassy of Cameroon said, "Go to the cafes and the bistros . . . See them in their European suits, reading the latest editions of European newspapers. The problem of African development was that the *educated elite never developed indigenous models, but instead tried to transplant Europe to Africa.*" It doesn't take long in Africa to see what the diplomat was talking about.

Basil Davidson, a renowned British scholar on Africa, writes in his new book, *The Black Man's Burden,* how European colonialism in Africa set out to deny and eventually eliminate the continent's precolonial history. And in that, the Europeans found willing accomplices among Africa's European-oriented elite, the "modernizers," who were in constant conflict with Africa's "traditionalists," including the acknowledged tribal chiefs.

These modernizing Africans clung to the notion that anything traditional was by definition primitive. And it was this elite that came to the forefront of the independence movements and proceeded to impose European models on their new African states. *Rather than seek to build on tradition, as the Confucianist societies of East Asia have tried to do even in their revolutionary phases, the new Africans often sought to purge what was deepest and most authentic in their cultures.*

That influence can still be seen today. Judges in Kenyan courts wear white wigs and speak in a flowery, archaic English that might be considered "quaint." Governmental institutions in the former British colonies—from parliaments to the "special branch" internal security forces—are near-duplicates of their counterparts at Westminster and Whitehall. Colonial governments in Africa were dictatorships backed by a top-heavy bureaucracy. Independence seems to have substituted black autocrats for the old white colonial governors, with little thought of Africa's traditions.

The suppression of indigenous cultures has been especially pronounced in the former French colonies of West Africa, which were treated as an overseas department of France, noted Pauline Baker, an Africa specialist with the Aspen Institute (in Colorado). "The French tried to have black Frenchmen," she said (*Washington Post,* July 12, 1992, A26); emphasis added).

African elites and governments were fascinated by shiny machines, industry, and new technology. In their selection of development projects, they displayed an abiding faith in the "religion of development"—a predisposition to castigate anything traditional and to exalt anything foreign as sanctified. Across Africa, industry was overemphasized to the neglect of agriculture. At independence, Nigeria, Sierra Leone, Tanzania, Zambia, and many other African countries used to feed themselves. Two decades later, they were importing food.

Agriculture was routinely denigrated by African elites as an inferior form of occupation. The late Kwame Nkrumah of Ghana was quite explicit:

Industry rather than agriculture is the means by which rapid improvement in Africa's living standards is possible. There are, however, imperialist specialists and apologists who urge the less developed countries to concentrate on agriculture and leave industrialization to some later time when their populations shall be well fed. The world's economic development, however, shows that it is only with advanced industrialization that it has been possible to raise the nutritional level of the people by raising their levels of income. (Nkrumah, 1957, 7)

Nkrumah was wrong. Five years into his presidency, food shortages had become serious and rampant in Ghana. In 1966, he was booted out of office in a military coup.

When African governments belatedly recognized the importance of agriculture, African leaders made mechanization the guiding principle of the agricultural revolution. Tons of expensive agricultural machinery were imported into Africa; combine-harvesters graced the landscape in Tanzania. Elsewhere, there was a persistent tendency to opt for capital-intensive and grand monuments. These are symbols of development or progress. But most of these "development projects" came to grief. Among the factors which accounted for their demise were construction delays, poor design, inadequate supervision, inappropriate technology (too capital-intensive), corruption, and pilfering. In its 1981 Report, the EEC noted that:

Many development projects failed in Africa because they were on too large a scale and were not adapted to the population and the environment they were supposed to benefit. . . . The projects of most lasting value are generally those which are simplest and directly benefit the local community concerned. (Cited in *West Africa*, Jan 18, 1982, 188)

By 1990, the African economic landscape was littered with a multitude of "black elephants": basilicas, grand conference halls, prestigious airports, new capitals, and show party headquarters. These projects failed for the simple reason that they did not fit into Africa's traditional setup.

Concentration of Too Much Economic Power

A great deal of economic power was invested in the state to under-take development. But the mistake or fatal oversight was the failure to attach countervailing checks or safeguards against such concentration of powers. The concentration of too much *economic* power in the hands of the state has the following pernicious effects:

1. It turns the state into a huge patronage machine. Factory locations, job creation, subsidies, and other goodies are dispensed by the state. It may use these to reward supporters, cronies, and sycophants as in Mexico, Brazil, Peru, and many African countries. In Mexico, for example, membership in the ruling PRI was necessary to secure a top government post. This practice creates the belief that one's success does not depend upon one's own ability but on how loudly one can sing the praises of the state.
2. It also fosters the erroneous belief that the state can solve *all* economic problems and this leads to politicization of almost every economic issue or problem. The state is called upon to intervene even when such intervention may not be necessary. For example, a tailor is overcharging and therefore the government must arrest him. The person making this call does not have the common sense to exercise his options by going to another tailor. The state *cannot* solve all economic problems. Unemployment, for example, will always exist and can never be reduced to zero. It is a pretentious state which seeks to eliminate it completely.
3. Concentration of economic power in the hands of the state encourages capital flight. Foreign exchange is controlled by the state and only top government officials, including the head of state himself, have access. Often, it is embezzled and looted.
   Capital flight has become a serious problem in the Third World. At least 15 billion dollars leaves Africa illegally. It is also a problem in Latin America. If rich Mexicans were to repatriate the 80 billion dollars they have hoarded abroad, more than half of Mexico's 110 billion dollars debt would be

repaid. Argentina and Venezuela also suffer capital hemor-
rhage.

It is equally serious in the Middle East. On March 24, 1991,
CBS "60 Minutes" reported that Iraqi president, Saddam Hus-
sein, had ten-twelve billion dollars stashed abroad.

4. It encourages all sorts of individuals, groups, tribes, or organizations to compete for control of the state. Such competition
often results in civil wars, with peasants caught in the cross-
fire. Those who win control of the state naturally use its instruments to further their own economic interests or welfare at the
expense of the others. Those excluded plot to overthrow the
government, and on and on the battle continues. In the end, it
is the military which emerges the victor because it has all
the guns.

Concentration of Too Much Political Power

This also has many undesirable consequences:

1. Concentration of political power in the hands of the head of
state often leads to abuse. Power corrupts and absolute power
corrupts absolutely, according to Lord Acton. Abuse of political
power is evident in election fraud, election rigging, and the
drift toward a one-party or one-man dictatorship.
2. It leads to brutal suppression of dissent or opposition. Ostensibly, the state had acquired broad powers to "develop" the
economy. Anyone who challenges such powers therefore must
be "an enemy" to be liquidated. Many "dissidents" have been
detained, murdered, or exiled. It may well be that the state
indeed needs broad powers. But common sense dictates that
there should be some *independent* mechanisms of checking such
powers. It is the height of lunacy, for example, to allow the
state to set up a Human Rights Commission to police its own
human rights violations.
3. It leads to censorship and denial of freedom of expression.
Development is actually a groping process. Economic conditions are not static. Prices are constantly changing on the world
market and consequently, development decisions must con-

stantly be reviewed to take advantage of changing circumstances. Mistakes are bound to occur. Such mistakes, however, are always embarrassing and the state may not want them exposed. It suppresses them by imposing draconian censorship laws. Journalists, editors, writers, and poets who expose any wrong-doing or mistakes are incarcerated. But then, if a problem is covered up, it only festers.

4. It encourages militarism. The state spends enormous amount of resources on the military to back its political legitimacy or add recognition and credibility to government. Military spending in the Third World has rocketed from only $1 billion in 1960 to nearly $35 billion by 1987, according to the World Bank. Obviously, these resources can be better put to real development.[2]

As remarked earlier, the state has now become *the problem* in Africa and the *enemy* of development. With so much power concentrated in the hands of the state, it induces all sorts of groups—racial, ethnic, and professional-to capture the state and advance their own group or individual interests.

In apartheid South Africa, the instruments of the state were captured and monopolized by the white minority tribe and used to promote the interests and welfare of whites. Nonwhites were effectively disenfranchised and excluded from partaking of the "public gravy." In Mauritania and Sudan, it was the Arab tribe which captured the powers of the state. In Angola, Central African Republic, Cameroon, Congo, Madagascar, Mozambique, Tanzania, Zambia, and Zimbabwe, the state was rigidly monopolized by one political party—the one-party state system. Nonparty members, just like the blacks in South Africa, were shut out. Under stratocracy, it was the military which usurped the powers of the state (Benin, Burundi, Ethiopia, Ghana, Mali, Niger, Nigeria, Rwanda, Somalia, and Uganda). Kleptocracy occurred when armed looters took over the state (Benin under Kerekou, Zaire).

Africa needs not just less government but also a situation where no individual or group can monopolize the state. In case one is looking for a solution to this problem, it would be useful to consider that adopted by many of Africa's "primitive and backward" tribes. They abolished the state!

Centuries ago, it occurred to many African tribes that the *state* was evil and not at all necessary for the maintenance of law and order. In fact, they decried the state as necessarily tyrannous and dispensed with centralized authority (a chief or king). Yet, they managed to preserve peace and order among their communities. They were called *stateless* or *acephalous societies,* and examples today include the Abesheini of Kenya, the Igbo and Tiv of Nigeria, the Nuer of Sudan, and the Tallensi of Ghana, to name only a few. They were the subject of intense early European curiosity in the olden days.

Baffled by the absence of the "state," European colonialists dismissed these people as "backward." The Europeans had it in their head that any community must have a political ruler. Since there was none in the "stateless" societies, the colonialists insisted on creating "chiefs" or "strongmen" (Saddams) for these backward people. But in "blissful ignorance," the people promptly "destooled" (removed) such "colonial" or "canton" chiefs. Such was the fate, for example, of the "government" *mantse* of the Ga people (Ghana) and the *akill* of the Somali. But the force of colonial arms prevailed and most of these "chiefs," feeling that they had the awesome colonial might behind them, became corrupt and despotic.

Now, the Europeans and other Westerners are singing a different tune. The *state,* while necessary for law and order and the suppression of predators at home and abroad, has shown itself to be a false god for all those who have looked to it to right civil wrongs, establish justice, remove poverty, educate children, curb inflation, cure unemployment, provide affordable housing, straighten out the business cycle, safeguard cultural values, and the like.

The "ubiquitous *state* has not ensured government of the people, by the people, for the people. It has not brought liberty, equality, fraternity, peace, land or bread to millions misled to trust it. It has disappointed the hopes of Marxists, democratic socialists, party political liberals and paternalistic conservatives in the West" (*Washington Times,* Jan 22, 1991, G3).

In Philadelphia, Mr. Edward Rendell, a Democratic candidate for the mayorship, complained bitterly, "Government does not work because it is not designed to. There is no incentive for employees to do their best, so many do not. There is no incentive to save money, so it is squandered" (cited in *Wall Street Journal*, June 18, 1991, A18). Maybe those *stateless* African societies were not backward after all. They were probably politically astute and far ahead of their time. Said a traditional chief: "Here in Lesotho, we have two problems: rats and the government" (*Health & Development*, March/April, 1989, 30).

Statism Is Alien

The economic systems established in postcolonial Africa under statism were grossly alien to indigenous African culture. The following description is drawn heavily from Ayittey (1991b).

As implied by "communal ownership," land in the African village did not belong to everybody. Land was lineage-controlled. The true owners of land were those who first settled on it—the ancestors. Although dead, their spirits were believed to be ever-present and guide the living.

The chief or the lineage head was a mere custodian of the land. His role was to hold the land in trust. He could not deny a tribesman access to the land. Even strangers could obtain use rights upon the provision of a token gift. Use rights were virtually perpetual so long as a small tribute was paid, voluntary in some cases, and the land was not abused. Crops raised on the land belonged to individual farmers, not to the village chief or headman. What types of crops to cultivate was an individual choice. All the means of production were privately owned, not held by the state. Even land was not owned by the state or the chiefs. Lineage heads exercised control over land in most villages.

The natives were free enterprisers, going about their economic activities on their own initiative, not at the command of chiefs. Profits made by them were theirs to keep, not for the chiefs to expropriate. There was *no* African law which prohibited the natives from making a profit or accumulating wealth in the course of their economic activities. Prosperity and wealth could be pursued but within the limits set by either Islam, or social norms, or both. The wealth of the rich was not sequestrated by the chief or king for equal distribution to all the people. All the wealthy were required to do was to *assist* their poor kinsmen.

There were few direct taxes. Only tribute was paid to the chief voluntarily. The size of the tribute was determined by how well the chief governed. The kings derived much of their revenue from their own royal estates and gardens. In essence, the kings looked after themselves.

In general, there were no state or tribal government enterprises, except in a very few cases such as in the Kingdom of Dahomey. A king or chief could operate a farm, a mine, or some commercial enterprise. But it was for his own benefit, not for the purpose of increasing the welfare of the people. It was not his traditional function to use his farm, if he chose to have one, to feed his people. The people fed themselves and provided for their needs.

In many indigenous systems, there was generally no direct interference with the production or distribution of commodities. Agricultural production and trading were activities dominated by women. What these women cultivated and traded were their own decisions to make.

Markets and trade were free and open. Though trade in some few commodities, such as slaves or ivory, was reserved for the king, in general no king or chief monopolized trade or markets to the total exclusion of his subjects. It would have been an *un-African* thing to do. Rather the chiefs encouraged their people to engage in trade and it was the traditional function of the chief to create a peaceful atmosphere for his people to engage in free trade. Prices on native markets were not fixed or controlled by the chiefs. They were, in general, determined by market forces—supply and demand. These principles were understood by the natives and they bargained over prices. Markets were well structured and organized in West Africa under 'Market Queens.'

Though some powerful merchants tried to control markets and fix prices, open competition was the rule. Nor could such competition be eliminated. There were numerous suppliers, middlemen, brokers, and trade routes, as well as substitutes. Trade in indigenous products could not be controlled, but the possibilities for control existed over "imported" items. However, even in these cases, control could not be complete, since alternative trade routes existed.

Kendall and Louw (1987, 21) also reached similar conclusions:

Pre-colonial African law and custom shared the following features with the free market system: Assets such as stock, crops, huts, handicrafts and weapons were privately owned and land was privately alloted and subject to private grazing rights;
• There were no laws against free contract and voluntary exchange;
• There was no coercive redistribution of wealth and almost no taxes;
• Chiefs and headmen had few autocratic powers and usually needed to obtain full consensus for decisions;
• Central government was limited, with a high degree of devolution to village councils, and there was no central planning structure;
• There were no powers of arbitrary expropriation, and land and huts could be expropriated under extreme conditions after a full public hearing.

Conclusions

Development planning failed in Africa for the simple reason that the state attempted to do what it should not have taken upon itself. As Bauer (1984, 23) put it:

Societies are made up of very large numbers of people. Their constituent persons and families perceive better than do others, or are even the only ones who can perceive, their own circumstances, attitudes, preferences, opportunities and prospects. They are also best qualified to judge their own likely responses to changes in these conditions. In the aggregate, they also possess a vast amount of other pertinent knowledge which the signals and mechanisms of the market order transmit and diffuse. Such transmission and diffusion of knowledge is indispensable for social, economic, scientific and technical innovation.

No centralized agency, however powerful, can perform these functions effectively, not even by coercion. Attempts to perform them by coercion go counter, moreover, to the widening of people's choice, the basic criterion of economic development.

Back in 1932, Kobina Sekyi, the Ghanaian lawyer and philosopher, expressed similar sentiments:

When each tribe or nation is enabled to develop along its own lines, the respective geniuses of the several distinguishable races will harmonise in the establishment of a settled state of peace and prosperity, where development, scientific and social, including moral and political, advance will be steady. (*West Africa*, third week of July, 1932)

But each ethnic group can develop along its own lines, *if and only if*, it is allowed the economic, political, and intellectual freedom to do so. Why? Because according to a proverb of Nigeria's Igbo clan, Efik: *"Enyene Idem ofiok oto nte Mfat edebede enye"* meaning, only an organism knows best its own needs and can best serve them. Yet, the pretentious state never consulted African "organisms" and sought to determine and serve their needs.

Now, African governments seem to have come to their senses. African leaders themselves at a historic conference at Arusha (February 1990) adopted the African Charter for Popular Participation in Development Transformation, which held that the absence of democracy has been a major cause of the chronic unemployment of Africa:

We affirm that nations cannot be built without the popular support and full participation of the people, nor can the economic crisis be resolved and the human and economic conditions improved without the full and effective contribution, creativity and popular enthusiasm of the vast majority of the people. After all, it is to the people that the very benefits of development should and must accrue. We are convinced that neither can Africa's perpetual economic crisis be overcome, nor can a bright future for Africa and its people see the light of day unless the structure, pattern and political context of the process of socio-economic development are appropriately altered. (*Africa Forum* 1, no.2, (1991), 14)

But then ask these same leaders to create the conditions necessary for full political participation of the people in development and they would perform the "Rawlings shuffle," "Moi masamba," "Kaunda twist," and the "Babangida boogie": one step forward, four steps back, a side kick and a somersault to land at the same place. Much ado about nothing.

Notes

1. There was a political motive for paying peasant farmers low prices. Most African governments derived their political support from urban elites: workers, students, etc. African governments pursued a "cheap

food" policy to ensure continued political support from this constituency. But this policy was economically stupid. As we have had the occasion to remark, price controls do *not* make food "cheap." Instead, they make food *more* expensive by creating shortages. This is true of *any* commodity whose price is controlled.

2. In 1990, the United States surpassed the Soviet Union and became the top arms supplier to the Third World. U.S. arms sales jumped from nearly $8 billion in 1989 to $18.5 billion in 1990, compared to Soviet arms deals worth about $12.1 billion in 1990 (*Washington Times*, August 12, 1991, A3). Although the blip in United States arms sales was attributed to the Iraqi threat and the subsequent Gulf War, the U.S. is expected to remain the leading arms supplier, with the former Soviet Union converting military establishments to civilian use.

References

Ayittey, George B. N. 1991a. "No More Aid for Africa." *Wall Street Journal,* Oct 18, 1991.

———. 1991b. *Indigenous African Institutions.* Irvington-on-Hudson, N. Y.: Transnational Publishers.

———. 1992. *Africa Betrayed.* New York: St. Martin's Press.

Bandow, Doug. 1986. "The First World's Misbegotten Economic Legacy to the Third World." *Journal of Economic Growth* 1 (4): 17.

Bauer, P. T. 1984. *Reality and Rhetoric.* Cambridge: Harvard University Press.

Kendall, Frances, and Leon Louw. 1987. *After Apartheid: The Solution for South Africa.* San Francisco: Institute of Contemporary Studies.

Killick, Tony. 1976. "Development Planning, Free Markets and the Role of the State." *Oxford Economic Papers* 41, no. 4 (October): 161–84.

———. 1978. *Development Economics in Action: A Study of Economic Policies in Ghana.* London: Heinemann Educational Books.

Mabogunje, A. 1988. "Africa after the False Start." Paper presented to the 26th Congress of the International Geographical Union, Sydney, Australia.

Nkrumah, Kwame. 1957. *Ghana: An Autobiography.* London: Nelson.

———. 1963. *Africa Must Unite.* New York: International Publishers.

———. 1968. *Handbook on Revolutionary Warfare.* London: Panaf Publishers.

———. 1969. *Dark Days in Ghana.* London: Panaf Publishers.

———. 1973. *Revolutionary Path.* New York: International Publishers.

Nyerere, Julius K. 1962. *Ujaama: The Basis Of African Socialism.* Dar es Salaam: Government Printer.

Taylor, D. R. F., and Fiona Mackenzie, eds. 1992. *Development from Within.* New York: Routledge.

Todaro, Michael P., ed. 1983. *The Struggle for Economic Development.* New York: Longman.

———. 1987. *Economic Development in the Third World.* New York: Longman.

Uphoff, Norman T. 1970. *Ghana's Experience in Using External Aid for Development.* Berkeley and Los Angeles: University of California Press.

Whitaker, Jennifer. 1988. *How Can Africa Survive?* New York: Harper & Row.

World Bank. 1984. *Toward Sustained Development in Sub-Saharan Africa.* Washington, D.C.

———. 1989. *Sub-Saharan Africa: From Crisis to Self-Sustainable Growth.* Washington, D.C.

———. Annually. *World Development Report.* New York: Oxford University Press.

World Bank/UNDP. 1989. *African Economic and Financial Data.* Washington, D.C.

Zinsmeister, Karl. 1987. "East African Experiment: Kenyan Prosperity and Tanzanian Decline." *Journal of Economic Growth* 2 (2): 28.

III

The Record on Foreign Aid and Advice

7

The World Bank and the IMF: Misbegotten Sisters

David Osterfeld

On opposite sides of 19th street in Washington, DC, stand two of the world's most powerful institutions. As lenders in their own right, they directly control billions of dollars each year; indirectly, tens of billions more. They sit in judgment on governments, using their financial clout to influence economic policy in scores of developing countries. The fate of hundreds of millions of people turns on the decisions these institutions make. The world they were created to serve no longer exists, yet their role is undiminished. (1991b, 5)

—Economist

Overview

One of these institutions is the World Bank, the other the International Monetary Fund, or IMF. Both were the outcome of the conference of the United States, Britain, and their World War II allies held at Bretton Woods, New Hampshire, in July 1944. The purpose of the conference was to construct and manage a postwar economic order.

Initially, the World Bank's task was to make long-term loans on a commercial basis for the purpose of European reconstruction in the aftermath of World War II. Very quickly, however, the focus shifted from reconstruction to development, with its first mission

185

to a Less-Developed Country (LDC), Columbia, coming as early as 1949 (Pomfret 1992, 133, 165). The IMF, largely the brainchild of John Maynard Keynes, was designed to insure monetary stability, that is, prevent devaluations except in emergencies, and promote freer trade by making short-term loans to countries experiencing balance of payments difficulties. The IMF was, as Pomfret has pointed out (1992, 113), the monetary counterpart to yet another postwar international institution, the General Agreement on Tariffs and Trade (GATT), whose purpose was to encourage negotiated reductions in trade barriers. Unlike the World Bank, the IMF was not intended to be an aid agency. Like GATT, it is a club. Member nations pay a quota, or "subscription," to the Fund, based on their relative economic sizes and are permitted to draw from this pool of "liquid reserves" (Harrod 1958, 171) when necessary in order to tide them over temporary balance of payments problems, thereby avoiding devaluations relative to other members' currencies. Similarly, a central tenet of GATT is nondiscrimination, that is, that every member-nation is to treat goods from all other members equally. It is implemented through the most-favored nation (MFN) principle, in which each member agrees to accord to all other members the same treatment it extends to that nation receiving its most favorable treatment.

The three pillars of the postwar economic world were the World Bank, intended to make long-term loans for the reconstruction of a Europe ravaged by war and to Third World countries to stimulate economic development by the creation of wealth (Krauss 1984, 165); the International Monetary Fund, designed to insure monetary stability through the use of short-term loans; and the General Agreement on Tariffs and Trade, whose purpose was to promote an open international trading order. Together, it was thought, the three institutions would prevent a return to the economic nationalism that characterized the depression years of the 1930s when many nations engaged in "competitive depreciation" of their currencies in order to stimulate exports while enacting tariffs in an effort to prevent imports, thereby, it was hoped, stimulating domestic production and reducing unemployment. The breakdown of international trade was the logical result and that contributed, many believe, to the outbreak of war (e.g., Mises 1969; Osterfeld 1972).

The Bretton Woods sisters, the World Bank and the IMF, have come to assume overriding importance, although not in the way intended by their founders.

The World Bank is, in fact, a quasi-autonomous group of four agencies: the International Bank for Reconstruction and Development (IBRD), the International Development Association (IDA), the International Finance Corporation (IFC), and the Multilateral Investment Guarantee Agency (MIGA).

The IBRD obtains its funds through paid-in contributions from member countries, commercial borrowing, and loan repayments. The bulk of its funding is obtained from bond sales on the international capital market. Because of its excellent credit rating, the volume of its business, and its large capital base, composed of both "paid-in capital," that is, money in hand, and "callable capital," that is, essentially loan guarantees or obligations from member countries to cover bad loans, the IBRD is able to borrow at very favorable rates—in 1987 its average rate was 7.73 percent. More than 90 percent of its approximately $170 billion capital base is callable capital. The IBRD then relends this money to developing countries at a slightly higher rate-8.78 percent in 1987 (Hancock 1989, 53; Goldman 1985, 94).

As Graham Hancock has written (1989, 53),

For the poorest nations—which are generally regarded as a "bad risk" by bankers—the IBRD is a source of finance which would simply never be forthcoming from commercial sources. On the other hand, for middle-income developing countries (Brazil and Indonesia, for example)—which take up the bulk of its loans—the terms that it offers are generally significantly better than those they themselves could obtain on the open market.

Moreover, IBRD loans come with five-year grace periods and twenty-year maturities. As the *Economist* (1991b, 9) recently put it, while "borrowers pay what the Bank calls a market rate of interest," almost "always this is, in fact, a lower-than-market rate; the Bank is charging a prime rate to non-prime borrowers." In short, while officially denying it, the Bank is in the business of supplying subsidized loans.

Established in 1960, the IDA serves as the "soft loan window" of the World Bank. It is financed by grants or "subscriptions" from World Bank member-states and makes "concessional" or subsidized loans, that is, loans at 0 percent interest and payback periods extending up to forty years, recently scaled back from fifty years, including a ten-year grace period. It's official purpose is to provide "development credits on special terms, with particular emphasis on projects not attractive to private investors" (Banks 1991, 933). These loans are targeted to the those LDCs with official per capita incomes of $835 or less in 1986 dollars, although the bulk of IDA loans go to countries with average annual per capita incomes below $400 (Banks 1991, 934).

The loans are restricted to governments only and during its thirty-year existence, cumulative approvals totaled $64 billion for more than 2,100 projects (Banks 1991, 934).

As of June 30, 1991, the IBRD's outstanding loans totaled $91 billion; the IDA's $45 billion. Throughout its history the loans from both the IBRD and the IDA were, as the *Economist* (1991b, 10) acknowledges, "overwhelmingly to government, government agencies and state-owned enterprises." This is hardly surprising since Article III, Section 4(i) of the Bank's *Articles of Agreement* requires all loans to receive an official, that is, a government, guarantee.

Interestingly, the IFC was created in 1956 with the specific charge of extending unguaranteed loans directly to private businesses in the Third World and to advise governments on how to privatize their state-owned enterprises (SOEs). However, the IFC has had little impact and as late as 1987 loan commitments to the IFC totalled a mere $920 million (*Economist* 1991a, 18; *Economist* 1991b, 10).

MIGA, established in 1985, began operations in 1988 with a capital subscription of $1.1 billion. It provides borrowers with protection against noncommercial risks such as war, and loses due to uncompensated expropriations and repudiation of contracts by host governments (Banks 1991, 929).

Since the IBRD's authorized capital was increased to $171 billion in 1988 while the IDA's currently stands at more than $180 billion (Banks 1991, 931, 944), it is clear that when one speaks of

the World Bank, for practical purposes one is speaking of the
IBRD and the IDA.

Evolution

As originally conceived, the division of labor between the World
Bank and the IMF was clear: the IMF was to concern itself with
short-term monetary stabilization; the Bank was to focus on long-
term economic development. Over time, this distinction became
increasingly blurred, as the World Bank has come to require such
things as exchange rate adjustments to facilitate monetary stabilization as part of its loan conditions, while the IMF now demands
such policy changes as trade liberalization in order to stimulate
long-term development. Biersteker has commented that the two
institutions operate "virtually interchangeably" (1990, 483);
Economist (1991b, 19) has written that "the IMF has taken on the
unaccustomed role of development lender," while the Bank "has
moved to meet the Fund from the other direction, . . . making
stipulations not just about the particular projects it finances but
about fiscal and monetary policy, trade policy, exchange-rate policy." The "overlap of the IMF's activities with those of the Bank,"
it concludes, "is all too obvious." In fact, loans from the Bank are
contingent upon membership in the IMF.
    How and why did this merger come about?

The World Bank

The World Bank's original mission dealt with the reconstruction
of war-ravaged Europe. Since this was quickly assumed by the
Marshall Plan, the Bank shifted its focus to Third World economic
development.
    Bank loans, both IBRD and IDA, are predominantly project-
oriented. Many of the Bank's projects are designed solely or almost solely by Bank officials on the ground that the LDCs do not
have the expertise to design their own development projects (see,
e.g., Hancock 1989, 124–28, and *Economist* 1991b, 10). Nevertheless, by the Bank's own accounts, a large percentage of its projects
were failing to achieve even its own criteria for success. The Bank

decided that the cause of its failure lay not with its projects but with the environment inside the borrowing countries. Regardless of its merits, an individual project was doomed to fail if it were being implemented in a environment characterized by price controls, inflation, tariffs, high taxes, huge budget deficits, and the like. Since "a good project in a bad economy was likely to be a bad project, it followed that loan conditions had to look beyond the project to the economy as a whole" (*Economist* 1991b, 13). The result was the development of "conditional" loans commonly known as Sectoral Adjustment Loans, or SECALs. Part of the loan would be earmarked for a specific project while the rest would be used to finance adjustments in the relevant sector, such as transportation, energy, or agriculture.

The difficulty with SECALs was that project loans tended to be both too small and, with the extensive paperwork entailed in project design and monitoring, too time-consuming to give the Bank much leverage over government policy making. The logical next step was to divorce the loans entirely from projects and attach them to policy. Hence were born Structural Adjustment Loans, or SALs. SALs are in essence a bribe in which the Bank lends on the condition that the recipient country adopt particular economic or financial reforms. This had the great merit, from the point of view of both the Bank and the recipient countries, of permitting loans to be both increased in size and disbursed quickly. Bank officials could now dispense loans faster and more easily, and the rulers in recipient countries obtained more or less discretionary control over large sums of capital. It is clear that SALs violate the spirit, if not the letter, of the Bank's *Articles* which stipulate that, "except in special circumstances" loans are to "be for specific projects of reconstruction or development" (Article III, Section 4[vii]. For this reason they constitute no more than 10 percent of Bank lending.

But this does not mean that they are unimportant. In many LDCs, World Bank and other aid money has come to total as much as 8 percent of their GNPs, or more than 50 percent of gross investment (*Economist* 1991b, 10). Since the Bank is a lending institution, but a lending institution that because of its quasi-governmental status is largely insulated from market forces, job promotions have come to be obtained more by meeting or exceeding lending targets than by worrying about the soundness of loans. It is much easier to meet the target with a few big loans than with many small ones. As a consequence, the incentive quickly became "lend big, lend fast" (Hancock 1989, 143). As one World Bank official admitted, "We're like a Soviet factory. The . . . pressures to lend are enormous and a lot of people spend sleepless nights wondering how they can unload projects. Our ability to influence in a way that makes sense is completely undermined" (cited in Bandow 1989, 115). And a World Bank consultant commented that anyone who stops to raise questions about the veracity of a particular loan "is considered an outcast—not a good team man" (cited in Lappe et al., 1981, 85–86. Also see Bartlett 1986, 5; Sowell 1983, 238; Tendler 1971, 91; Irwin 1990b, A10).

In addition, the focus of World Bank activities changed fundamentally during the 1970s. Under Robert McNamara, president of the Bank from 1968 to 1981, the Bank shifted its focus from creating wealth by stimulating development to transferring wealth by initiating social welfare programs (see Clark 1981). As Ann Hughey commented (1980, 123.), McNamara

seemed almost possessed with redistribution of income. He seems to have turned away from the concept of helping the poor by raising overall national economic standards. He seems to feel that dams and roads and ports and steel mills . . . may help the economy but they don't necessarily put extra food into the stomachs of the teeming poor.

As a result, while increasing only modestly during the decade prior to McNamara's tenure, Bank lending ballooned from $934 million in 1968 to $12.3 billion in 1981, nearly a thirteen-fold increase (Bandow 1989, 74; Bartlett 1986, 3). Significantly, the percent of Bank lending going for such social services as slum improvement, population control, education, and construction of residential sites, increased from 3.6 in 1968 to 14.5 by 1981 (Bandow 1989, 74; Krauss 1984, 166). At best, such projects are only tangentially related to the Bank's official purpose of stimulating economic development.

According to its *Articles*, the purpose of the Bank was to stimulate self-sustaining economic development by promoting "private foreign investment by means of guarantees or participation in loans and other investments made by private investors" (Article I[ii]). Over the years, however, it has evolved into an agency focusing on promoting development by supplying capital to governments at well below market rates of interest, and then into an institution that concerned itself not so much with the creation of wealth at all as with its transfer. In the process, with the emergence of SECALs and SALs, the Bank's role has evolved from being a facilitator of private capital flows to the LDCs to a would-be policy maker in the LDCs, concerning itself with such IMF-related matters as exchange rates and balance of payments problems.

The IMF

The IMF's primary responsibility was to insure exchange rate stability, thereby promoting international trade. Under the IMF system the U.S. dollar served as the primary international reserve asset. The dollar was pegged to gold at the rate of $35 per ounce. Nations were willing to hold dollars so long as they had confidence that they could convert the dollar to gold at that rate. The system of fixed exchange rates works, Melvyn Krauss has observed (1984, 178–79), "only when the domestic monetary authority behaves responsibly.... [I]t is the practice of fiscal control, not the exchange rate regime, that really counts for economic health."

Once President Lyndon Johnson decided in the mid-1960s to finance the foreign War in Vietnam and the domestic War on Poverty by inflation, that is, resort to the printing press, rather than taxation, it soon became apparent that continued convertibility of the U.S. dollar at the official rate of $35 per ounce would be impossible. Originally, the official rate was raised and, when that proved insufficient, President Richard Nixon suspended convertibility in August 1971. By 1972 many nations were floating their currencies in violation of the IMF *Articles*. The Bretton Woods system was essentially dead and the IMF an agency without a purpose. As Robert Aliber wrote (in the *Economist* 1991b, 8)

Within a few years all that remained of the IMF system was the IMF—a pool of currencies modest in size and largely irrelevant in function, given the rapid growth in international reserves, and 1,800 highly paid international civil servants to police a set of rules that no longer existed.

The IMF responded by easing the conditions for its loans. In 1974 it created the Special Oil Facility, a separate "borrowing window" allowing members to cover that part of their balance of payments deficits attributable to higher oil prices (Banks 1991, 941–42). In the same year it also established an Extended Fund Facility (EFF) to aid countries experiencing payment problems stemming from "structural difficulties." In the process, it lengthened repayment periods from three-to-five years to five-to-ten years. And in 1976 it created a Trust Fund for the specific purpose of lending to LDCs subject to "conditionality," a practice of questionable legality since conditionality was not envisioned by the Fund's original agreement (Reynolds 1992, 5). While EFF loans were not concessional, as the *Economist* noted, "income per head became a criterion for the first time." Not surprisingly, IMF lending skyrocketed, increasing thirteen-fold between 1971 and 1976 (*Economist* 1991b, 9, chart 3).

Since the economies in many LDCs stagnated or even deteriorated during this period, they found themselves unable to repay the loans as they fell due by the late 1970s and early 1980s. In response, the IMF "liberalized" its "compensatory facility" by creating a new loan window in 1985, the Structural Adjustment Facility (SAF). The SAF provided loans for ten-year periods at 0.5 percent interest and a five-and-a-half-year grace period. In contrast to the Bank's SALs, SAF loans were targeted specifically to the poorest countries. SAF was followed two years later by the Enhanced Structural Adjustment Facility (ESAF), permitting borrowers to obtain twice the amount they could get through SAF, but on stricter conditions (Banks 1991, 943; *Economist* 1991b, 18). Thus, over time IMF loans became more concessional and carried longer maturities. Everyone agreed that by the 1980s there was little difference between the Bank and the Fund.

Evaluation

The World Bank

What has been the overall impact of the World Bank and IMF? The evidence strongly suggests that on balance the Bank has failed either to stimulate development or to raise living standards in the LDCs. This is so even if one looks at the Bank's own reports.

A 1986 World Bank study concluded that the Bank-funded enterprises "represent a depressing picture of inefficiency, losses, budgetary burdens, poor products and services and minimal accomplishment of the noncommercial objectives so frequently used to excuse their poor economic performance" (cited in Bovard 1988, 185). Following independence, sub-Saharan Africa has been the major recipient of World Bank attention. Between 1973 and 1980 alone, the World Bank invested $2.4 billion in Africa for the stated purpose of boosting agricultural output. Yet, between 1960 and 1985 per capita food output in Africa declined by 20 percent. A 1987 World Bank study admitted that fully 75 percent of its African agricultural projects had failed (Hancock 1989, 145). Another 1987 World Bank study classified nearly 60 percent of its projects around the world as either having "serious shortcomings" or being "complete failures." It also concluded that 60 percent of those judged to be successes were not sustainable after completion (Bandow 1989, 77–79; Hancock 1989, 145). The World Bank data (1983, 18) show that official development assistance (ODA) totaled just 5 percent of the gross domestic investment of the low-income countries of South Asia but more than 40 percent in the low-income countries of Africa. They also indicate (1980, 11, table 2.8) that for the decade of the 1970s per capita income in South Asia's low-income countries grew over five times faster than it did in the low-income countries of Africa.

If anything, the Bank's success rate is exaggerated. This is so for two reasons. First, "funds are fungible." This means that the project that the Bank has approved and is *officially* funding may be economically sound, but that project would have been financed even in the absence of a Bank loan. The loan, therefore, frees up domestic money which can now be spent on another project. Thus, the project that the Bank is *actually* funding is likely to be a marginal, or economically unsound one which would not have been funded had that project been advanced for approval. If so, Bank loans should be judged by the rates of return on the projects it *actually* funds rather than by the ones it *officially* funds. The problem is, as the *Economist* (1991b, 10) points out, these projects "are unknown, and possibly unknowable." One thing, however, is clear: basing accounting figures on the *officially* funded projects rather than those the Bank *actually* funded exaggerates the success rate of World Bank loans (see Osterfeld 1992, 159). And second, in a study generally friendly to the Bank, Robert Ayres (1983, 108) acknowledges that in order to make themselves and their programs look good, "some Bank officials admitted that they cooked up the evidence."

Not only has the Bank failed in its mission to stimulate Third World development, one can probably conclude that, on balance, the Bank's impact on both development and living standards in the LDCs has been negative. There are several reasons for this assessment.

Distortions. Within a market system, priorities are set by consumers' buying and abstention from buying. Entrepreneurs, anxious to maximize profits, will tend to produce those goods and services with the greatest discrepancy between total revenue and total cost. It is through the fluctuation of prices and costs that the unhampered market system is able to disseminate the relevant information to market participants. If consumer demand for a good or service increased or its supply decreased, then, ceteris paribus, its price would rise, thereby encouraging increased production. Conversely, if consumer demand decreased or the supply increased, the price would fall, thereby discouraging production of that particular good. Thus, the market process works in such a way as to produce those goods and services that consumers wish to buy in the quantity and quality desired by them.

The problem of the efficient allocation of resources is handled in the same way that the problem of priorities is handled: the price system. To produce their goods the entrepreneurs must bid for the factors they need. They therefore stand in the same relation to the factors of production as consumers do to the sellers of final goods. Thus, prices for the various factors of production reflect the demand for them by entrepreneurs. Since what entrepreneurs can bid is limited by their expected yield from the final sale of their products, factors of production are spontaneously channeled into the production of those goods most intensely desired by consumers. Those who best serve the consumers earn the most profits and are therefore able to offer the highest bids for the factors they need. If returns are not high enough to cover the costs of a particular operation, this means that, from the standpoint of the consumers, there is a more productive use for those factors elsewhere. The free market therefore allocates factors to their most value-productive point, relative to the priority system that the consumers have established.

It follows that it is economically rational to pursue a project only when the (expected) revenues exceed the costs. The rule holds for any country interested in economic development. This poses a serious difficulty for the recipients of ODA. As pointed out above, World Bank loans, whether from the IBRD which are moderately concessional, or the IDA, which are essentially free, are in fact subsidies. Since the transferred resources are scarce, their transfer at reduced or even zero costs *to the recipients* seriously distorts cost data. Thus, even assuming that public officials are honest and have the best interest of their citizens at heart, the artificial lowering of costs entailed in the Bank loans make many economically unsound projects *appear* profitable. Trying to determine whether costs exceed benefits in the absence of accurate cost data is a lot like trying to cut a piece of paper with a single scissors blade. Inevitably, numerous mistakes will be made and the waste of resources will be enormous.

Moreover, private investors risking their own capital are under the economic constraint of serving consumers. Public officials to whom resources are transferred are largely relieved from this constraint. In fact, since they receive resources at *zero costs to themselves*, they are able to treat these as free goods. Even when public officials are not corrupt, they are human. Relief from the economic constraint of serving consumers enables public officials to substitute their own priorities, however well intentioned, for those of the consumers. The World Bank, itself, is certainly aware of this. In its 1989 report (55) the Bank observed that in Pakistan fully 70 percent of all new lending was "targeted" by the government; in Yugoslavia the figure was 58 percent; and in Brazil it stood at 70 percent.

Since economic development is often confused with industrialization, the result has been the diversion of resources from the satisfaction of consumer wants to use in capital-intensive projects even when there is no real demand for such products or they can be produced more cheaply elsewhere or by private companies. In the same report (1989, 57), the Bank noted that a large portion of government-directed credit went to state-owned enterprises (SOEs). In Guyana 56 percent of all nongovernmental borrowing was by SOEs; in Mexico it was 43 percent, in Nepal 25 percent, and in Brazil 18 percent. Even though many are legal monopolies, they operate so inefficiently, and are so corrupt, that they still manage to lose money and can be kept in operation only with continued subsidies and directed credits (Hudgins 1989, 7).

It is hardly surprising to find the Third World littered with ultramodern steel mills, hydroelectric dams, modern airports, double-deck suspension bridges for nonexistent railroads, giant oil refineries in countries that neither produce nor refine oil, huge crop-storage depots that have never been used because they are not in locations that are accessible to farmers, and numerous other white elephants (Ayittey 1987, 210–11; 1988; Bauer 1987, 15; Chapman 1986; Fitzgerald 1980, 284–85). Although undertaken in the name of development, they do not contribute to economic growth. They are the modern counterpart of the Egyptian pyramids: colossal, impressive, and a wasteful drain on the resources of the country.

Incentives. By making loans to SOEs or to sectors that are failing because of government policies, the Bank not merely removes whatever incentive recipient governments might have to introduce market-oriented reforms, it actually rewards them for pursuing economically detrimental policies. To cite just a few examples, Tanzania has been one of the largest recipients of Bank money. Yet, even following a Bank report that blamed the collapse of

Tanzanian agricultural production on oppressive domestic tax policies, Tanzania received another $6.8 billion from the Bank for agricultural projects. One finds similar situations in Ghana, Ethiopia, Romania, the Philippines, and numerous other countries (Bandow 1989, 79–80; Waters 1985, 7; Hudgins 1989, 7).

SECALs and SALs have not altered the situation. In fact, a 1986 Bank report on the ten largest SAL recipients concluded that none had introduced serious policy reform (in Bandow 1989, 84). The reasons are not difficult to uncover. First, only about 10 percent of Bank lending is in the form of SALs. This clearly limits the amount of leverage the Bank could have over the domestic affairs of recipient countries. Moreover, the pressure to lend—most SAL proposals *originate* with the Bank—further undermines the ability of the Bank to entice market reforms in the recipient country. Recipient countries know full well that the Bank is unlikely to cut off loans to a nonperforming country—Zaire, for example, has been "adjusting" for years. In fact, by adopting the reforms demanded by the Bank, a country would effectively reduce its chances of receiving future Bank loans. There would be no reason to extend an SAL to a country that has already reformed itself. Thus, despite its free-market rhetoric, the incentive created by the method of disbursing Bank loans has the unfortunate effect of penalizing countries adopting free-market reforms.

ODA entails other untoward incentives. Michael Irwin, former director of the Health Services Department at the World Bank who recently resigned in disgust at the Bank's "bloated, overpaid bureaucracy, its wasteful practices, and its generally poor management," has stated that "public proclamations to the contrary, poverty reduction is the last thing on most World Bank bureaucrats' minds" (Irwin 1990a, 2). Unless, perhaps, the poverty reduction they are concerned with is their own. In a response to increasing complaints about its excessive staff, World Bank president Barber Conable launched a major reorganization effort in 1987. At the time the Bank staff totaled 6,150, with an administrative budget of $816 million. At the end of the reorganization effort in 1989, the staff had been reduced to 6,100. The cost of the reorganization was $148.9 million (Irwin 1990a, 2). By the end of 1991 the Bank staff totaled over 6,200, more than when the reorganization began.

World Bank salaries are not only high, they are tax free. Hundreds of vice-presidents, directors, and even "technical advisers" earn in excess of $100,000 per year. Moreover, their annual increases regularly exceed the inflation rate in the United States. Further, every staff member whose spouse earned less than $10,000 the previous year was entitled to a $3,000 salary supplement. In addition to free medical care and life insurance, every member is eligible for $5,480 in education grants per child ages 5 to 24, home-leave travel for themselves and their family including $1,070 in pocket money for themselves and $534 for a spouse and each child per trip (Irwin 1990a, 5). Finally, about 10 percent of its total administrative budget is spent on travel, first class, Irwin adds, "never economy" (1990a, 7).

Moreover, the Bank's incentive to "lend big, lend fast" has redounded to the benefit of large Western-based multinational corporations (MNCs). For example, a $15 million high-tech irrigation project built on the banks of the Niger River in Africa was financed by an IDA grant and built by Western contractors. It has been abandoned by the Niger government because it cannot afford the extraordinary operating costs of the project. Yet, just a few miles away IDA money is being spent to finance the construction of another, identical, project. The only beneficiaries of such multi-million-dollar projects are the Western consultants and contractors (Hancock 1989, 155). The World Bank acknowledges that 70 percent of the money it loans out to Third World governments is actually spent on goods and services provided by businesses in the wealthy industrialized countries (Hancock 1989, 159; Lappe et al. 1981, 90).

And finally, it is important to understand that ODA "goes not to the pitiable figures we see on aid posters or in aid advertisements" (Bauer and Yamey 1983, 125), it goes to their rulers. Dispensing aid on the basis of need, as has become increasingly the case with the IBRD and the IDA, creates a truly perverse incentive: it provides Third World rulers with a vested interest in perpetuating the poverty of their own subjects. If the recipient country were actually to develop, its rulers would lose their aid money. Thus, the incentive for the Bank to lend is in part responsible for the enormous corruption common in so many Third World countries.

It is not an accident that some of the world's wealthiest individuals were or are rulers of some of the world's poorest countries. The figures reach into the billions of dollars: an estimated $10 billion for the Marcoses in the Philippines, $5 billion for Mobutu in Zaire, and more than a $1 billion for Duvalier in Haiti. This is done, it should be noted, with the implicit approval of the agencies involved. The official name for such larceny is "leakage."

In brief, foreign aid brings together three separate groups whose interests lie in perpetuating rather than eliminating Third World poverty: the aid bureaucracy itself, giant corporations in developed countries, and rulers in recipient countries.

Crowding out Capital. Finally, there can be little doubt that the World Bank has retarded development by crowding out private capital. It has done this in a number of ways. First, by retarding market-oriented reforms, it has discouraged private investment by permitting governments to maintain environments hostile to private enterprise. Second, ODA has politicized the economy, thereby diverting energy from productive economic activity into lobbying for political largess. And third, the World Bank has regularly financed projects, and entire sectors, that would have been developed by private capital. For example, the World Bank has spent millions of dollars to finance the Bombay High oil project in India. Since the most likely lands for finding oil have been taken by the government, the result is that private capital has been dissuaded from entering the area (Krauss 1984, 169–70). The same is true not only of Bank-financed energy projects in general, but of many other projects as well, such as Bank-financed SOEs in the cement business in Algeria, steel in Brazil, and fertilizer in India, to cite just a handful of examples. It is hardly surprising that while LDC borrowing skyrocketed during the 1970s and 1980, foreign direct investment (FDI) in the LDCs actually declined (Tammen 1989, 2).

Not only do such projects inhibit the Bank's official goal of facilitating the flow of private capital to the Third World, the inefficiency resulting from the capital crowd-out retards economic development and lowers the standard of living of the average individual in the recipient countries. Thus, the Bank is at least in part responsible for both the "debt crisis" and the economic stagnation experienced by so many Third World countries during this period.

As Alan Waters, former chief economist for the U.S. Agency for International Development, has summarized (1985, 7):

> Foreign aid is inherently bad. It retards the process of wealth economic growth and the accumulation of wealth (the only means of escape from poverty and degradation); it weakens the coordinating effect of the market process; it pulls entrepreneurship and intellectual capital into nonproductive and administrative activities; it creates a moral ethical tone which denies the hard task of wealth creation. Foreign aid makes it possible for . . . societies to transfer wealth from the poor to the rich.

The IMF

The record of the IMF is no better than that of the World Bank. Ironically, created to avoid devaluations, the IMF has become their single most prominent proponent.

Following Mexico's 1982 default on its foreign loans, the IMF, desperately searching for a new role following the collapse of the Bretton Woods system in the 1970s, assumed the responsibility of managing the Third World debt crisis of the 1980s. The IMF developed a standard package of policy requirements as conditions for receipt of an IMF loan. The conditions were (1) currency devaluation in order to reduce balance of payments difficulties; (2) restrictions on the amount of credit and a reduction in the public-sector deficit, both intended to curb inflation by reducing domestic demand, and (3) removal of restrictions on foreign trade and capital movements, designed to facilitate economic growth through trade (Reynolds 1992, 5–6).

The basic idea is that since less money and credit would be available, the price of foreign goods relative to domestically produced goods and services will rise, thereby reducing the demand for them. Conversely, since domestic production costs will fall relative to foreign costs, the position of the devaluating country will "improve," that is, its goods will become less costly, thereby stimulating the demand for its products abroad. Thus, imports will fall at the same time that exports increase, thereby alleviating its foreign debt "problem" by running a huge trade surplus.

Significantly, a review of thirty-four nations pursuing IMF-prescribed devaluation policies found that inflation increased significantly *following* devaluation and that economic activity dropped measurably, as well. For example, Mexico's money base was expanding at a rate of 11.6 percent in 1976, when it devaluated the peso. By 1978, that rate had jumped to 108.9 percent (Reynolds 1992, 6–7). This suggests that the IMF theory contains a serious flaw. It does. Governments burdened by debt must raise taxes, which is encouraged by the IMF, anyway, in order to dampen the demand for foreign goods. This has two effects: it taxes away domestic savings at the same time rendering foreign capital goods more expensive. The result is a reduction in investment, and thus productivity. Significantly, the justification of the domestic austerity program is that it stimulates exports. The problem is that exports' costs rise, or do not fall, in spite of the austerity measures, since the costs of the capital goods necessary to produce the exports rise as the price of foreign capital goods, or domestic capital-competing goods, increases following devaluation. Thus, IMF-imposed devaluation has generally failed in its goal of stimulating increased exports. Moreover, the reduction in domestic economic activity reduces the tax base. The resulting government deficits require increased taxes, which further retard economic activity. Where this is not politically feasible, the only option is the printing press, and massive inflation. All of this is the exact reverse of what the IMF intended (Reynolds 1992, 5–8).

The key question is: Why is a current accounts deficit bad? The IMF had put much emphasis on "export-led growth." But as Alan Reynolds (1992, 10–11) points out, what it fails to note is that practically all of the world's developed countries began as debtor nations, that export led-growth *followed* import-led investment.

In order to understand the folly of the IMF devaluation policy it is necessary to examine the causes of the so-called Third World debt crisis of the 1980s. The oil-price shock of 1973–74 resulted in a massive surplus of savings in the oil-producing nations, which were recycled to banks in the developed countries. Since the recession caused by the oil-price shock reduced the demand in developed countries for investment capital, interest rates declined dras-

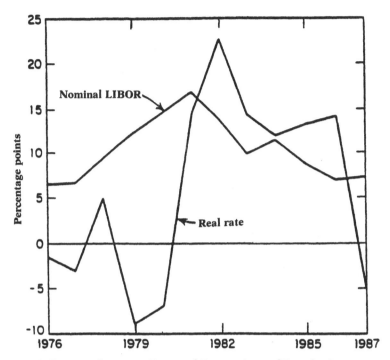

Figure 1. Interest Rates on External Borrowings of Developing Countries, 1976–1987

LIBOR = London interbank offered rate. The nominal rate is the average six-month dollar LIBOR during each year: the real rate is the nominal LIBOR deflated by the change in the export price index for developing countries.
Source: World Bank, *World Development Report 1988*, Fig. 1.9, p. 29

tically, with real rates at times actually below 0 percent (figure 1). The 1974 U.N. Resolution on the Establishment of a New International Economic Order deliberately discouraged foreign investment and applauded the nationalization of MNCs as the means to liberate LDCs from dependence on the developed countries of the world. The result was a massive increase in lending to the LDCs, encouraged, it must be noted, by the availability of concessional loans from the World Bank and the IMF. Significantly, "loans to central governments and state owned enterprises were especially

favored by commercial banks. Because of their sovereign status
these entities were considered to be low risk. Developing countries
were happy to take advantage of this unaccustomed access to
cheap loans with few strings attached" (World Bank 1988, 28–29).
The result of the confluence of these two factors was to reinforce
the decline of FDI's share of total foreign capital flows to the
LDCs. The problem was that borrowing and investment decisions,
for reasons outlined above, were "often imprudent and resulted in
excessive indebtedness in a number of countries. And in a number
of countries borrowing fueled a flight of capital that drained the
pool of resources for investment even as the burdens of foreign
debt mounted" (Whitehead 1987. Also see World Bank 1988, 29).

One tragic consequence of this is that the burden of debt repayment fell precisely on the shoulders of those least able to manage
it: the poor citizens in the LDCs. They shouldered it in the form of
higher taxes and cutbacks in services. The irony is that, far from
liberating the LDCs, the switch from FDI to Bank loans, from
equity or investment to loans or debt, placed the LDCs in a position of even greater dependency on the developed world.

The problem is not so much an external accounts debt, as the
IMF believes. After all, every developed country except England
became developed only by importing capital from abroad. In fact,
as the *Economist* (1984) pointed out, the United States in the
nineteenth century was, relative to its gross domestic product,
even more in debt in terms of capital flows, than countries such as
Brazil and Mexico were in the mid-1980s. The difference, however,
is twofold: (1) the flow of capital was primarily in the form of
equity rather than bank loans, and (2) the flow of capital was
primarily to private investors rather than to governments. The
advantage to the LDCs of allowing MNC investment in their countries is that if the MNC fails, it is the stockholders in the home
country, and not, as is the case with bank loans, the citizens in the
LDCs, who must bear the loss.

As Reynolds has summarized (1992, 10),

Developing countries can clearly benefit by exploiting investment opportunities beyond those that can be financed by their own past accumula-
tions of wealth. Therefore, it is not inherently sinful for growing economies to remain debtor nations—that is, run a current account-deficits—

for many years or even decades. If current-account deficits are financed by voluntary, private capital inflows, they reflect improved opportunities for profitable investment and production, and make such improved production possible (e.g., by financing imports of high-tech equipment). In turn, it is growth-oriented policies that make the financing of current-account deficits possible, because the prospect of enlarged output in the future can be discounted in higher prices of equity and bonds today.

In brief, the current account deficit with which the IMF seems so obsessed is not a very meaningful figure. If anything, by comparison with both the developed countries during their formative years and such current Third World success stories as the "Asian NICs," the deficits are too small, not too large (Reynolds 1992, 18–19). The critical issue is not the size of the deficit but its composition.

Conclusions

The World Bank and the IMF were both established in 1944. The former was created to promote self-sustaining economic development by facilitating the flow of private investment capital; the latter was established to promote an environment of free trade by insuring monetary stability.

Neither succeeded. The World Bank has, on balance, probably retarded rather than promoted development, and supplemented private capital rather than facilitated its flow to the LDCs. Despite its free-market rhetoric, throughout its history Bank loans have gone overwhelmingly to parastatals and SOEs which the Bank, itself, has repeatedly acknowledged to be drains on the economy. The IMF has not only failed in its efforts to maintain monetary stability, but has pursued a policy that has inflicted needless suffering on some of the poorest peoples of the world.

Neither was needed. A special institution was not needed to insure that the LDCs had enough capital. It is hardly an accident that some of the nations of the world are highly developed while others lag far behind. Those countries that have pursued what Richard Richardson and Osman Ahmed (1987, 23) have termed an "enabling environment" have prospered; those nations that haven't, have remained mired in poverty (see, e.g., Moore and

Simon 1989). An "enabling environment" is nothing more nor less than a traditional nineteenth-century liberal economic order. The essential component of a liberal order was the limitation of the government's functions to the protection of the person and property of each individual. The laws or rules imposed in the liberal order were essentially *negative*, that is, they told individuals what they could *not* do. This meant that in a such an order each individual possessed a "protected domain" (Hayek 1969, 167) within which he or she had complete autonomy. No one, not even the state, was permitted to intervene. Individuals had the right to do anything they wished as long as they did not violate the protected domain of other individuals. It followed that all interactions between individuals were voluntary; they were the result of mutual consent and thus redounded to the mutual benefit of all parties involved.

In such an environment access to capital was not a problem. Since investors did not have to fear that their capital would be seized by the governments, they were willing to invest as long as they had a reasonable expectation that the investment would produce a positive return. The American railroads in the nineteenth century, for example, were built with British capital, and America was a debtor nation until World War I. To the extent that capital became a problem, it was traceable to a country's own domestic policies of government interference with private property and the market process.

Nor was a special institution necessary to avert balance of payments "difficulties." A nation buying more abroad than it was importing saw its gold reserves dwindle, causing prices to fall. The lower prices reversed the flow of gold as foreign buyers began purchasing domestic products at bargain prices. Thus, balance of payments problems were self-correcting. Similarly, monetary stability was also encouraged, since domestic inflation not only discouraged foreign investment but encouraged capital flight.

Finally, neither the Bank nor the Fund is needed now. As already pointed out, both have become, in essence, institutions in search of purposes. The Bank was originally established to facilitate the flow of private capital and to make long-term commercial loans for development purposes. Its loans are now often highly concessional and have the effect of crowding out private capital. Moreover, the Bank increasingly concerns itself with short-term balance of payments problems. The IMF was created to deal with balance of payments issues and to make short-term loans to facilitate monetary stability. It now makes longer-term loans for what are, for practical purposes, long-run development purposes. Countries seriously interested in economic development must, likewise, move to adopt an "enabling environment" by limiting government, protecting private property, reducing taxes, and allowing the free market to allocate resources (see, e.g., Osterfeld 1992; Asman 1992; Hudgins 1990).

Neither the Bank nor the Fund was necessary in 1944; neither is needed now. Both have caused far more harm than good. They should be abolished.

References

Asman, David. 1992. "Wealth of Naciones." *Policy Review* (Spring): 38–45.
Ayittey, George. 1987. "Economic Atrophy in Black Africa." *Cato Journal* (Spring/Summer): 195–222.
———. 1988. "Africa Doesn't Need More Foreign Aid; It Needs Less." *Hartford Courant* (August 4): B–12.
Ayres, Robert. 1983. *Banking on the Poor.* Cambridge, Mass.: MIT Press.
Bandow, Doug. 1989. "What's Still Wrong with the World Bank?" *Orbis* (Winter): 73–89, 115.
Banks, Arthur. 1991. *Political Handbook of the World 1991.* New York: CSP.
Bartlett, Bruce. 1986. "Barber Conable at the World Bank: New Hope for World Economic Growth." *Heritage Foundation Backgrounder*, April 4.
Bauer, Peter. 1987. "Creating the Third World: Foreign Aid and Its Offspring." *Journal of Economic Growth* (Second Quarter): 11–22.
Bauer, Peter, and Basil Yamey. 1983. "Foreign Aid: What Is at Stake?" In *The Third World*, ed. Scott Thompson, 115–35. San Francisco: ICS.
Biersteker, Thomas. 1990. "Reducing the Role of the State in the Economy: A Conceptual Exploration of IMF and World Bank Prescriptions." *International Studies Quarterly* 34: 477–92.
Bovard, James. 1988. "The World Bank vs. the World's Poor." *Freeman* (May): 184–87.

Chapman, Stephen. 1986. "The Futility of Aid to Africa." *Chicago Tribune,* June 8, section 5, 3.

Clark, William. 1981. "Robert McNamara at the World Bank." *Foreign Affairs* (Fall): 167–84.

The Economist. 1984. "Beggaring the Poor." February 18, 15–16.

———. 1991a. "Aid and Enterprise." May 25, 18.

———. 1991b. "The IMF and the World Bank." October 12: special supplement, 1–48.

Fitzgerald, Randall. 1980. *When Government Goes Private.* New York: Universe Books.

Goldman, Morris. 1985. "Multilateral Institutions and Economic Development." In *U.S. Aid to the Developing World,* ed. Doug Bandow. Washington, D.C.: The Heritage Foundation.

Hancock, Graham. 1989. *The Lords of Poverty.* New York: Atlantic Monthly Press.

Harrod, Roy. 1958. *International Economics.* Chicago: University of Chicago Press.

Hayek, F. A. 1969. *Studies in Philosophy, Politics and Economics.* New York: Simon & Schuster.

Hudgins, Edward. 1989. "Why the World Bank Should Read Its Own Report." *Heritage Foundation Backgrounder,* September 22.

———. 1990. "Private Property: The Basis of Economic Reform in Less Developed Countries." *Heritage Foundation Backgrounder,* May 24.

Hughey, Ann. 1980. "Is the World Bank Biting Off More Than It Can Chew?" *Forbes* May 26, 122–23, 127–28.

International Bank for Reconstruction and Development. 1989. *Articles of Agreement.* Washington, D.C.: World Bank.

Irwin, Michael. 1990a. "Banking on Poverty: An Insider's Look at the World Bank." *Cato Institute Foreign Policy Briefing,* Washington, D.C., September 20.

———. 1990b. "Why I've Had It with the World Bank." *Wall Street Journal,* March 20, A10.

Krauss, Melvyn. 1984. *Development without Aid.* New York: McGraw-Hill.

Lappe, Frances, Joseph Collins, and David Kinley. 1981. *Aid as Obstacle.* San Francisco: Institute for Food and Development Policy.

Mises, Ludwig von. 1969. *Omnipotent Government.* New Rochelle: Arlington House.

Moore, Stephen, and Julian Simon. 1989. "Communism, Capitalism, and Economic Development: Implications for U.S. Economic Assistance." *Heritage Foundation Backgrounder,* December 8.

Osterfeld, David. 1972. "The Nature of Modern Warfare." *Freeman* (April): 205–11.

———. 1992. *Prosperity versus Planning: How Government Stifles Economic Growth.* New York: Oxford University Press.

Pomfret, Richard. 1992. *Diverse Paths of Economic Development*. Hemel Hempstead, England: Harvester-Wheatsheaf.

Reynolds, Alan. 1992. *The IMF's Destructive Recipe of Devaluation and Austerity*. Indianapolis: Hudson Institute.

Richardson, Richard, and Osman Ahmed. 1987. "Challenge for Africa's Private Sector." *Challenge* (January/February): 16–25.

Sowell, Thomas. 1983. *The Economics and Politics of Race*. New York: William Morrow.

Tammen, Melanie. 1989. "Energizing Third World Economies: The Role of Debt-Equity Swaps." *Heritage Foundation Backgrounder*, November 8.

Tendler, Judith. 1971. *Inside Foreign Aid*. Baltimore: Johns Hopkins University Press.

Waters, Alan. 1985. "In Africa's Anguish, Foreign Aid Is a Culprit." *Heritage Foundation Backgrounder*, August 7.

Whitehead, John C. 1987. "Third World Dilemma: More Debt or More Equity?" Address to the Council on Foreign Relations, New York City. Washington, D.C.: Department of State, October 21.

World Bank. Various years. *World Development Report*. New York: Oxford University Press.

8

Does Eastern Europe Need a New (Marshall) Plan?

Steven Horwitz

With the collapse of the Soviet Union and the Soviet-style economies of Eastern Europe, the question of reform has come to the forefront. More particularly there has been much discussion of the role of the West in any reform program. Though most people feel that there is something Western countries can do for Eastern Europe, there is a sense of loss or confusion about exactly what should be done. One idea that has been the focus of some significant discussion is to devise another version of the so-called Marshall Plan, officially the "European Recovery Program" (ERP), implemented in 1948 to rescue the war-torn economies of post-World War II Western Europe. Proponents of this idea suggest that a new Marshall Plan could provide the resources and policies that the former Soviet-style economies need to make the transition to market economies.

Before adopting a new Marshall Plan, it is crucial that we understand the old one a bit better. In particular, we need to examine three aspects of the Marshall Plan: (1) why Western Europe needed American help; (2) the form such help took; and (3) the political and economic ideas that informed the Plan and its creators and implementers. With this understanding of the Marshall Plan, we can turn to the present situation in Eastern Europe and explore the implications of a new Marshall Plan there. What we will find is that the ideas that informed the original Marshall Plan, namely that conscious, planned political intervention and design are needed to create economic institutions and guide economic growth, are the very same ideas responsible for the current economic disaster in Eastern Europe. Given this, proposing a new Marshall Plan to solve its problems can be likened to giving free liquor to an alcoholic.

Economic Development and Economic Planning

As a number of other contributors to this volume have indicated, there are important links between how one views debates over the relative merits of markets and planning and how one views the appropriate policies for economic development. For defenders of planning, government, perhaps in combination with business and labor, both can and should play a major role in directing the path of economic development through particular policies and strategies. For defenders of markets, no such direction is necessary. By simply ensuring the rule of law and the protection of voluntary contract and exchange, governments can cultivate a fertile soil for economic growth and development. As a result, it is crucial to understand theoretical debates over the feasibility of planning before one prescribes development policies.

These issues become even more relevant in discussing development in Eastern Europe. For fifty years or more, the economies of Eastern Europe had been guided by the ideology of economic planning. The official economic philosophy stated that markets were both exploitative and inefficient and that only conscious, collective planning guided by the enlightened Party leadership could ensure both economic growth and some notion of social justice. However, both the actual experiences of these economies and the theoretical discussions among economists lead to a different conclusion. Despite apparently acceptable growth as measured by GDP, Eastern European economies have been unable to provide the average citizen with a standard of living close to that of the West. This lack of economic growth is one key factor in fueling the political and economic changes currently taking place.

Although the economics profession in general saw no reason to believe that planning was doomed to fail, some economists had long argued that planning would be unable to match the efficiency of the market. The original argument was made by Ludwig von Mises ([1920] 1935).[1] Mises argued that the efficient allocation of resources required some standard by which to compare the values of their alternative uses. Such a standard could be provided by money prices because all goods traded in markets exchanged against money, which provides the standard of comparison. However, for money prices to be meaningful they had to result from true market exchange, and true market exchange required private ownership of resources, particularly the means of production. Thus, the planned economy, which almost by definition excludes the private ownership of production goods, would not have exchange, markets, or money prices. Lacking money prices, Mises claimed, planners would be unable to know whether they had rationally allocated their resources. As a result, one would not expect planned economies to achieve rates of growth and standards of living equal to those of market economies.

F. A. Hayek followed up on Mises's original insights by arguing that the real issue was epistemological. The advantage that markets have over planning is that they can make use of more knowledge. In a series of papers in the 1930s and 1940s, Hayek argued that markets, through the process of exchange, could incorporate and disseminate knowledge that could not be communicated through social coordination processes based on language alone (Hayek 1948). Much that human beings know (and that is relevant for the allocation of resources) is not known in a form that can be articulated. Yet this knowledge can still be utilized by others when it is embodied in social institutions such as prices. Mises's original point concerning the indispensability of prices is amplified by Hayek, who pointed out that this indispensability was based on the ability of prices to communicate knowledge.

The problem for planning is that the attempt to centrally marshal economic knowledge cannot possibly incorporate as much knowledge as can a decentralized price system. The prices formed from unhampered market exchange enable actors to use more of the knowledge of others, heightening economic coordination and order. The key to economic development is to give the pulls and tugs of the market maximum feasible freedom to drive the formation of prices and the allocation of resources. To the extent prices are established by markets, economic systems will be able overcome the inevitable dispersion of knowledge that plagues human attempts at social interaction.

What this argument implies is a different way of looking at how economies achieve growth and development. Once one gets beyond directed planning as the means to growth, one should ask what kinds of institutional arrangements are more likely to lead to prices best performing their coordinative role. Economic development, on this view, refers to the ability of individuals to form increasingly reliable sets of expectations based on the signals embodied in market prices and profits. The more prices are able to accurately reflect the knowledge of others, the more easily can individual economic actors make use of that knowledge to form expectations about others. The more reliable are expectation-formation processes, the easier it is for individuals to coordinate their decisions with each other. It is this coordination, in combination with the increasing complexity and creativity it brings, that constitutes economic growth and increasing economic order.[2] The very bottom line for economic development is whether individuals are more easily achieving more of their ends. If they are doing so, then the economy is developing.

It is also important to point out that this argument is not simply a critique of *comprehensive* attempts at planning; it applies to more piecemeal types of intervention as well. Economic regulation, central bank policy, and other macroeconomic tools, as well as antitrust policy, are all plagued by smaller, but no less intractable, versions of this knowledge problem.[3] This order-based perspective on economic growth can also explain the problems Keynesian-type activist policy has faced over the last thirty years and why using such policies in the pursuit of economic development is likely to fail. With these ideas in mind, we turn to the Marshall Plan and Eastern European recovery more specifically.

The Goals, Ideology, and Policies of the Marshall Plan

The circumstances that gave rise to the Marshall Plan are fairly straightforward. At the end of World War II, Western Europe was in ruins, in terms of both physical and human capital. Political systems had been undermined by the war and the events prior to it, and economic resources had been destroyed or had dramatically deteriorated. The task facing the victorious Allies was rebuilding and revitalizing Western Europe to bring it back into the world economy. In addition, that rebuilding process could not overlook the threat posed by the apparent military and economic power of the Soviet Union. One great fear among the architects of the Marshall Plan was that if the United States did nothing for Western Europe, it would quickly fall under Soviet military and/ or economic domination. The task then was to provide funds for rebuilding the resources destroyed by the war.

Aside from a general rebuilding of their economies, postwar analysts were very concerned that the nations of Western Europe be reintegrated into the world economy. As historian Michael Hogan (1987, 26) argues, "Policymakers in the Truman administration were convinced that a 'dynamic economy' at home required American trade and investment abroad, which in turn required the reconstruction of major trading partners in Europe and their reintegration into a multilateral system of world trade." There were two major reasons behind the push for integration. One was that Western Europe was an important source for U.S. trade and that only healthy economies there could provide the resources that Americans desired. The second was that the more Western Europe became integrated into the world economy, the stronger it became and the more able it would be to hold its own against the Soviet threat from the east.

In addition to this type of integration, U.S. policy makers wanted to see Western Europe *internally* integrated. This internal integration would also be an effective barrier against Soviet incursion and would heighten the prospects for a strong European economy. Important to this integration was the model held by the architects of the Marshall Plan. As Hogan (1987, 27) notes, "The Marshall Planners would replace the old European state system

. . . by applying the American principle of federalism and using it to create an integrated European economy similar to the one that existed in the United States." This view was part of a more general strategy on the part of American policy makers. That strategy envisioned an exporting of the U.S. political economy of the 1940s to Western Europe. The kinds of changes that had taken place in the United States during the Progressive Era and the New Deal, specifically the building of a corporatist economic system based on various types of private-public mixes, were to be extended across the Atlantic through the vehicle of the Marshall Plan.[4]

Hogan (1987, 3) describes the American political economy in question as

founded on self-governing economic groups, integrated by institutional coordinators and normal market mechanisms, led by cooperating public and private elites . . . [which] married the older traditions . . . [of] individualism, privatism, competition, and antitrust, to the twentieth-century trend toward an organized capitalism characterized by national economies of scale, bureaucratic planning, and administrative regulation.

The result became an economy somewhere in between a genuine market economy and the attempts at more comprehensively planned systems emerging in the Soviet Union and China. Crucial to understanding the evolution of the U.S. political economy was that the increase in government intervention was generally welcomed by the corporate community who saw government as a force for stability, order, and security against the uncertainty of intensifying competition. As Kolko, Wiebe, and Weinstein document, much of the Progressive Era legislation, and later the New Deal, was seen by corporate interests as a way to lock in their wealth and status, because it would be they who would have the most expertise, and therefore influence, in the newly created regulatory structures.

With these changes and their apparent popularity and success as the backdrop, the Marshall Plan became an obvious way to extend American ideas into a reconstructed Western Europe. In particular, this effort was infused with an optimistic (in retrospect, naive) sense of what conscious reconstruction could do. Hogan (1987, 19) captures this spirit when he argues that "American Marshall Planners . . . tried to transform political problems into technical ones that were solvable, they said, when old European ways of conducting business and old habits of class conflict gave way to American methods of scientific management and corporative collaboration." One major set of players in this process were private foundations and research institutions such as the Ford Foundation. As Sallie Pisani (1991, 47) describes it, "The Ford Foundation was established on the principle that the behavioral sciences provided a scientific basis for experts to help the citizens of underdeveloped nations improve their standard of living." Pisani points out that a number of Marshall Plan personnel had connections with the Ford Foundation and that it was attempting to be an additional arm for implementing U.S. development policy. More specifically, Ford people thought that the key to U.S. economic success was that it had a class of small businessmen who were supportive of government intervention. As a result, Ford "attempted to recreate America, as they imagined it, in foreign lands. This type of mythological handling of whole classes of individuals appeared in Marshall Plan efforts in Europe" (Pisani 1991, 48). For the intellectuals behind the Marshall Plan, it was a chance to make Europe in their own image: the corporatist state.

An example of this mix of scientistic planning and private-public combination would be the investment guarantees provided by the U.S. government under the Marshall Plan. U.S. corporations could submit investment projects to Plan officials and, if they were consistent with the aims of the Plan and approved by the Plan bureaucrats, the U.S. government would provide a guarantee for the value of the project (Wexler 1983, 88). If the project should fail, the U.S. government would pay back the private investor. Under the guidance of knowledgeable plan implementers, private sources of capital could be tapped and redirected toward "proper usages" with little effective risk to the investor. Ironically, the program was a failure, as only about 10 percent of the funds allocated for guarantee purposes were actually used. Immanuel Wexler (1983, 89) argues that even with the guarantee, U.S. firms were reluctant to have their investment projects overseen by both the administrators of the Marshall Plan and the various European governments.

In essence, the Marshall Plan was an attempt at noncomprehensive economic planning. Enlightened and experienced economists, businesspeople, and administrators from the United States would formulate and implement a series of proposals that would provide the concrete steps toward European economic recovery. In addition to the general trend toward governmental planning in that era, it was also the height of the Keynesian revolution in economics. The management of macroeconomies was deemed to be amenable to the same principles of scientific management and public-private cooperation that was happening at the industry level. Many of the specific provisions of the Marshall Plan dealt with financial integration and macroeconomic management and were based on explicitly Keynesian premises.[5] We can get a flavor for the planning aspect of the Marshall Plan by looking at both the general direction it set forth and some of the specific policy directives it initiated. We will conclude this section with some brief remarks on its successes and failures.

While acknowledging that the long-term goal of the European Recovery Program was integration based on generally market-oriented principles, the short-term strategies adopted by the implementers of the Marshall Plan were anything but market-oriented. Their broad approach included a "supranational planning authority with the power to allocate resources, set production targets, and foster integration" (Hogan 1987, 57) The Marshall Plan explicitly did not wish to allow European recovery and integration to take place through spontaneous market mechanisms, rather the plan wanted "a European order superintended by central institutions with the power to coordinate national economies" (Hogan 1987, 328). As Nicholas Eberstadt (1991, 27; emphasis in original) observes, "the ERP actually *required* recipient states to engage in economic planning in order to obain aid."[6]

The most obvious example of these attempts at economic planning, and their ultimate failure, revolved around the use of production targets as recovery goals. Production plans and targets were central to the ERP. European leaders were expected to plan for strategic economic decisions and use "indicative economic planning" to steer the path of recovery (Hogan 1987, 151–52). The Economic Cooperation Administration (ECA), which ran the Marshall Plan in Europe, proposed using its control over the local currency disbursement of American grants "to bring the Europeans into line with its production, trade, and financial objectives" (Hogan 1987, 152). This confirms Eberstadt's linkage between U.S. aid and planning. These production targets were set not simply for overall output, but also for various individual commodities, such as coal, iron, steel, etc. For example, Wexler (1983, 75) reports that after the first year of the ERP only three of twelve major commodity production targets had been exceeded, those for coarse grains, tin, and sugar beets.

Not surprisingly, the process of setting production targets was not the objective scientific planning process that the planners might have hoped for. As Wexler (1983, 82ff.) notes, meeting those targets was complicated by various special-interest provisions that the U.S. Congress had incorporated into the Marshall Plan. For example, there was a requirement that at least 50 percent of cargo financed by the ERP and procured in the United States be shipped in vessels flagged in the United States. Not only did this add an additional regulatory burden on the plan's administrators, it made achieving production targets more difficult if the requisite ships could not be found.

There was also a requirement that a quarter of all wheat exports financed by the ERP had to be exported as flour milled in the United States. Another gave the Department of Agriculture the ability to declare that the United States had surpluses of various agricultural commodities, forcing the ECA to purchase the commodity in question from U.S. farmers for use in Western Europe. These purchases were also subsidized by the U.S. government "by as much as 50 percent of the market cost" (Milward 1984, 121). Milward concludes that "it is very likely that the ERP induced a higher level of United States food exports to Western Europe than would have otherwise been the case." Although this policy might have help U.S. farmers, what it did for Western European recovery, and U.S. taxpayers, is questionable. Tyler Cowen (1985, 71–72) also discusses various special-interest provisions for Virginia tobacco growers, U.S. dried fruit manufacturers, pasta producers, truck manufacturers, and oil companies. The latter were able to sell oil through the ECA at prices well over the cost of production, thanks to Marshall Plan aid provisions.

A further problem with production targets was that they were inevitably quantitative and aggregative. The Marshall Planners were infatuated with meeting aggregate production targets and paid little if any attention to the composition of output.[7] Success of the Plan was to be determined by whether these aggregate goals were met, independent of how that production might relate to the demands of consumers. Given our previous discussion of the importance of coordination for economic growth, this result should not be surprising. To the extent that planners cannot acquire the detailed knowledge needed to perform these coordinative functions, the best they can do is to rely on aggregate targets. Even if such production targets are met, there is no assurance that they relate to the wants of the public. One can easily increase output as measured by GDP by producing items that people do not really want. The question is whether we want to call this economic growth and use it as an appropriate strategy for developing an economy.

One of the major strategies for integrating the European economy was to break down the national barriers against free trade and organize some form of currency payments process. The implementers of the Marshall Plan attempted to do so through various negotiating strategies and a sequential process of moving toward genuine multilateral trade. Rather than allow trade agreements and payments institutions to emerge through spontaneous market processes, the planners attempted to rationally construct various schemes, a number of which proved to be less than successful. Eberstadt (1991, 27), for example, mentions the system of bilateral drawing rights established by the Marshall Plan.[8] This was intended to be an intermediary step toward true multilateralism, but wound up "subsidizing governments with overvalued currencies and large trade deficits and . . . penalized governments that attempted to maintain discipline in their accounts." Belgium, for example, which held the line on fiscal policy, lost four-fifths of its dollar aid during this bilateral drawing system. Once again, a well-intentioned attempt at constructing economic institutions was disrupted by unforseen and unintended consequences.

One last point should also be noted. As the ERP continued on, the nature of much of the direct aid changed. With the outbreak of the Korean War in 1950, and generally heightened fear of the Soviet military, much of the direct aid became tied to military considerations. The Marshall Plan slowly evolved into an attempt to rearm Western Europe to forestall the Soviet threat. Many of the plans and production targets were altered to fit this new direction. In thinking about future Marshall Plan-type aid packages, the possibility of this kind of outcome should be considered. This result should also not be a surprise. As some authors have argued, any attempt at economic planning will have to involve the coerced mobilization of people and resources, not unlike how one might prepare for war. Don Lavoie (1985b, 320; emphasis in original) makes this point quite clearly: "Planning does not accidentally deteriorate into the militarization of the economy; it *is* the militarization of the economy."

These are just a few examples of the planning aspects of the Marshall Plan. My purpose here is not to discuss this point exhaustively; rather I want to give a flavor for the kinds of policies and attitudes enforced by the Plan's creators and implementers. I also want to touch briefly on whether the Plan was a success. If by a success we mean did the economies of Western Europe recover to prewar levels, the answer is yes. But how much of that recovery is due to the ERP? Scholars are unclear on the answer to this. The general consensus in recent years seems to be that the effects of the Marshall Plan were marginal. Whether that margin was the crucial margin is the issue. Alan Milward (1984, 91) argues that Marshall Plan aid simply sped up a recovery that was already under way: "quantitative measures of [ERP's] impact on the European economies suggest that the contribution was greatly exaggerated by Cold War historians."[9] Hogan (1987, 437ff.) is a bit more positive, arguing that although the effect of the Marshall aid was marginal, it was a margin that made a difference.[10] However the success, or lack thereof, of the Marshall Plan is independent of whether it is a useful model for Eastern Europe today. As we shall see below, the circumstances, goals, and especially the ideology have changed, and so has the relevance of a Marshall Plan-type of aid package.

A New Marshall Plan for Eastern Europe?

Fundamentally, the problem faced by a new Marshall Plan for Eastern Europe is that the Marshall Plan was a plan. The condition that Eastern Europe finds itself in is the result of the failures of economic planning as discussed earlier. Why should we now believe that a *new* plan will be any better than the old one(s)? As the history of the Marshall Plan indicates, it was not simply a package of pure financial assistance. It involved the use of economic planning and intentional macroeconomic coordination in the countries that received ERP aid. With a less naive view of what can be accomplished through economic planning, we can be notably more skeptical concerning the success of any aid package modeled after the Marshall Plan.

That having been pointed out, we can also see that the circumstances and needs of Eastern Europe are very different from those faced by the Western European economies after World War II. Those economies were once *developed* economies that had been destroyed by the war. The aim of the Marshall Plan was to help them "reattain their prewar levels of output" (Eberstadt 1991, 27). The plan was clearly not a program for economic development; instead "the Marshall Plan financed Western Europe's *return to normalcy*. It did not sponsor its progress to some new stage in economic or political development" (Pfaff 1987, 72; emphasis in original).[11] One explanation is that although the war destroyed resources, it did not destroy a history of economic institutions and practices that could fairly easily be recovered once resources were back in place.[12] More specifically, Western Europe was disconnected from the broadly liberal institutions of property rights and freedom of contract and exchange for only a few short years. Eastern Europeans have had at least two generations pass since those institutions were even a small part of the fabric of their societies.[13] The task facing reform in Eastern Europe is not merely acquiring resources, but discovering an institutional framework within which resources can be used efficiently and economic growth can take place. The important point is that no matter how well or how poorly the Marshall Plan worked at the time, the problems facing Eastern Europe are vastly different from those of

Western Europe after World War II. Add to that the critique of economic planning and the Marshall Plan becomes a doubly dubious model for economic development in Eastern Europe.

Given this perspective, the question facing Eastern Europe concerns how liberal institutional frameworks grow and evolve. One answer to this question comes from the same thinkers who were so influential in arguing that economic planning was doomed to fail. For Hayek (1988), the flip side of the impossibility of conscious social planning is that beneficial social institutions have and should arise as sets of unintended consequences driven by humanity's constant search for new knowledge and new ways of improving itself. Hayek and other Austrian School economists have argued that these spontaneous evolutionary processes apply not just to the economic activities that take place in a society under the rule of law and bounded by a stable monetary system, but to the very institutions of law and money themselves.

If a precondition for economic growth is a strong legal framework protecting property rights and contracts, then such a framework can best be found through a process of legal evolution, not through a conscious attempt at design. The same can be said for a monetary order. A stable monetary framework can best be discovered by allowing monetary arrangements to evolve within the rule of law.[14] For Eastern Europe to recover what it has lost, Western attempts to "create" legal and monetary institutions will have to be abandoned in favor of allowing the discovery processes of the market, as they emerge in each of the reforming countries. Only these evolutionary processes can make use of the knowledge needed to effect economic coordination and enhance economic growth. Given the state of the U.S. legal system and financial system, sending lawyers and central bankers to the former Soviet Union to assist in designing legal and monetary systems there is highly questionable.

These arguments are not limited to microeconomic planning and the planning of institutions, they also apply to the kinds of Keynesian macroeconomic policies used by the Marshall Planners. In the same way that microeconomic coordination cannot be produced by conscious design, neither can macroeconomic coordination. Western market economies have learned the lessons of attempts at Keynesian demand management. The inflation and stagnation in the United States in the 1970s should caution Eastern Europeans against attempts to imitate those policies in the reform process. The same kinds of knowledge problems that led to the downfall of planning in those countries are likely to plague less comprehensive attempts to "manage" (i.e., plan) the macroeconomy. How, for example, are macroeconomic managers to know the demand for money, or the "appropriate" level of aggregate demand? What industries should be the recipients of attempts to boost aggregate demand through government expenditures? What is to ensure that the chosen industries are ones that will deliver the goods that consumers want?[15] And, how are such policies different from the planning processes responsible for the current economic situation in Eastern Europe?

Rather than focusing on U.S. financial aid or immodest attempts at designing new social and economic institutions, reforming Eastern Europe requires the export of ideas and practices. What the West has to offer is not money and capital but a model of how to achieve economic growth by giving as much scope as possible to the spontaneous forces of entrepreneurial discovery. Of course, the United States is not perfect in this regard, but the history of the last two hundred years is not to be taken lightly, and the Western traditions of private property, freedom of contract, and market exchange have revealed themselves to be the true causes of economic growth. As Cowen (1985, 73) argues, "The basic problem with foreign aid is that economic growth is not a creature of central planning and direction. Growth is the result of individual initiative and enterprise within a sound legal and economic framework."

Critics might respond by granting those ideas, but still claiming that Eastern Europe needs capital to kick the process into motion. However, as Peter Bauer has argued, this is a fallacy. If the acquisition of capital preceded economic growth, "the world would still be in the Old Stone Age."[16] Rather the acquisition of capital is the effect of economic growth and not the cause. The cause is the set of ideas and practices that allow the creation of capital and thus increase the productivity of human labor and total human wealth. We emerged from the Stone Age, by unintentionally conforming to certain traditional and largely *moral* practices, many of which men tend to dislike, whose significance they usually fail to understand, whose validity they cannot prove, and which have nonetheless fairly rapidly spread by means of an evolutionary selection—the comparative increase of population and wealth—of those groups that happened to follow them (Hayek 1988, 6).

The driving force of economic development is the set of ideas embodied in the moral restraint that permits spontaneous processes of social and economic discovery to take their course and lead us into an unknown future. These ideas, and the institutions that result from them, cannot be bought with U.S. tax dollars. In fact, the very premise of using tax dollars to "guide" development directly contradicts those ideas. Rather, those ideas will be imitated to the extent they are practiced by the West and deliver success.

In fact, as Eberstadt points out (following a number of recent thinkers, especially Peter Bauer), the relationship between U.S. aid and economic development is a very tenuous one. Eberstadt (1991, 25) argues that "American development-assistance policies, for many years, have been more likely to lead a prospective beneficiary toward an Eastern Europe-style economic morass than to help it escape from one toward economic health and self-sufficiency." He also points out that the current problems facing Eastern Europe are strikingly similar to the conditions found in other Western and African countries that *have already been receiving* U.S. development aid for ten or twenty years. If so, "why should U.S. aid be expected to help Eastern Europe evolve *away* from its current characteristics?" (Eberstadt 1991, 25).

It can be added that the likely beneficiaries of any Western aid are not going to be the citizens of Eastern Europe. Potential beneficiaries include Western firms who can effectively lobby for special-interest clauses and industrial guarantees like those of the original Marshall Plan. Other likely winners are the *governments* of Eastern Europe. Most U.S. aid has historically been government-to-government aid which assumes that the recipient government not only knows where to use the funds, but in fact does use them on the citizenry rather than enhancing its own wealth. Finally, the biggest beneficiaries may be Western politicians who can both sell their influence to domestic special interests and claim that they "did something" to help Eastern Europe. To re-state Eberstadt's point, Western politicians have been "doing something" for much of the underdeveloped world for twenty years with very little to show for it. The question is really "who are they doing something *for?*"

Conclusion

The problem with developing a new Marshall Plan for Eastern Europe is that it seems to assume that the crisis faced in that part of the world is that the old plans were bad plans and that the solution is a new plan. To the contrary, the argument above is that the problem is the whole notion of planning, and that the original Marshall Plan suffered from the same false belief in the power of conscious direction of economic processes as did the failed governments of the former Soviet Union and Eastern Europe. For countries ravaged by over forty-five years of plans, plans, and more plans, the last thing needed is a new plan. This is not to deny that the West should do something for Eastern Europe. Instead, we need to understand that what drives our own economy, and its history of productivity, are the ideas embodied in its legal and monetary institutions. The ideas of the rule of law, freedom of exchange and contract, and private property combined with the moral restraint to not subject such institutions to the hubris of "scientific" planning are the best aid package for Eastern Europe. Anything else will only repeat the most fundamental and tragic errors of the twentieth century.

Notes

1. The debate that Mises's article sparked is best summarized in Lavoie (1985a).
2. On the idea of economic order as involving creativity, complexity, and coordination, see Horwitz (1992, chapter 2).
3. On regulation generally, see Kirzner (1985). On central bank policy, see Selgin (1988) and Horwitz (1992). On antitrust, see Armentano (1982). For a general discussion of the problems of noncomprehensive planning, see Lavoie (1985b).

4. This corporatist political economy (called "political capitalism" by some) is best explored in various revisionist histories of the Progressive Era. See Wiebe (1962), Kolko (1963), and Weinstein (1968).
5. See Hogan (1987, 23): "Supplementing the planners' approaches was a commitment to Keynesian techniques of macroeconomic management."
6. See also Cowen (1985, 66ff.) and Hogan (1987, 71).
7. See Wexler (1983, 95–96), where he quotes a high-ranking Plan administrator as making this point after assessing the Plan when it concluded.
8. Also see the discussion in Cowen (1985, 68).
9. Also see Cowen (1985, 73): "At best, its effects on postwar Europe were mixed."
10. The reader might also want to see the combined review of the Hogan and Milward books in Diebold (1988).
11. Also see Eberstadt (1991, 27).
12. See Cowen (1985, 73–74): "Not only was the European economy already industrialized and fairly well integrated, but Europe had a long tradition of capitalistic institutions."
13. See Eberstadt (1991, 29): "The populations of Eastern Europe have been separated from that framework [of legal protections for individuals] for more than four decades. The majority have no memory of firsthand exposure to it, to say nothing of personal familiarity."
14. For a spontaneous order view of law, see Benson (1990). On money, see Hayek (1978), Selgin (1988), and Horwitz (1992).
15. See Lavoie (1985b, chapters 4–6), for more on this point.
16. Peter Bauer, as quoted in Pfaff (1987, 72).

References

Armentano, Dominick. 1982. *Antitrust and Monopoly: Anatomy of a Policy Failure*. New York: Wiley.

Benson, Bruce. 1990. *The Enterprise of Law*. San Francisco: Pacific Research Institute.

Cowen, Tyler. 1985. "The Marshall Plan: Myths and Realities." In *U.S. Aid to the Developing World*, ed. Doug Bandow. Washington, D.C.: Heritage Foundation.

Diebold, William. 1988. "The Marshall Plan in Retrospect: A Review of Recent Scholarship." *Journal of International Affairs* 41 (Summer): 421–35.

Eberstadt, Nicholas. 1991. "How Not to Aid Eastern Europe." *Commentary* 92 (November): 24–30.

Hayek, F. A. 1948. *Individualism and Economic Order*. Chicago: University of Chicago Press.

———. 1978. *The Denationalisation of Money*. London: Institute for Economic Affairs.

———. 1988. *The Fatal Conceit: The Errors of Socialism*. Ed. W. W. Bartley III. Chicago: University of Chicago Press.

Hogan, Michael. 1987. *The Marshall Plan: America, Britain, and the Reconstruction of Western Europe, 1947–1952*. Cambridge: Cambridge University Press.

Horwitz, Steven. 1992. *Monetary Evolution, Free Banking, and Economic Order*. Boulder: Westview.

Kirzner, Israel. 1985. "The Perils of Regulation: A Market Process Approach." In his *Discovery and the Capitalist Process*. Chicago: University of Chicago Press.

Kolko, Gabriel. 1963. *The Triumph of Conservatism*. New York: The Free Press.

Lavoie, Don. 1985a. *Rivalry and Central Planning: The Socialist Calculation Debate Revisited*. Cambridge: Cambridge University Press.

———. 1985b. *National Economic Planning: What Is Left?* Cambridge, Mass.: Ballinger.

Milward, Alan. 1984. *The Reconstruction of Western Europe, 1945–51*. Berkeley: University of California Press.

Mises, Ludwig von. [1920] 1935. "Economic Calculation in the Socialist Commonwealth." In *Collectivist Economic Planning*, ed. F. A. Hayek. Clifton, N.J.: Augustus M. Kelley.

Pfaff, William. 1987. "Perils of Policy: The Marshall Plan Only Worked Once." *Harper's* 274 (May): 70–72.

Pisani, Sallie. 1991. *The CIA and the Marshall Plan*. Lawrence: University of Kansas Press.

Selgin, George. 1988. *The Theory of Free Banking: Money Supply under Competitive Note Issue*. Totowa, N.J.: Rowman and Littlefield.

Weinstein, James. 1968. *The Corporate Ideal in the Liberal State, 1900–1918*. Boston: Beacon Press.

Wexler, Immanuel. 1983. *The Marshall Plan Revisited: The European Recovery Program in Economic Perspective*. Westport Conn.: Greenwood Press.

Wiebe, Robert. 1962. *Businessmen and Reform*. Chicago: Ivan R. Dee.

IV

The Political Economy of the Asian Miracle

9

Industrial Policy as the Engine of Economic Growth in South Korea: Myth and Reality

Young Back Choi

The rapid transition of the South Korean economy from a "hopeless basket case" in the 1960s to an "economic miracle" in the 1980s has become a subject of much discussion, in popular as well as academic media. Many marvel at the fact that South Korea has pulled itself up from a major U.S. aid recipient to the twelfth-largest trading nation in the world, from a largely agrarian nation to a major exporter of manufactured goods, and from a per capita GNP of a mere $100 in 1960 to over $6,000 in 1991. Along with other rapidly growing economies in Asia such as Taiwan, Hong Kong, Singapore, and Thailand, the Korean experience keeps one hopeful that industrialization and prosperity are not impossible for non-Europeans, latecomers, or resource-poor countries.

Some go beyond admiration and perceive South Korea as a potential threat, if not already a threat. Those who see the country as a next "Japan, Inc." fret over the fact that South Korea has become the second-largest shipbuilder in the world after Japan, or that it is one of the four producers of large-scale random-access memory chips, with 13 percent of the world market share. The perceived threat is enhanced with the possibility of the unification of the two Koreas generating a substantial regional power with a combined population of almost seventy million.

There are also those who are intent on learning from South Korea, finding the experience paradigmatic both for less developed countries (LDCs) and even for the United States (Amsden 1989). Different people draw different lessons from the South Korean experience, depending on their views on how and why the country has enjoyed such rapid economic growth in recent decades. The most common and popular view, by far, is that government *dirigisme* is responsible for the South Korean growth (Wade 1990, 8). Robert Wade defines dirigisme as the directional thrust by government to strongly influence the market. Others think that, while government involvement has been very pervasive, policies have tended to be market friendly (Agarwala 1983; Lal 1988). They argue that despite all the government interventions, price distortions in South Korea have been much less than in other countries that have been less successful in economic growth. Then, there are those who see other factors as significant in explaining the South Korean experience, for example, such cultural factors as Confucianism, the Japanese colonial experience, the large U.S. aid, or education.

The purpose of this chapter is to critically evaluate some of these commonly held views and offer what I would regard as a more balanced position. The apparent success of industrial policy in South Korea in the 1960s and 1970s was a result of many fortuitous events which are neither easy to replicate nor necessarily desirable. I will first examine the "uniqueness" view that resources, Confucianism, colonial experience, and foreign aid are responsible for South Korea's recent growth. Next, I will examine the "active government," (or industrial policy argument), and the "relatively little price distortions," (or pro-market), propositions. After criticizing these views, I will suggest an alternative explanation that is compatible with pervasive government involvement in South Korea and the market process theory by using Mancur Olson's (1982, 47–53) notion of "encompassing organization." I will conclude the chapter with a number of conjectures on questions that need further clarifications.

Record of Economic Development

A better sense of the magnitude and the pace of economic development in South Korea can be gained from the following considerations. It is apparent that per capita GNP has far surpassed the almost tripling of the population in about three decades. Per capita GNP, expressed in U.S. dollars, has increased more than eighty times in nominal terms since 1962 which is equivalent to a roughly twenty-fold increase in real terms (Song 1990; Bank of Korea, 1991). In 1962, South Korea was poorer than Zaire, Congo, or Sudan (Wade 1990, 35), but in 1991 it was richer than Czechoslovakia, Portugal, or Greece. Though still a relatively poor country compared to Western Europe, North America, or Japan, Korea has improved its standing in the international community significantly.

In little more than two decades, the proportion of the work force in agriculture declined from almost 60 percent to around 20 percent. In value terms, agriculture declined from almost 40 percent of GNP in 1960 to about 10 percent in 1989, while manufacturing increased from some 12 percent to more than 30 percent during the same period. The value of exports increased more than two hundred-fold, in nominal terms, during this period. In 1989, South Korea became the tenth-largest trading nation in the world, and is currently the seventh-largest trading partner of the United States (World Bank 1991).

Social indicators also attest to significant improvements in South Korea. For example, during the same period, life expectancy increased from less than 60 to more than 70, closer to the level of North America or Western Europe. Other indicators, for example, literacy, infant mortality, education, and so forth, show equally impressive improvements. Few, therefore, would dispute the fact of social and economic growth in South Korea. There are disparate views, however, on why and how this state of affairs has come about.

Resources, Confucianism, Colonial Experience, and U.S. Aid

Before we move on to the issue of dirigisme, let us briefly consider the role of (1) natural resources, (2) Confucian legacy, (3) colonial experience under Japan, and (4) U.S. aid in South Korean economic development. The discussion of the role of education is postponed to a later section.

(1) Natural resources are the least likely candidate in explaining South Korean economic development, unless one regards its poor resource endowments as a blessing in disguise. South Korea is a small, densely populated, and resource-poor country. It is one-fourth the size of California and has the third-highest population density after Bangladesh and Taiwan (ignoring city states.) Since the South Korean terrain is mountainous, only 20 percent of its land is suitable for agricultural or urban use. It is also mineral resource-poor, with the exception of tungsten and limestone. South Korea, therefore, has to import most of its raw materials, along with food stuff.

(2) To some people the Confucian legacy, which the South Koreans share with the Japanese and Chinese, seems a little more promising. This supposed Oriental counterpart of "Protestant ethics" emphasizes diligence, education, and harmonious relationships within family and hierarchy. This proposition seems to make sense in light of the fact that Confucianism was the state ideology of the Lee Dynasty in Korea for five hundred years until the turn of this century.

Two facts militate against this proposition. First, Confucianism, at least as it was practiced in Korea, was not very supportive of industry or commerce. In fact during the Lee Dynasty (A.D. 1392–1910), artisans and merchants were accorded a lower status than peasants and only higher than slaves. If Confucianism seems to exert a positive influence on the enterprising spirit of people in South Korea, as well as in other Asian countries, it must be in a significantly altered form from the traditional (Mason et al. 1980, 284–85; see also Song 1990, 48–53). Secondly, South Korea is no longer dominated by Confucianism. In fact, religious believers in South Korea, who account for the great majority of people, are roughly equally divided among Confucianism, Buddhism, and Christianity. That is, one might as well describe South Korea as a Buddhist or a Christian nation.

(3) Some people believe that the Japanese colonial rule over Korea (1910–45) has had something to do with the latter's recent

economic development (Woo 1991, 207–8). The suggestion is that Japanese colonialism transformed Korea from a feudal economy into a capitalist one, if only in embryonic form. Some go further to suggest that Japan left Korea in an advantageous position amongst LDCs in terms of infrastructure and some key industries, such as textiles, chemicals, and machinery.

This suggests that somehow Japan had intentions different from those of other colonizers. Colonial rule is based on forceful annexation, not on voluntary consent; the colonized do not see the benefit of colonization that the colonizers anticipate. Initially, the Japanese intended to turn Korea into a "rice bowl" for Japan, as well as to keep it dependent on manufactured goods from Japan. It was not the Koreans who chose to specialize in growing rice, however. Through cadastral survey, land registration, and expropriation of the state land, large tracts of land were transferred to Japanese colonist-farmers. Driven off the land, millions of Korean farmers migrated to bandit-infested Manchuria and the communist dominated Soviet Far East for better luck. Lest enterprising Koreans might venture into manufacturing, they were not permitted to start factories (Woo 1991, 31). To keep Koreans ignorant, the Japanese discouraged Koreans from establishing schools, keeping only one university open in Korea, mainly to educate the sons of Japanese colonists. At the time of their liberation from Japan, Koreans were in dire poverty (Song 1990, 39; see also Mason et al. 1980). To argue that somehow Japanese colonialism helped Koreans to prepare for later economic development is to argue that the belated growth of a child after getting rid of parasites that infected him since his infancy was made possible by the parasitic infection.

After 1930, admittedly, Japan built heavy industrial plants in Korea, to better manage its growing empire and to turn it into a competing economic bloc, as Western nations became more protective of their own markets. This, however, helped South Korea precious little in its later economic development for the following reasons. First, Koreans had been systematically kept at the level of menial work, reserving managerial and engineering posts for Japanese. Secondly, since much of what the Japanese had built between 1930 and 1945 was located in northern part of Korea, when Korea was divided into two countries, few of the industries they had built were located in South Korea. Thirdly, the three years of devastating war in Korea (1950–53), responsible for the deaths of over two million Koreans, left few urban and industrial structures intact. South Korean economic development, moreover, began in earnest almost twenty years after its liberation from Japan and almost ten years after the terrible Korean War. Perhaps a better case can be made of the U.S. aid.

(4) South Korea received massive foreign aid, largely but not exclusively from the United States Military and economic aid from the United States from 1945 to 1976 was more than twelve billion dollars (Woo 1991, 45). Before the Korean War, U.S. economic aid to South Korea was about sixty million dollars a year. After the war, upon President Eisenhower's urging that "all eyes would be on South Korea after the armistice," the U.S. economic aid to South Korea jumped to two hundred million dollars a year (cited in ibid., 57; Parry 1988, 98). To get a proper sense of the magnitude of U.S. aid to South Korea, one must remind oneself that U.S. federal nondefense spending was less than five billion dollars in 1950 and about nine billion dollars in 1953. More importantly, U.S. economic aid represented over 10 percent of South Korean GNP in 1950s, or over 25 percent if military aid is included. The U.S. economic aid of 383 million dollars in 1957, for example, was equivalent to 70 percent of South Korean government revenue (Woo 1991, 46).

The economic impact of U.S. involvement in South Korea was probably even greater than the U.S. aid figures might indicate. For instance, in 1956 the United States gave South Korea over four hundred million dollars in military aid, in addition to over three hundred million dollars in economic aid. Moreover, the U.S. spent another three hundred million dollars in that year to cover the costs of the U.S. troops stationed in South Korea, some of which must have been used in purchasing local goods and services. The massive U.S. aid, along with other foreign aid, did help South Koreans survive and rebuild as they emerged poverty stricken from Japanese colonialism, and in even greater destitution from the utter destruction of the Korean War where armies from nineteen nations fought up and down the peninsula for over three years. Economic hardship was made worse by over two million refugees from North Korea swarming down on South Korea, when twenty million South Koreans themselves were on the verge of starvation. Despite the massive U.S. aid, South Korea seemed to be doomed as a development project. Syngman Rhee's government exacted a high price from the United States for being an outpost in the Cold War, but refused to trade with Japan in the name of anticolonialism or to adopt measures recommended by the experts from the United States to stabilize the economy on the ground of political expediency. Rhee used his control over the U.S. aid flow to further his own political aims, resulting in rampant corruption. The frequent verdict on the South Korean economy, up to the middle of 1960s, was that it was "a bottomless pit," "a permanent U.S. ward," or that the massive aid doused South Koreans with "a welfare mentality" (ibid., 46).

Active Government

More promising is the proposition that governmental policies have been instrumental in the rapid growth of South Korea in the past three decades. The start of rapid economic growth coincided with a radical shift in government policies from around 1963, with the inception of President Park's Third Republic after the military coup he led in 1961. Compared to the earlier Republics that meddled through by distributing foreign aid, while attempting to develop import-substitution industries, the Third Republic was conscious of its role as a regime of economic development. President Park, who did not hesitate to violate human rights and suspend political freedom, placed all his political bets on economic development. His mottos were "Nation building through export," "Alleviation of poverty through economic development," and "Political freedom is a luxury the starving can ill-afford," and the like. He undertook ideological campaigns to reform people's attitudes, and rounded up *lumpens* and thugs and sent them to labor camps. He nationalized banks and kept politicians and businessmen under a tight leash, vanquishing those who did not comply with his wishes. He assembled a corp of technocrats to plan for economic development and personally attended monthly meetings where export strategies were discussed amongst bureaucrats and businessmen. Park personally awarded those who exceeded the export targets set by the government, but export encouragement went beyond his personal appreciation; it involved low-interest loans and the granting of rights to import goods to a tightly protected consumer goods market for extra profits. By 1979, when President Park was assassinated, South Korea had experienced an average annual growth rate of almost 10 percent for over fifteen years and seemed to be well on its way to industrialization. South Korea seemed to have been radically transformed since 1960, when many experts decided that it was a "basket case," into an economy where rapid growth is the norm, thanks to President Park's policies, one may observe.

With a few popular anecdotes, the case for the efficacy of industrial policies in South Korea seems to be closed. For example, South Korea is currently one of the lowest-cost producers of steel. When the South Korean government decided to build an integrated steel mill in the late 1960s, however, a World Bank study team advised the government that such a project was not economically feasible, given South Korea's lack of iron ore, coking coal, steel-making skills, domestic market, and capital (Amsden 1989, 291). Going against the experts' advice, the South Korean government invested almost four billion dollars to create the Pohang Iron and Steel Company, Ltd. (POSCO) in 1968, appointing a retired general as its president. Many expected POSCO to become another white elephant project found in LDCs. In five years, however, POSCO began production with an annual capacity of about one million tons, and after several expansions, the mill reached an annual capacity of over nine million tons of crude steel in 1983, feeding steel into the then expanding shipbuilding, automobile, and construction industries. In 1986, POSCO entered a joint venture with U.S. Steel to modernize the latter's plant in California, providing half the capital, the basic design of the facility, and the training of American managers and workers in operations and maintenance (ibid., 291–92).

Consider another example. In 1991 South Korean producers had over 13 percent of the world market share in dynamic random-access memories (DRAM) (*Wall Street Journal*, July 14, 1992,

B1). The semiconductor industry was started when the government established a research institute to cultivate it in 1976 and provided investment incentives in 1982 and thereafter. Late in 1988, Samsung, the leading South Korean semiconductor producer, introduced engineering samples of 4 Meg DRAM, only six months behind Toshiba, the world leader, and began shipping in bulk in late 1989 (Wade 1990, 313–17). Anecdotal evidence such as this seems to demonstrate very convincingly that well-conceived and executed industrial policies can do wonders for economic development. The late President Park, who viewed his own role in Korean history as similar to that of Emperor Meiji of Japan, could not have agreed more with this proposition.

The Pro-Market Proposition

Such arguments, however, do not establish the effectiveness of government in managing economic growth. For at one end of the spectrum, there are many examples of failed economies despite industrial policies to stimulate economic growth. On the other side, there are those economies such as Hong Kong that have grown rapidly without much government prodding. To observe that South Korean government policies have been effective because its economy grew fast, without showing how, is circular. In addition, even if it is established that government policies can be helpful in economic growth under certain general conditions, one cannot automatically assume that the government has the will or the ability to undertake the necessary policies. For the proponents of industrial policy to be persuasive, therefore, they must show (1) how government policies uniquely contributed to industrialization, (2) how the government avoided being swarmed by rent-seeking, special-interest groups, and (3) that the correlation between economic growth and government policies is not spurious by showing that there is no other factor that can sufficiently explain the growth. In this section, I will address the first and the last issues, leaving the second for the next section.

To show how governmental policies help develop the economy one must show the existence of conditions under which private enterprises cannot, singly or jointly, take advantage of potential gains. As far as orthodox economics is concerned, there are three kinds of situations under which government involvement in the economy is in principle justified—public goods, market failure due to externalities, and increasing returns to scale. The proponents of the efficacy of South Korea's industrial policies as the engine of economic development have in mind mainly the latter two categories (Westphal 1990). For example, it is often observed that the protection of domestic markets, together with export subsidies, ensures infant industries operate on a sufficiently large scale, developing viable industries that otherwise would not have taken roots. Often cited are the successful South Korean shipbuilding, automobile, steel, and semiconductor industries. Along the line of externalities, it is observed that the South Korean government policies helped Korean firms to obtain technologies which they themselves would not have obtained because of multinational firms' unwillingness to transfer important technologies and the excessive competition amongst local firms. Similarly, it is observed that government could overcome the externalities that stem from the foreign lender's inability to assess the credit-worthiness of local firms in the absence of sufficient information (Krauss 1991). Or alternatively, some hold to Alexander Gerschenkron's thesis of the "economics of backwardness" that, given the relative scarcity of skilled manpower in less developed countries, the latecomers have to rely on capital-intensive projects to economize on skilled manpower. This trend is more and more pronounced. Since only the state can mobilize such large resource, so the argument goes, economic development increasingly involves the state (Amsden 1989).

While the above arguments seem to support the proposition that government policies played a crucial role in the industrialization of South Korea, upon close examination things do not seem as simple. First, when the state acts as the conduit of foreign credit on the ground of externalities, or imperfect information, credit does not necessarily come cheaply. It has been reported that as much as 10 percent of all foreign loans were retained by President Park's government for discretionary use, political and personal.[1] In addition, in many public projects it was discovered that the pricing of foreign capital goods was much higher, anywhere between 20 percent to 100 percent higher than the norm, the difference being remitted to the key figures in the ruling party as kickbacks. Moreover, the manner of allocating credit (remember banks had been nationalized) cannot be said to be an ideal form of picking winners. The owners of big business bribed their way to gain access to the government-rationed credits, that are priced much below the market, or rather the black-market, rates.

Secondly, even when an industry promoted by government seems to be successful, it may not be necessarily due to government policies. South Korean semiconductor firms are doing better in recent years, but it is due to factors beyond their wildest imagination—the U.S. protectionism. Import restrictions on Japanese DRAM since 1986 have not been extended to South Korea because it was not a significant producer of DRAM at the time. As a result, Japanese firms producing 4 Meg DRAM are operating at 50–60 percent capacity whereas their South Korean counterparts are producing at full capacity, unhampered by the U.S. regulation. The whim of U.S. protectionism, however, can change at any moment.

Thirdly, a "successful" creation of an industry where economies of scale are important is not necessarily beneficial. In less than two decades since it began exporting ships, for example, South Korea has become the second-largest shipbuilding nation in the world, producing more than the EC and COMECON combined (Amsden 1989, 270; see also Woo 1991, 135–38). But South Korean shipbuilders need periodic government bail-outs to stay in business. So what is the point of having a large-scale industry except the fact that they tend to be "too big to fail"?

Fourthly, the industries where the economies of scale and externalities are important, the industries for which government may in principle be called upon to act, are neither necessary nor sufficient for economic development. Among the latecomers, Taiwan, Singapore, and Hong Kong, for example, have done as well as South Koreans without shipbuilding, automobiles, semiconductors, and so forth. These countries have done it mostly with consumer products such as toys and electronics in which production economies of scale or externalities are less significant. If industrialization is possible without ever more massive projects for latecomers, as it seems to be the case in these countries, Gerschen-kron's thesis of the economics of backwardness and its implication for the necessity for a greater role of the state in the development of a latecomer are suspect. Gerschenkron's thesis is based on the assumption that latecomers adopt the same kinds of industries that developed countries had to develop. But that is shown not to be the case. The modern economic skepticism about the willing-ness and the ability of the state to pursue common goods, namely, the failure of socialist planning and rent seeking, only reinforces this view.

Finally, there is a sufficient explanation for economic develop-ment—education. A recent study by Robert Barro shows that much of the observed growth rates of different countries can be explained by the gap between the actual level of per capita GNP and the per capita GNP expected based on the level of education (Barro 1991). That is, much of the high rates of growth in East Asian countries can be explained by inordinately low levels of income in 1960 relative to their level of education. In a way, these countries have grown fast to catch up with the level of income expected of them based on their level of education. Although Barro reports an underestimation of growth rates in the case of South Korea and Taiwan (ibid., 418), that is, they grew faster than they were expected based on their educational level, this can be explained. It is not necessary to attribute the remainder to govern-ment dirigisme. The massive inflow of refugees in both countries, who represented above the average quality of human resources, is a far more promising candidate. In other words, the measure of educational level, not reflecting the special circumstances of Ko-rea or Taiwan, understated the level of human capital. If the level of education is sufficient, as I think it is, to explain the recent growth rates in East Asia, including South Korea, the case for industrial policy becomes even more tenuous.

Encompassing Organization

If the South Korean government, nevertheless, seemed to be more effective in promoting industrialization than other LDCs, it is because the ruling elites acted as the "encompassing organization." Mancur Olson defines the *encompassing organization* as an entity that has incentives "to make the society in which [it operates] more prosperous" not because it is altruistic, but because it expects disproportionate gains from it (Olson 1982, 53). That is, the late President Park and his political allies ran the economy as if they were the owners/managers of Korea, Inc.

To better understand my characterization of President Park's rule as an encompassing organization, one must understand the circumstances around the military coup in 1961 that brought Lieutenant General Park to power for the next nineteen years. Only a year before the coup, President Rhee's government (1948–60) had been overthrown in popular uprisings led by students. The major grievance was the stealing of the presidential election through vote rigging, but the uprising reflected the popular discontent with deteriorating economic conditions as well. President Rhee was mainly known for his anticommunism, anticolonialism, and stubbornness. In the context of the Cold War, and the destructive war in Korea, President Rhee used his anticommunist rhetoric and stubbornness to exact from the United States large sums of aid. The aid helped the war-ravaged South Koreans to survive and to rebuild. But President Rhee's policy of pursuing, against the wisdom of U.S. economic advisers, import-substitution industrialization on the cushion of the U.S. aid and his version of anticolonialism, created a system of market protection, import licenses, and monopoly rights, a classic setting for rent seeking. A change of mood in Washington, brought about by the worry that South Korea was "a bottomless money pit," as well as by Washington's own growing budget deficits, insisted on a stabilization policy in South Korea and began to reduce aid (Woo 1991, 69–72). These led to a prolonged recession in South Korea and to the eventual overthrow of Rhee's government.

Prime Minister Chang's government that came to power in the aftermath of the student uprising lacked authority, and remained paralyzed in the face of conflicting demands from various interest groups and ideologues. Hugh Farley, a CIA field officer in South Korea, wrote in March 1961: "The Republic of Korea is a sick society [with an] endemic Oriental problem of graft, corruption and fraud" (cited in ibid., 78). In less than a year, the Second

Republic was overthrown in the military coup led by General Park.

The leaders of the coup were full of revolutionary zeal, professing to get rid of corruption, to reform society, and to alleviate economic hardships. But their authority was precarious—the military junta consisted of relatively obscure and marginal figures, unknown to the general public. And the idea of being ruled by a military junta, let alone a junta of obscure generals and colonels, did not appeal to South Koreans steeped for centuries in the ideology of the Lee Dynasty that put civil order above the military. Policy makers in the United States were very suspicious of the nature of the junta. (Some, including officials in Washington, even thought General Park was a Communist.) In short, many did not believe that the military junta could last.

To solidify political power, General Park tried to win people's hearts and gain legitimacy by a two-pronged approach—a populist anticorruption campaign and a campaign for economic development. The two were not meant to be separate. Expropriate the rich, whose fortunes were regarded as being accumulated by illicit means under Rhee's regime, and use the proceeds to finance economic development. Two of the anticorruption campaigns are noteworthy. One was a currency reform, claimed to be fashioned after that of West Germany. It was intended to register and confiscate idle cash hoards, but was only successful in worsening inflation. The other was the rounding up of the wealthiest men in South Korea on charges of corruption and treason. Rounding up corrupt politicians is one thing; rounding up business leaders, whether or not corrupt, is another. With the most prominent businessmen in jail, the economy deteriorated even further. Out of desperation, General Park made a deal with the businessmen: in exchange for the exemption from criminal persecution and the expropriation of property—commercial banks were nationalized anyway—the business leaders were to redeem themselves by establishing industrial firms and donating shares to the government (Woo 1991, 84; see also Haggard et al. 1991, 859).

From this initial attempt to reform society, the military junta emerged as the *encompassing organization*, after utterly destroying the old political network often through brutal repression, publicly shaming the business leaders and charging them with a new patriotic duty to industrialize and export, having nationalized banking to tightly control credits, and having placed all stakes in the political game on economic development. The members of the junta were not ascetics, or inordinately public minded, but they realized that their political survival, as well as material gain as the major stakeholders, depended on the overall performance of the South Korean economy.

Park's Export Promotion

In the face of declining U.S. aid, the desire to earn foreign exchange to purchase the capital goods needed for industrialization and to build up the military, therefore, was translated into an *all-out war on export promotion*. The junta that soon became a civilian government upon the general's retirement from the army ran the country as a military commander might in directing an army unit—setting goals, in the manner of "Take that hill," with relatively little concern for the costs, or "casualities." Out of the blue, it would declare "This year GNP shall grow by 9 percent and exports shall double." As faithful soldiers might, businessmen and bureaucrats scrambled to meet the targets.

President Park's government did everything in its power to create an environment favorable to meet the targets. While the domestic consumption goods market was still heavily protected, the exporters could import duty free all the necessary goods for the production of exports. Additional incentives were provided to exporters in the form of import licences, monopoly franchises in domestic consumption goods markets, and so on, as mentioned above. Moreover, the government was in general goal-oriented, for example, the goal of meeting certain export targets, and left it to the private sector to decide how the goals should be met, in terms of choosing the line of business, organizing production, and finding the buyers, and so forth.

The pragmatic approach of South Korean government in largely limiting itself to setting goals, in allowing exporters to trade freely, and in providing them with export subsidies has led some people to observe that South Korea has grown fast because its governmental policies were "market friendly," or "market conforming." What could one possibly mean by government economic policies being market friendly? There seem to be three versions of this proposition: (1) The degree of intervention, as measured by the degree of price distortions, has relatively been small; (2) The government promoted exports; and (3) The government did not persist in supporting industries or projects once they were found to be unsuccessful in the world market. Let us consider each in turn.

1. Ramgopal Agarwala's cross-section alaysis of thirty-one countries—including South Korea—finds a negative correlation between the level of price distortion and the long term growth rates (Agarwala 1983).[2] Although South Korea's case is consistent with the above findings, it is unwarranted to conclude that its government intervened relatively little. The price distortion index, which is based on broad categories, can be misleading because there have been two production regimes in South Korea—one for domestic markets and another for exports. Domestic markets had been heavily protected.[3] In order not to handicap the export industries in the world market, the government has permitted firms in the export-oriented industries to import all raw materials, intermediate products, and capital goods duty free. This means that price distortions were significant in some categories and nil in others. The averaging of the two sets caused the price distortion to appear to be relatively low. Therefore, to conclude that government policies entailed little price distortion or were even market friendly is misleading.

2. South Korean government has actively promoted exports since the early 1960s. But export promotion is not equivalent to being market friendly by any means. Since South Korea started out with heavy protection, unless exempted from duties on necessary inputs in export industries, exporters would have been severely handicapped in the world market. But export promotion went beyond exempting such inputs. If successful in meeting export targets, exporters were often given the rights to import goods duty free in excess of their own use in the production for export and to sell them in domestic markets for high markups. In addition, large exporters were often given the rights to operate a mo-

nopoly or a quasi-monopoly firm in the protected market for extra profits. Moreover, exporters had privileged access to government-rationed credit at even negative real rates of interest. Some observe that this could be interpreted as merely counteracting distortions caused by tariffs on other goods that kept wages and other costs of doing business higher than they would have been otherwise (Lal 1988, 213–14). But who could tell whether the supposed countermeasures were exactly right, or too much? To speak of export promotion policies as market friendly is to stretch the term beyond recognition.

3. The South Korean government policies may be described as market friendly only in the sense that regardless of how a firm got started—subsidies, low-interest loans, monopoly rights in domestic markets, etc.—if that firm was judged to be generating insufficient profits after a nurturing period, in general it was allowed to fold by withholding privileged credits. That is, the government regularly subjected business firms it promoted to the market tests (with exceptions of course). I argued in the preceding section that this tendency is generated by the ruling elites as the encompassing organizations.

In a way, South Korea was able to grow because the rulers were able to pursue what they defined as the national goal, disregarding much of special-interest pleas, and to mobilize the people with a combination of incentives and exhortation, as well as brutal repression. This was possible because an obscure group, unconnected to the existing interest groups, took power by force, destroyed the then existing old-boy network, and publicly shamed all existing authorities in its populist anticorruption campaigns, and then still lacking legitimacy, placed all political bets on economic growth. The junta's survival depended on growth.

Further Factors Influencing Growth

Still, the idea that an economy straddled by an authoritarian ruling group acting as an encompassing interest can grow fast may seem less than fully believable in light of the fact that government may not command enough information to plan or direct the economy as well as a free economy. I offer two factors that might explain this: the level of technology, timing, and proximity to growing economies, and certain governmental actions such as sending troops to Vietnam.

The level of industrial production in South Korea was so low that it was easy to import technologies, in the form of turnkey projects or capital goods, or through foreign direct investments, that were no longer economical in many developed countries because of rising labor costs, or that were no longer tolerable because of pollution. Given the dire economic conditions in South Korea in the early 1960s, and the corresponding low wages, many declining industries in more developed countries became economically viable, and even profitable when transplanted to South Korea. South Korean businessmen, in fulfilling their "patriotic duties to build the nation through export," imported all necessary inputs for production—raw materials, machinery, and even foreign technicians and engineers to teach them how to produce, all of which were obtained on credit—hired local labor, and exported the finished products to the largely known markets in the West. Despite all the calls for a higher "domestic content," much of what South Korean businessmen did is *arbitrage*, pure and simple. It is precisely because it took no genius to replicate the process that South Koreans nowadays worry that their labor-intensive industries are threatened by such latecomers as mainland China, Indonesia, Malaysia, Bangladesh, Sri Lanka, and India.

Also important is the timing of the earnest attempts at economic development. South Koreans had many contemporary examples in close proximity to study and imitate. In addition to Japan that was growing at a phenomenal pace thanks to the booms created by the U.S. war efforts in Korea and Vietnam, Taiwan, Hong Kong, and Singapore began to show significant growths from the mid-1950s onward. With the combination of plentiful examples to follow, many projects with proven markets to pick from, and the general tendency of the South Korean government to be content with the fact that export targets were met, or exceeded as often was the case, and that businessmen made regular contributions to the ruling party, it was difficult not to grow.

Two of the South Korean governmental actions in the 1960s are particularly noteworthy: the normalization of relations with Japan, and the participation in the Vietnam War as a U.S. ally. The normalization of relations with Japan, concluded in 1965 twenty years after the Korean liberation from Japan, had the effect of opening the flood gate of trade that had been kept shut by President Rhee's anticolonialism, permitting the inflow of Japanese investment and capital goods. Some 800 million dollars in extra funding from Japan as reparation came in handy in financing initial development projects, including the aforementioned POSCO (Woo 1991, 87).[4]

Dispatching troops to Vietnam, over three hundred thousand soldiers between 1965 and 1972, proved to be critical to South Korean economic development, as well. In return, the United States not only increased military aid to South Korea, and equipped and paid its troops stationed in Vietnam, but bestowed many civilian contracts on South Korean firms, worth up to a billion dollars, providing critical outlets for Korean infant industries and enabling South Korean firms to gain experience in overseas contracts (ibid., 85, 93–97).[5] President Park's government not only charged businessmen and bureaucrats to meet targets in exports, GNP growth rates, and so forth, but tried to provide funding and even to secure markets. At the height of the credit crunch in 1971, the government even declared a moratorium on all corporate debt owed to (Korean) private lenders for three years, to relieve business firms from the crushing burden of debt service on foreign loans (ibid., 113). In keeping with the tradition of helping out business, when South Koreans faced another severe credit crunch in the early 1980s, President Chun demanded and obtained four billion dollars of extra funding from Japan (he initially demanded ten billion dollars!), for shouldering much of the defense of North East Asia from communism (ibid., 187). This is why the South Korean government's approach to economic development is best described as *enterprising*. It is not that South Koreans avoided rent seeking, but that the dominant group monopolized it, claiming the lion's share of the gains from economic growth.

Costs of Authoritarian Rule

The heady experience of nearly a decade of fast growth and some unbelievable feats such as POSCO and the shipbuilding industry, however, made President Park very confident about his ability to direct economic development in South Korea.[6] Consequently, from the mid-1970s, the government became more interventionist and chose to develop "heavy and chemical industries," identified as winners, to steer South Korea into a truly industrialized nation and to become self-sufficient in armaments in the face of an enhanced threat from the belligerent communist North Korea and the decreasing U.S. commitment to South Korean defense (during the Carter administration.) The government borrowed heavily from overseas to construct massive projects in heavy and chemical industries, causing inflation and the problem of servicing the foreign loans. And it turned out to be impossible to plug holes of this magnitude, even for a government as resourceful and enterprising as that of South Korea. There were many doubts about the government's ability to service its debts as the then fourth-largest indebted nation after Brazil, Mexico, and Argentina. Foreign investors even began to shun South Korea as a place of investment. Furthermore, by the time these projects were completed in the late 1970s, many of the factories built remained idle for lack of demand, causing high unemployment. The ambitious economic plans of President Park, who wanted to be remembered as "bearer of the historical mission of rebuilding Korea," thoroughly undermined his legitimacy, which he himself placed exclusively on the track records of economic success. In 1979, in the midst of severe recession, massive riots, and protests all over South Korea, President Park was assassinated by the chief of KCIA.

A discussion of the Korean experience would be grossly deficient if the costs of the authoritarian rule that forcefully mobilized people are left out. Too many sacrifices were forced upon the ordinary citizens of South Korea in the name of economic development. For example, when inflation was almost 20 percent a year throughout the 1960s and 1970s, government forced citizens to buy long-term bonds that quickly became worthless, and at the same time gave favored businessmen interest-free loans, or low-interest loans. When big business firms complained about the difficulty of remaining solvent during recession, for example in the wake of the oil crisis in the early 1970s, government declared a moratorium on private loans (unofficial loans since all banks were nationalized) to corporations for three years, de facto forcing ordinary citizens from factory workers and maids to small investors to give interest-free loans to big corporations for three years! On top of that, South Koreans had been forced to pay exorbitant prices for shoddy products in protected consumer goods markets dominated by government-sanctioned monopolies and oligopolies. At the same time, members of the ruling party enriched themselves by selling to themselves large tracts of land for next to nothing, in the name of privatization, knowing full well that the government-financed projects being planned would drive up the value of the real properties in question. People are not stupid when it comes to the issue of someone getting rich at their expense. The people who protested the unfairness of the way the economy was managed were brutally suppressed on the charges of sedition and even treason. Over two decades of this type of shady side of industrial policy made many men and women, some of whom do not have visible means of earning a living, let alone amassing a great fortune, very wealthy, while making many more others resentful.

The ruling elites took a personal interest in the growth of the South Korean economy because they claimed a lion's share of the gain, while forcing the general public to bear the costs of adjustments and their mistakes. This has left lingering doubts about the legitimacy of the status quo. Many South Koreans seem to have a sense of lawlessness and doubt the legitimacy of the fortunes of the rich. For example, in the early 1980s, a certain thief, Cho DaeHyung, became a sensation by robbing wealthy neighborhoods over an extended period. Whenever he narrowly escaped a police pursuit, citizens cheered and wished him well. When Cho was finally captured and many stolen goods recovered, no one came forward to reclaim his or her goods for months, to the amazement of the police. It was later revealed that the people robbed by Cho were too embarrassed to acknowledge that the stolen goods belonged to them. It was impossible to own such goods—millions of dollars worth of diamonds, for example—based on their known income sources. The lingering sense of the illegitimacy of fortunes is the gravest threat to the orderly development of the Korean economy in the future.

Conclusions

What are the lessons from the South Korean experience? One may still insist that industrial policy may work *if it is done skillfully under certain circumstances.* A usurper of political power in a poor country may provide a background where one may try to replicate the Korean experience based on the following considerations: (1) industrial policy may be best promoted as a means of promoting the common good, defined by an encompassing organization, immune from the pleas of special interests as well as genuine dissents; (2) industrial policy should consist of setting broad goals and providing an environment conducive to the achievement of the goals, instead of picking winners or directly regulating and managing projects; and (3) the government should maneuver diplomatically to gain access to markets created by others' follies, for example, war.

One should realize that the first of these involves *dictatorial rule.* The third factor makes one wonder whether there is likely to be another United States that single-handedly financed two major wars in Korea and Vietnam. For without the demands created by both wars, the Japanese economy would not be what it is today. And without the Vietnam War, the South Korean economy would not be what it is today. Even though there seem to be some generalizable features in the Korean experience that can be applied to other LDCs, I am less than confident that other LDCs would be able to replicate the Korean experience since there are so many features that are crucial yet unique to Korea.

Moreover, the apparent benefits of the industrial policies must be judged against harms they have caused. For the industrial policies that exacted enormous sacrifices from people also planted a cancer that may kill the social covenant. We ought to be very cautious in suggesting that industrial policy is desirable for economic development.

But others may observe that a free economy with less government intrusion in the form of industrial policy is preferable on the
following grounds. After all the export promotion schemes, all the
five-year plans, all the efforts to secure the outlets for industrial
products from hastily created industries, even by sending nearly
half a million troops thousands of miles away (many of whom
never returned), and all the sacrifices forced upon ordinary citizens, the South Korean economic development record is nothing
special *when compared to* those of Taiwan, Singapore, or Hong
Kong. These countries embarked on the course of rapid economic
growth earlier than South Korea and they kept themselves well in
front with their per capita GNP ranging from 50 percent to more
than 100 percent higher than that of Korea. Since the governments of these countries have been *in varying degrees* less intrusive
in the economic sphere, Hong Kong being the closest to free trade,
without doing any less spectacularly than South Korea, one wonders whether all the raving and ranting about economic development strategies sponsored by government had been necessary.

Moreover, as Korea has narrowed the gap between itself and
the more developed countries, and the gap between its potential
and actual attainment, it has become more and more difficult for
discretionary policies of the government to be of much use. If
anything, dirigiste governments tend to be hindrances, rather
than a help, to entrepreneurs wishing to exploit opportunities
they discover. The gradual realization of this has led a great many
South Koreans to seek to lessen the government domination in the
economy and to call for liberalization. In part responding to U.S.
demands to liberalize the economy, and in part adopting the advice of free-market-oriented economists-technocrats, South Korea
has since the early 1980s liberalized gradually and steadily.

Notes

1. Woo (1991, 108) reports even higher estimates at 10–15 percent, or
even up to 20 percent.
2. Barro (1991) confirms the finding in a study with a much larger
sample.
3. The prevalence of contraband and counterfeits of foreign products only

testifies that there were significant price distortions in many product categories. Until very recently, one could see at Kimpo International Airport (near Seoul) that the luggage of people entering South Korea—both that of Koreans and of foreign nationals—was inordinately large, full of valued foreign goods that could be sold beyond customs for fat profits. With increasing liberalization, travelers entering Korea now tend to travel much lighter.

4. It consisted of 300 million dollars in grants, 200 million in government loans, and 300 million in commercial credits.

5. For example, Vietnam absorbed almost 95 percent of total Korean steel exports, and over 50 percent in transportation equipment exports, etc.

6. About this time Nam, a U.S. trained economist and one-time prime minister, publicly confessed that he was awed by President Park's "innate economic knowledge."

References

Agarwala, Ramgopal. 1983. "Price Distortion and Growth in Developing Countries." *World Bank Staff Paper* No. 575.

Amsden, Alice H. 1989. *Asia's Next Giant: South Korea and Late Industrialization.* New York: Oxford University Press.

Bank of Korea. 1991. *Economic Statistics Yearbook.*

Barro, Robert J. 1991. "Economic Growth in a Cross Section of Countries." *Quarterly Journal of Economics* (May): 407–43.

Datta-Chaudhuri, Mrinal. 1990. "Market Failure and Government Failure." *Journal of Economic Perspective* (Summer): 25–39.

Haggard, Stephan, Byung-Kook Kim, and Shung-In Moon. 1991 "Transition to Export-led Growth in South Korea: 1954–1966." *Journal of Asian Studies* 50 (November): 850–73.

Hayek, F. A. 1945. "The Use of Knowledge in Society." *American Economic Review* (September): 519–30.

Hogendorn, Jan S. 1992. *Economic Development.* 2d ed. New York: Harper-Collins.

Kirzner, Israel M. 1979. *Perception, Opportunity, and Profit: Studies in the Theory of Entrepreneurship.* Chicago: University of Chicago Press.

Korea Development Institute. 1992. *Quarterly.* (Spring).

Krauss, Lawrence. 1991. "Japanese Capitalism: A Model for Others?" *International Economic Insight.* (Nov./Dec.): 6–10.

Krueger, Anne O. 1990. "Government Failures in Development." *Journal of Economic Perspective* (Summer): 9–23.

Lal, Deepak. 1988. "Ideology and Industrialization in India and East Asia." In *Achieving Industrialization in East Asia,* ed. Helen Hughes, 195–240.. New York: Cambridge University Press.

Lim, Youngil. 1981. *Government Policy and Private Enterprise: Korean Experience in Industrialization*. Korea Research Monograph No. 6. Institute of East Asian Studies, University of California.

Mason, Edward, et al. 1980. *The Economic and Social Modernization of the Republic of Korea*. Cambridge: Harvard University Press.

Nassar, Sylvia. 1991. "Industrial Policy: The Korean Way." *New York Times*, July 12.

Olson, Mancur. 1982. *The Rise and Decline of Nations*. New Haven: Yale University Press.

Parry, Thomas G. 1988. "The Role of Foreign Capital in East Asian Industrialization, Growth, and Development." In *Achieving Industrialization in East Asia*, ed. Helen Hughes, 95–128. New York: Cambridge University Press.

Song, Byung-Nak. 1990. *The Rise of the Korean Economy*. New York: Oxford University Press.

Srinivasan, T. N. 1990. "Development Thought, Strategy and Policy: Then and Now." Unpublished background paper for *World Development Report 1991* (October).

Wade, Robert. 1990. *Governing the Market: Economic Theory and the Role of Government in East Asian Industrialization*. Princeton: Princeton University Press.

Westphal, Larry E. 1990. "Industrial Policy in an Export-Propelled Economy: Lessons from South Korea's Experience." *Journal of Economic Perspective*. (Summer): 41–59.

Woo, Jung-en. 1991. *Race to the Swift: State and Finance in Korean Industrialization*. New York: Columbia University Press.

World Bank. Various years. *World Development Report*.

10

The Political Economy of Post–World War II Japanese Development: A Rent-Seeking Perspective

Shigeto Naka, Wayne T. Brough,
and Kiyokazu Tanaka

Introduction

After World War II Japan experienced very rapid economic growth while maintaining a stable democratic political regime.* When the American Occupation of Japan ended in 1952, Japan was economically insignificant. Today Japan is a not only democratic, but also a rich and technologically advanced nation, with its per capita income exceeding those of many Western countries.

Many attempts have been made to explain postwar Japan's economic and political miracles. Broadly speaking, two schools of thought have emerged (see Patrick and Meissner 1986). The first emphasizes the uniqueness of Japan's sociopolitical institutions in coordinating Japan's industrial policies. It maintains that Japanese bureaucrats provided the optimal mix of a market system and a command system. The second school of thought focuses purely on the technical relationships among economic variables to explain Japan's growth. Its proponents assert that the growth of postwar Japan was mainly a market phenomenon. Neither of these views is satisfactory. The sociopolitical approach falls short because of its methodological inconsistency, while the neoclassical-economic-growth approach is weak because of its institutional vacuum.

In this chapter, we use an alternative framework to analyze and explain the growth of Japan's political economy.[1] Our analysis draws upon the theory of public choice. This theory utilizes the rational-choice model to analyze the interactions between private and political markets. It holds that the state is a nexus of contracts in which self-seeking individuals interact with one another for personal gain, an assumption consistent with the behavior of market participants. Further, because such interactions take place from within a constitutional framework, an analysis of institutional structures is necessary.

In the case of modern Japan, the rules of the game were significantly altered by the Occupation forces (1945–52) as a result of World War II. The change destroyed the nexus of contracts that had comprised the Japanese state and created institutional instability; Japanese political operatives were forced to adjust their behavior. However, once these adjustments were made, a stable nexus of contracts emerged, as observed by the stability of the political regime in the subsequent postwar years. It can be said that the sociopolitical stability in postwar Japan was structurally induced by the Occupation forces.

How did Japan move from disequilibrium to a stable, new equilibrium? In this process, what role did the Occupation forces play? What did Japanese political operatives do to gain or protect their interests? In analyzing these questions, we introduce the main thesis of this chapter: that is, under the structure of the new equilibrium, rent seeking became relatively more efficient than in other industrial nations. By efficient rent seeking we mean that the social costs of wealth redistribution are relatively lower than in other countries. This does not mean, however, that efficient rent seeking is a desirable goal from a societal point of view. By definition, any rent seeking entails a decrease in social wealth. In addition to redefining the rent-seeking game, the Occupation forces strengthened market institutions. These points should be considered significant variables contributing to the growth of the Japanese economy.

An Overview of the Japanese Political Economy

Japan's postwar history began in August 1945 when Japan surrendered to the Allied Powers. Three periods are identified in postwar Japanese economic history: the recovery period (from 1945 to the early 1950s), the high-growth era (from the early 1950s to the early 1970s), and the era of economic slowdown (from the early 1970s to the present).

The recovery period roughly coincided with the occupation period (1945–1952), in which the United States took the initiative in occupying Japan. General MacArthur became the Supreme Commander of the Allied Powers (SCAP) and established the General Headquarters (GHQ) to demilitarize and democratize Japan. While establishing the new democratic constitution of Japan, MacArthur implemented three important social reforms: (1) labor reform, (2) land reform, and (3) economic deconcentration or zaibatsu dissolution. These reforms significantly affected the subsequent development of postwar Japan.

Japan regained her sovereignty in April 1952, which marks the beginning of the high-growth period. The high-growth period was characterized as an era of modernization and rapid technological progress. As shown in table 1, Japan's real GNP grew at an average annual rate of about 10 percent between 1951 and 1973, representing a seven-and-a-half-fold increase in production. In 1952, the per capita GNP of Japan was only $188, ranking the country lower than both Brazil and Malaysia (Patrick and Rosovsky 1976, 11). By 1973, Japan's per capita GNP grew to about $3,700, a figure which was greater than per capita GNP in Italy and Great Britain, and about three-fifths of that in the United States. In the mid-1960s Japan's GNP exceeded that of West Germany, becoming the third largest economy in the world.

The high-growth period brought not only an improvement of living standards, but also a shift in the international account balance. Exports began to grow in the 1960s and full employment was attained with a mild inflation. These achievements were said to be made possible by a high investment rate that, in turn, was supported by a high personal savings rate. Hayashi (1986) reports that personal saving rates in Japan have been roughly 10 percent-

Post–World War II Japanese Development 259

Table 1. Gross National Product of Japan, 1951–1975
(1970 = 100)

Year	Real GNP (hundred million yen)	% Increase	Real GNP Per Capita (yen)
1951	126,130	—	52,479
1952	140,829	11.7	60,822
1953	151,636	7.7	69,001
1954	155,841	2.8	74,734
1955	172,680	10.8	81,797
1956	183,299	6.1	90,689
1957	197,594	7.8	102,918
1958	209,366	6.0	104,827
1959	232,728	11.2	119,038
1960	261,832	12.5	142,084
1961	297,115	13.5	167,174
1962	316,151	6.4	186,363
1963	355,746	12.5	214,618
1964	393,495	10.6	240,820
1965	415,913	5.7	265,951
1966	462,177	11.1	308,038
1967	522,568	13.1	361,654
1968	589,042	12.7	423,126
1969	653,668	11.0	486,190
1970	721,444	10.4	570,459
1971	774,003	7.3	627,456
1972	849,780	9.8	710,841
1973	904,235	6.4	845,503
1974	901,788	−0.3	1,033,004
1975	932,596	3.4	1,139,271

Source: Ministry of Finance, Showa Zaiseishi (Tokyo: Toyo Keizai Shinpo-sha, 1978), 29.

age points higher than those of the United States, even after adjusting for the accounting differences in these nations.

Three main factors are considered to have ended the postwar Japanese miracle when Japan entered the 1970s: (1) the oil crisis, (2) the decrease in investment demand, and (3) the slowdown in technological progress (see Kosai [1981] 1986; Lincoln 1988; Ito 1991). The oil crisis raised the cost of production and reduced expected earnings in the business sector, resulting in a decline in investment demand. This decline, in turn, placed downward pressure on the equilibrium level of income. Together, these factors decreased the demand for advanced technologies and slowed the economic growth of Japan. Since the 1970s Japan has entered an era of "economic maturity" (Lincoln 1988).

Alternative Views

Japan's remarkable economic development during the high-growth era has sparked many theories of its rapid growth. A glance at the literature on the Japanese economy reveals the following as commonly accepted explanations:

1. Japan has been a highly market-oriented economy, using market mechanisms rather than the command system to allocate resources;[2]
2. Japan has adopted industrial enterprise groups—the so-called "keiretsu" structure—for its industrial organization;[3]
3. Japanese firms tend to utilize indirect financing over direct financing and the capital market was heavily regulated and underdeveloped until recently;[4]
4. The Japanese labor market tends to be less mobile and internalized within firms, utilizing enterprise unions and employing long-term job contracts; this led to what is now called Japanese-style management;[5] and
5. The Japanese political system, dominated by the conservative Liberal Democratic Party (LDP), seems very stable despite the prevalence of factionalism, and the government seems to have maintained cooperative rather than adversarial relationships with business.[6]

Each aspect of the above characterizations of Japanese political economy has been examined extensively.[7] For example, focusing upon the harmonious labor-management and cooperative business-government relationships in Japan, one popular school of thought asserts that these characteristics arise from the unique culture of Japan. It emphasizes the group-oriented behavior among the Japanese, and attributes Japan's economic success to the willingness of the Japanese people to endure personal sacrifice to maintain the harmony of the group.[8]

As noted earlier, two main schools of thoughts have emerged (Patrick 1986). One school of thought is characterized by the neo-classical economic paradigm and focuses upon the analysis of Japan's market system. Observing Japan's large private-market economy, this school analyzes the sources of Japan's success purely from the perspective of an economic growth model. Theorists conclude that Japan's economic growth is explained by the usual macroeconomic variables. As a result, in explaining the development of the Japanese economy, they discount the effectiveness of direct government assistance and control of Japanese industries as well as many cultural elements in Japan. Instead, they focus on the Japanese government's ability to maintain a stable macroeconomic environment.

The alternative school of thought, more popular among political scientists, emphasizes the role of Japan's sociopolitical institutions.[9] Focusing upon management by Japanese economic bureaucrats, this school attributes the economic success of Japan to direct government planning and control (e.g., Johnson 1982). Its proponents maintain that Japan's economic success was largely engineered by well-disciplined and public-minded economic bureaucrats. Thus, this school not only maintains a public-interest view of the state, but assumes that the bureaucratic system has information-processing capacity superior to that of the market system.

The debate between the two schools focuses on which resource allocation method—the market system or the command system—is more effective for promoting economic growth. To date, the issue has not been resolved. We contend that the debate must be elevated to a higher level that includes a broader examination of the institutional framework. As long as researchers rely upon different behavioral systems and split the analysis of economic and political market transactions, there is no common ground to compare and evaluate their results. A meaningful comparative study must begin with the premise that the political economy represents a nexus of contracts of self-seeking individuals. The theory of public choice offers such a paradigm.

The Framework: The Theory of Public Choice

Public choice employs a rational-choice model to analyze the interactions of private and political markets. The state is viewed as a nexus of contracts in which self-seeking individuals engage in exchanges with one another for personal gains; this is very similar to market behavior, but the constraints are different. A stable regime implies the existence of stable contractual relationships. This, in turn, implies the existence of effective institutional enforcement mechanisms. In this exchange paradigm of the state,[10] the primary function of the state is to redistribute wealth among different sets of individuals or groups.

We assume that rational individuals engage in exchanges with one another by choosing the best available institutional alternative to write and enforce contracts. In this, we deemphasize the distinction not only between the market and hierarchies but also between market institutions and political institutions because all these institutions represent alternative mechanisms for writing and enforcing contracts.[11] This methodology enables us to analyze consistently both economic and political market transactions.

One important implication here is that any significant regime change, such as a foreign invasion or revolution, will lead to disequilibrium by altering the relative price structure of institutional choice. When such a disequilibrium occurs, rational individuals must adjust their behavior to reach a new equilibrium by adopting and inventing new institutions.

In addition, we assume that in choosing between different institutional arrangements, rational individuals utilize institutional comparative advantages derived from within the fundamental rules of the game (i.e., constitutional structure). The constitutional framework, bargaining strength, and nature of contracts are considered major determinants for a choice of institutional alternatives.

Finally, the choice among institutional arrangements is considered to have welfare implications because it affects the resource allocation in the political economy. In this we emphasize the deadweight losses of wealth transfers. Rent-seeking costs—the costs imposed upon society through political exchanges—are a part of these losses. Following the theory of pressure groups developed by Becker (1983), each interest group is assumed to have the incentive to maximize its private gains by minimizing its own deadweight losses from wealth transfers. This incentive is one of the driving forces for rational actors choosing between different institutions.

Based upon the above framework, we propose the following hypotheses concerning the development of the political economy of postwar Japan:

1. The American Occupation of Japan initially induced disequilibrium in the nexus of contracts in the Japanese state by significantly altering the fundamental rules of the game;
2. The stability of the postwar regime in Japan was induced by the shift in Occupation policy which established new institutional choices within a new constitutional order for a market economy over a command economy; and
3. The incentives of Japanese interest groups to maximize their own private gains by minimizing their own deadweight losses from wealth transfers promoted an institutional structure that reduced the overall deadweight losses at social level; thus, contributing to its economic growth.

Each of these hypotheses is examined in sections below.

The U.S. Occupation and the Structural Disequilibrium

For transactional reasons (see Olson 1965), three major interest groups dominate a political economy. These are bureaucrats, politicians, and special-interest groups. The general public supplies wealth to these groups via coercion (taxation) and functions merely as a constraint upon politicians (Mackay and Weaver 1981).

In prewar and wartime Japan, the Japanese bureaucracy appeared to have exercised vast power in Japan's resource allocation. However, there is substantial evidence to suggest that the bureaucracy was significantly constrained by politicians and economic special-interest groups.[12] For instance, Curtis (1988, 4–5) examined the Japanese party system during the war and concluded: "wartime totalitarianism in Japan was never quite total, and some of the old party leaders continued to be politically active" Similarly, Friedman (1988, 38) examined the prewar development of Japan's machine tool industry and concluded: "The prewar government and the zaibatsu were locked in a power struggle that prevented either side from implementing its favored industrial policy."

These conclusions suggest that the political equilibrium in prewar Japan was maintained by the balance of power among the three dominant interest groups—bureaucrats (including the military), dominant economic special-interest groups, and conservative politicians at local and national levels. Each of these groups engaged in exchange with one another by constraining one another's behavior. When the Occupation began, the balance was significantly altered, resulting in disequilibrium.

The initial disequilibrium was created by SCAP's policies to promote the civil liberties of the Japanese people and decentralization of the government. These policies changed the relative price structure of institutional choice for Japanese political operatives by lowering the cost of political participation and by increasing social mobility. Initially, these policies weakened Japanese capitalists, conservative politicians, and militarists, while strengthening civil bureaucrats, socialists, and unions. In particular, economic bureaucrats gained vast power over other groups and began to dominate the Japanese political economy.[13]

Three policies by SCAP are responsible for the dominance of the command system. They are labor reform, antitrust reform, and land reform. Labor reform strengthened the bargaining powers of labor unions, the Japan Socialist Party (JSP), and the Japan Communist Party (JCP). By their nature, these groups preferred collective ownership to private ownership, thus contributing to a stronger state. Table 2 shows a dramatic increase in the percentage of unionized workers during the Occupation.

Zaibatsu dissolution weakened the bargaining powers of traditional capitalists by separating ownership from control (see Hadley 1970). Prewar Japanese markets were dominated by wealthy capitalists who controlled family-owned holding companies known as zaibatsu. Zaibatsu dissolution began in October 1945,

Table 2. Growth of Unions for Selected Years, 1945–1955

Year	Number of Unions	Number of Union Members	Number of Labor Disputes	Number of Participants
1945.6	0	0	0	—
1945.12	707	378,481	—	—
1946.6	11,579	3,748,952	0	—
1946.12	17,265	4,849,329	920	2,772,582
1947.6	23,323	5,692,179	—	—
1947.12	28,014	6,268,432	1,035	4,415,390
1948	33,926	6,677,427	1,517	6,714,843
1949	34,688	6,655,483	1,414	3,307,407
1950	29,144	5,773,908	1,487	2,348,397
1951	27,644	5,686,774	1,186	2,818,688
1952	27,851	5,719,560	1,233	3,383,435
1953	30,129	5,842,678	1,277	3,398,667
1954	31,456	5,986,168	1,247	2,635,426
1955	32,012	6,185,343	1,345	3,748,019

Source: Junnosuke Masumi ([1983] 1985, 19, Appendix).

which marked the beginning of Japan's antitrust policy. The Holding Company Dissolution Commission was formed in 1946 to dispose of the stocks of zaibatsu-owned companies.[14] In 1947, the Law for the Elimination of Excessive Concentration of Economic Powers and the Anti-Monopoly Law were passed to eliminate excessive concentration. Antitrust reform weakened the powers of traditional capitalists who favored private ownership.

Land reform, together with the dissolution of the Agricultural Association (Nokai) that controlled the allocation of foodstuffs and credit in the countryside, weakened the bargaining powers of traditional rural elites who supported conservative politicians.[15] With the economic and political purge that removed many capitalists and conservative politicians from public office,[16] land reform further weakened the power of traditional conservatives.

By contrast, the bargaining power of economic bureaucrats was greatly strengthened because SCAP kept the civil-bureaucratic system relatively intact to implement its policies. The government adopted a central planning system to control the Japanese economy and established the Economic Stabilization Board and fifteen public corporations (Kodan) to control commerce. Attempts were made to nationalize the coal industry. During this period, tax rates reached a maximum of 85 percent on individual incomes and 52.5 percent on corporate profits (Packman and Kaizuka 1976, 320). Wildes (1954, 92) reported that Japan's bureaucracy expanded its size by 84 percent, as measured by the number of government employees.

The Occupation altered the structures of virtually all political institutions, including the Parliament (Diet), court system, police system, education system, electoral system, and local governments. It generated uncertainty and changed institutional constraints under which each special-interest group operated. Overall, it strengthened the power of anticonservative groups and the economic bureaucracy by removing previous institutional constraints. As a result, the initial institutional arrangements of postwar Japan became biased in favor of state allocation of resources rather than market allocation. During the immediate postwar period, those who could gain from a command system rather than a market system dominated the Japanese political economy.

The Path toward the New Equilibrium

By 1948, it had become apparent that the Cold War would intensify. Confronting the possibility that Japan would fall into Communists' hands, the U.S. decided to rebuild Japan as a bulwark nation and changed its Occupation policy (Masumi 1985; Schaller 1985). This shift is known as the "reverse course," which once again altered the balance of power among Japanese political operatives by repealing many of the recent liberalization programs (see Masumi 1983). Unionization was discouraged rather than encouraged. The Red Purge expelled many radicals while reinstating previously purged conservatives. The attack on big businesses was weakened and antitrust enforcement was relaxed. Joseph Dodge— a Detroit financier—was dispatched to Japan to revive the Japanese economy. With the implementation of the so-called Dodge policy in 1949, the exchange rate was fixed to foster international trade; bureaucrats' fiscal and monetary powers were restrained, central planning was terminated; all Kodans were abolished (see Shiraishi 1983; Kosai [1981] 1986); and a free economy was revived (Kosai 1986).

As a result, the political economy of Japan was altered in favor of those who could gain from a market system rather than a command system. This shift once again affected the relative price structure of institutional choice and produced mutually beneficial exchange opportunities for those reinstated economic and conservative political actors. The reverse course laid the foundation for Japan's industrial organization during the high-growth era.[17] Japan's reliance on the market system was strengthened by the reverse course. In this respect, the role of the U.S. Occupation of Japan was forcibly to change the relative price structure of institutional choices for Japanese political operatives by acting as a decisive agenda-setter and enforcer (see Naka 1990; Brough and Naka 1990).

As we shall see, the structure of Japan's political economy during the high-growth era reflected the institutional choices of these reinstated actors to extract maximum gains from new exchange relationships by minimizing their own deadweight losses.

The Nature of the New Equilibrium

Because the exchange relationships between major economic and political actors that emerged through the Occupation's reverse course were relatively stable, many political scientists and foreign observers used a corporatist model (triad-model, power-elite-model, Japan Incorporated model, or bureaucracy-led-model) to describe the economic growth of Japan.[18] This may be why so many researchers assert that Japan had a "dual" industrial structure in which efficient, large-scale businesses dominated inefficient, small businesses (see Miwa 1990).

In fact, in 1963, "the 100 largest nonfinancial corporations controlled 53.2 percent of all paid-in corporate capital" (Caves and Uekusa 1976, 470). Moreover, many large Japanese firms belonged to enterprise groups that developed around banks. This structure underlies Japan's capital and product markets, as well as its distribution channels, and is commonly referred to as "keiretsu."[19]

Each keiretsu group has a semihierarchical structure with a main bank at the core that is encircled by large manufacturing or trading firms; many small-to-medium-sized subcontracting firms comprise the outer level.

In addition, Japanese politics has been almost continually dominated by the conservative Liberal Democratic Party (LDP). A powerful, autonomous bureaucracy also existed, with economic bureaus such as the Ministry of International Trade and Industry (MITI) seeming to have exercised vast control over industrial policy in Japan. All these observations suggest that the Japanese political economy was dominated by a triad of power-elites. However, subsequent studies have raised questions as to the accuracy of such depictions.

Table 3 shows comparative statistics of concentration ratios in Japanese and U.S. industries. The weighted average concentration ratio for U.S. manufacturing firms in 1963 was 40.9 percent, compared to 35.4 percent for Japan (Caves and Uekusa 1976, 471–72). Similar studies show that Japan's industrial structure was technologically not unique when compared with other Western industrial nations.[20] Further, various statistical studies have shown that keiretsu affiliation did not result in significantly higher profit rates on equity or on assets; in fact, it even lowered them (Caves and Uekusa 1976; Nakatani [1984] 1990; Miwa 1990). If Japanese industrial organization represented a biased structure in favor of large corporations in collaboration with ruling LDP politicians and elite economic bureaucrats, then the profits of those keiretsu firms should be higher on average than those of nonmember firms (Caves and Uekusa 1976; Miwa 1990; Ito 1991). A monopoly or monopsony explanation, or a power-elite hypothesis, cannot adequately describe postwar Japan's political economy.

We propose the following alternative hypothesis: The Occupation's reverse course altered the structure of rent seeking in Japan.[21] The reverse course generated: (1) relatively longer-term political contracts, (2) a relatively more effective system of political contracts that includes a set of prime contractors and subcontractors, and (3) a relatively more encompassing political contracting system, compared to other industrial nations. Because of

Table 3. Number of Industries and Values of Shipments, by Concentration Ratio for the Four Largest Firms, United States and Japan, 1963

	By Number of Industries			
	United States		Japan	
Concentration Ratio	Number	Cumulative Percent	Number	Cumulative Percent
80–100	27	6.5	46	9.0
70–79	18	10.8	21	13.1
60–69	29	17.8	29	18.8
50–59	43	28.1	61	30.7
40–49	49	39.8	56	41.6
30–39	80	59.0	63	53.9
20–29	81	78.4	79	69.3
0–19	90	100.0	157	100.0
Total	417	—	512	—

	By Value of Shipment			
	United States		Japan	
Concentration Ratio	Billions of Dollars	Cumulative Percent	Billions of Dollars	Cumulative Percent
80–100	50.9	12.2	3.7	5.6
70–79	14.3	15.6	3.5	10.8
60–69	23.8	21.3	1.8	13.4
50–59	49.3	33.2	10.6	28.9
40–49	31.9	40.9	8.5	41.3
30–39	72.8	58.4	7.6	52.5
20–29	90.5	80.2	9.7	66.7
0–19	82.4	100.0	22.7	100.0
Total	415.7	—	68.2	—

Source: Caves and Uekusa (1976, 471).

these characteristics, Japan's rent-seeking structure during its high-growth period was not only relatively more efficient, but wealth-enhancing, compared to other rent-seeking industrial nations. We argue that this structure emerged because those reinstated economic and political actors sought to maximize their own rents by minimizing the deadweight losses of wealth transfers. To derive this conclusion, we examine the incentives of three major groups of Japanese political operatives when the reverse course began.

The following incentives for bureaucrats, politicians, and interest groups are considered to have emerged when the reverse course began.[22] First, the incentive of bureaucrats was to maintain or even to increase control of resource allocation. This behavior may best be described as "takings" in the form of taxes or the attenuation of private property rights in favor of accruing rents for bureaucrats.[23] However, because the new constitution of 1947 made Japan's parliament (Diet) the highest law-making organ in the state, majority coalitions of politicians could effectively constrain bureaucratic takings.[24] Moreover, because the reverse course promoted a free economy rather than a controlled economy, bureaucrats had to alter the form of their intervention.

Second, because the new constitution increased social mobility by decentralizing the government and by assuring civil liberties, politicians became more susceptible to the preferences of voters, including special-interest groups. Politicians became residual claimants of rent seeking. Politicians had the incentive to increase their residual income through political brokerage activities; that is, arbitrating property rights arrangements between the bureaucrats and special-interest groups (see McCormick and Tollison 1981). However, because income levels in Japan were low, only economic special-interest groups had the capital necessary to engage in rent-seeking behavior and generate residual income for conservative politicians. Assuming that these groups had only a fixed amount of rent-seeking capital,[25] takings by bureaucrats would reduce the politicians' residual income by reducing the capital available to economic interest groups. Thus, politicians had the incentive to control bureaucrats to reduce their takings from economic special-interest groups. Ceteris paribus, both politicians and interest groups could gain more by creating mutually binding arrangements to constrain bureaucrats' taking activities.[26]

Each of these three groups of actors had incentives to expand its power by utilizing its own institutional comparative advantage.

However, agency problems emerged, which made contract enforcement among groups more difficult. Initially, the Occupation created significant levels of uncertainty in Japan's political market. Agency problems were substantial in any contractual relationship. The bureaucrats, politicians, and interest groups reneged on contracts with one another; opportunism manifested itself even within each group. Even though the reverse course decreased the power of economic bureaucrats by dismantling the controlled economy, the foremost agency problem was still caused by bureaucrats. Because initial Occupation policies demolished many organizations, effective institutional mechanisms to enforce contracts with government bureaucrats did not exist. The committee system in legislature was ineffective,[27] and party organization was also in a state of flux (see Masumi [1983] 1985; Curtis 1988). Virtually all legislation was initiated and drafted by bureaucrats (see Johnson 1982). To put it simply, the bureaucrats dominated all other groups.[28]

With the Occupation's reverse course, industrialists regained lost ground. However, as Dodge's stabilization policies progressed, not only did competition in the marketplace intensify, but capital scarcity was created by decreasing industrial subsidies.[29] Industrialists demanded political protection through legislation in the political market (see Samuels 1987, 102–104). To assure a favorable regulatory environment, industrialists had to pay brokerage fees (campaign contributions) to conservative politicians and give up some industrial controls to bureaucrats (effective taxes/fees) in return for regulations that provided preferential financing, tax breaks, and protection from foreign competition. To insure this exchange, mechanisms were needed, however, to ensure that bureaucrats would not renege on contracts created by politicians and industry.

At the same time, takings by bureaucrats from industrialists reduced the levels of expenditures available for campaign contributions to politicians. Conservative politicians had an incentive, therefore, to decrease takings to protect their campaign contributions from industrialists. Politicians strengthened their organizations to offer high-quality and reliable services to industrialists.

Mutual incentives existed between conservative politicians and industrialists to create binding institutional arrangements to facilitate political exchange.

The binding institutional arrangements were maintained through a continual legislative majority in the Diet. The imminent threat from the left-wing urged both conservative politicians and industrialists to invest their resources in the unification of two conservative parties (see Masumi 1983). A legislative majority would also enable politicians to monitor bureaucrats more effectively by increasing their veto power and by controlling the prime minister's office. As a result, the LDP was formed in 1955. While both parties continued to invest their resources to sustain the legislative majority, these investments became nonsalvageable assets for both politicians and industrialists (see Klein and Leffler 1981; Crain, Shughart, and Tollison 1988, for the theory). To maintain the net discounted future values of these intangible and nontransferable assets, mutual incentives to create "longer-term" political contracts were generated.

Industrialists and conservative politicians also moved to constrain the power of bureaucrats. Two institutions emerged to perform this function. As we shall see, these two institutions characterize the political economy of postwar Japan.

First, industrialists and politicians moved to reduce the frequency of negotiations with bureaucrats. Frequent negotiations penalized industrialists by increasing transactions costs; moreover, they reduced the supply of campaign contributions to politicians. The greater the risk of moral hazard in the political market, the larger the penalty the industrialists had to pay. Because enforcement mechanisms were still underdeveloped, the incentive to reduce the frequency of negotiations was generated, further strengthening the incentive to maintain longer-term political contracts (see Naka, Brough, and Tanaka 1992).

Second, to reduce takings by the state, a dual-system of political contracting represented by prime and subcontractors was developed (see Naka, Brough, and Tanaka 1992). Industrialists who sought private gains from the Occupation's reverse course faced two choices for writing and enforcing their contracts with others They could either write and enforce contracts privately or they could rely on political mechanisms. To maximize gains from their contractual engagements, rational individuals would choose the method which minimized transaction costs. Considering the existence of a dominant state that excised takings, and weighing the risk of moral hazard in the political market due to underdeveloped political enforcement mechanisms, private contracting was the least-cost alternative.

At the same time, because Dodge's stabilization policy decreased industrial subsidies, a new method to allocate financial resources—the so-called the main bank system—was developing in the financial market (Shiraishi 1983). This development had various spillover effects.[30] To reduce moral hazard among lendees, the main bank system promoted interlocking shareholdings (see table 4) and interlocking directorates between lenders and lendees. As described by many, this led to the emergence of the keiretsu system. Moreover, to stave off radical labor influences, industrial managers began to develop enterprise-based unions. The enterprise-based union is a company-specific organization containing not only blue-collar, but also white-collar employees (Aoki 1988).[31] This institutional arrangement reduced private contracting costs with respect to labor-management relations.

In short, an efficient system of private enforcement mechanisms was developing in Japanese industrial markets, while political institutions were evolving. The existence of private enforcement mechanisms generated the incentive for industrialists to first contract privately among themselves, then, bring their predetermined matters to the legislative market. In this way, industrialists could not only economize on transaction costs, but could reduce their payments to bureaucrats. This institutional choice was made possible because cross-shareholdings and cross-board-memberships of the keiretsu, as well as the use of enterprise-based unions among large keiretsu firms, lowered contracting costs in the market relative to those in alternative institutions. This dual-system of political contracting was also beneficial to ruling politicians because it increased their residual income by reducing fees imposed by bureaucrats upon their clients.

This structure permeated Japan's keiretsu system and the en-

Table 4. Corporate Stock Ownership by Classification in Japan, 1949–1980

Year	Govern- ment	Finance firms	Trust firms	Security firms	Other firms	Individ- uals	Foreign
1949	2.8	9.9	—	12.6	5.6	69.1	—
1950	3.1	12.6	—	11.9	11.0	61.3	—
1951	1.8	13.0	5.2	9.2	13.8	57.0	—
1952	1.0	15.8	6.0	8.4	11.8	55.8	1.2
1953	0.7	16.3	6.7	7.3	13.5	53.9	1.7
1954	0.5	16.7	7.0	7.1	13.0	54.0	1.7
1955	0.4	19.5	4.1	7.9	13.2	53.1	1.8
1956	0.3	21.7	3.9	7.1	15.7	49.9	1.5
1957	0.2	21.4	4.7	5.7	16.3	50.1	1.5
1958	0.3	22.4	6.6	4.4	15.8	49.1	1.5
1959	0.2	21.7	7.6	3.7	17.5	47.8	1.5
1960	0.2	23.1	7.5	3.7	17.8	46.3	1.4
1961	0.2	21.4	8.6	2.8	18.7	46.7	1.7
1962	0.2	21.5	9.2	2.5	17.7	47.1	1.8
1963	0.2	21.4	9.5	2.2	17.9	46.7	2.1
1964	0.2	21.6	7.9	4.4	18.4	45.6	1.9
1965	0.2	23.4	5.6	5.8	18.4	44.8	1.8
1966	0.2	26.1	3.7	5.4	18.6	44.1	1.9
1967	0.3	28.2	2.4	4.4	20.5	42.3	1.9
1968	0.3	30.3	1.7	2.1	21.4	41.9	2.3
1969	0.3	30.7	1.2	1.4	22.0	41.1	3.3
1970	0.3	30.9	1.4	1.2	23.1	39.9	3.2
1971	0.2	32.6	1.3	1.5	23.6	37.2	3.6
1972	0.2	33.8	1.3	1.8	26.6	32.7	3.5
1973	0.2	33.9	1.2	1.5	27.5	32.7	2.9
1974	0.2	33.9	1.6	1.3	27.1	33.4	2.5
1975	0.2	34.5	1.6	1.4	26.3	33.5	2.6
1976	0.2	35.1	1.4	1.4	26.5	32.9	2.6
1977	0.2	35.9	2.0	1.5	26.2	32.0	2.3
1978	0.2	36.6	2.2	1.8	26.3	30.8	2.1
1979	0.2	36.9	1.9	2.0	26.1	30.4	2.5
1980	0.2	37.3	1.5	1.7	26.0	29.2	4.0

Source: Okumura (1990, 55).

terprise-based union of every large firm. As such, the system became necessarily encompassing.[32] Contractual settlement made at the subcontracting level covered many small -and medium-sized firms. To avoid exploitation by large firms, further "backward" or "forward" integration was common within interlocking keiretsu groups. When agreements were brought to the political stage by prime contractors, they reflected the majority interests of all firms involved.[33] Accordingly, distributional gains were widely shared by a large number of members, while costs were dispersed to outside groups (mostly consumers and foreign producers). This is one reason why it was difficult to explain Japan's industrial dual-structure based upon a simple monopoly or monopsony model.

The following welfare implications emerge from this analysis (these implications should be interpreted in a relative sense rather than in an absolute sense): First, industrial policies emerging through this system of rent seeking are likely to be efficiency-enhancing for the encompassing keiretsu system. Costs are likely to be externalized outside the groups. In this respect, one major function of the prime contractors is to maintain intra group coordination while internalizing intergroup externalities. The continual existence of very encompassing and very broad economic associations such as Keidanren (the Federation of Economic Organizations) suggests the existence of such functions.

Second, following the first implication, the total amount of rent-seeking expenditures spent in this system is smaller due to less rent-avoidance activities, in terms of their frequency and number. Because many contracting decisions are made at subcontracting level, decision-making costs at this level became higher (e.g., longer working hours). However, once decisions are made, less rent-seeking and rent-avoidance activities would occur at the national level. On balance, the total amount of rent-seeking expenditures may be lower than in other industrial countries.

Third, the deadweight losses of rent-seeking expenditures may be smaller due to the longer durability of political contracts and the extensive use of private contracting rather than political contracting. As such, efficiency losses are likely to be reduced. Further, the incentive to use private contracting at the subcontracting level induces the Japanese economy to remain largely a market economy in which the price system and name-brand capital function as enforcement mechanisms.

Fourth, a longer market-time horizon is likely to result from a longer political-time horizon due to the relative stability and durability of political contracts.[34] The Japanese economy may be more conducive to longer-term business investment decisions partly because the political time horizon may be longer and more stable, not because bureaucrats and industrialists are far-sighted.

Finally, there are opportunity costs associated with this institutional framework. Resources have been allocated to private contracting rather than political contracting. As a result, the development of political contracting has been deterred.[35] This may be the reason why so many political scientists comment that postwar Japan's democracy is "immature" compared to that of the United States. From an efficiency point of view, however, this institutional choice would reduce rent-seeking and rent-avoidance costs at the social level.

These implications together suggest that the structure of rent seeking in postwar Japan during the high-growth era was relatively efficient and relatively more wealth-enhancing, compared to other industrial nations. Further, this structure reduced deadweight losses in the political economy by largely utilizing market institutions for the allocation of resources. We argue that this structure is an important explanatory factor for Japan's rapid economic growth.

Conclusion

In this chapter, we used the theory of public choice to analyze the post–World War II political economy of Japan. We focus on how Japan's nexus of contracts was altered by the American Occupation, and how Japanese political operatives reacted to such alterations. We argue that Japan achieved a new political equilibrium with the help of the Occupation forces. Finally, we examined the nature of the new equilibrium based upon Becker's (1983) theory.

The main conclusion of this chapter is that Japan placed more emphasis on markets rather than command elements to allocate resources, not because Japanese bureaucrats ingeniously calculated the optimal balance between the market and the government, but because, quite simply, the costs of negotiating and enforcing contracts in private markets were lower than those in the political markets, due to the peculiar development of Japan's industrial organization after the American Occupation of Japan. We suggest that these contractual arrangements generated lower deadweight losses, contributing the economic growth of postwar Japan.

Finally, because the exchange relationships between reinstated economic and political actors are the foundation of Japan's postwar industrial organization, any changes in these relations will induce changes in the foundation of Japan's industrial structure. Such changes have been occurring since the beginning of the 1970s when Japan entered the era of economic slowdown. Various factors have caused such changes, including: (1) the emergence of a variety of special-interest groups which could supply residual incomes to politicians (see Sato and Matsuzaki 1986; Inoguchi and Iwai 1987); (2) the growth of per capita income and the resulting change in the tastes of voters, including special-interest groups (see Yakushiji 1987); (3) shifts in industrial comparative advantages caused by changes in technologies; (4) further specialization and division of labor in the political market (see Sato and Matsuzaki 1986; Inoguchi and Iwai 1987); and (5) shifts in the international environment, with increasing foreign pressure to open the Japanese economy.

Our analysis suggests that these changes will cause efficiency losses in allocating resources through the political economy of Japan, gradually producing larger deadweight losses in Japan. As the structures of keiretsu and enterprise-based unions change, the relative price structure of institutional choice will also change. Political contracting rather than private contracting may become the dominant strategy of interest groups. Future research must outline these changes, explain how they occur, and derive the welfare implications from such changes.

Notes

* We would like to thank Peter Boettke, Tyler Cowen, Bill Shughart, and Bob Tollison for encouragement and helpful comments. Henry Butler also provided useful comments on an earlier draft.
1. Previously, we have attempted to explain postwar Japan's political economy based upon the theory of public choice. See Naka (1990); Brough and Naka (1990, 1991); Naka and Brough (1991); and Naka, Brough, and Tanaka (1992).
2. See, for instance, Patrick and Rosovsky (1976); Trezize and Suzuki (1976); Kosai ([1981] 1986); Takahashi (1986); and Noguchi (1986). McCraw (1986, 19) writes; "Most outside observers, looking back on the miracle, tend to overemphasize the role played by the government, and commensurately to understate the degree to which Japan was, and remains to this day, a company-oriented society characterized by intense inter-corporate rivalry."
3. See Noguchi (1986); Okumura (1983); Aoki (1988); Kawasaki and McMillan (1987); Hodder (1988); Asanuma (1989); Nakatani ([1984] 1990) and Miwa (1990).
4. For Japanese financial markets, see, for instance, Wallich and Wallich (1976); Suzuki (1986); Hamada and Horiuchi (1987); and Cargill and Royama (1988).
5. See Koike (1977); Aoki (1988); Ito (1991); and Ozaki (1991) for a general discussion.
6. Almost all students of the political economy of modern Japan have mentioned this. See, for instance, Baerwald (1986); Johnson (1982); McCraw (1986); Ouchi (1984); and Curtis (1985).
7. See Vogel ([1975] 1985); Patrick and Rosovsky (1976); Kodansha International ([1979] 1987); Thurow ([1985] 1986); Patrick and Meissner (1986); McCraw (1986); Yamamura and Yasuba (1987); Shoven (1988); and Komiya, Masahiro, and Kotaro (1988) for editorial works on each of these aspects.
8. Cultural norms create constraints upon human behavior. As such, analysis of cultures is important. However, researchers who rely on culture tend to assume cultural norms as given. No clear explanations as to the sources of these norms are offered.
9. See Vogel ([1975] 1985); Curtis (1985); Johnson (1982); and Ouchi (1984). See Murakami (1987) for a survey of Japanese models.
10. The exchange view of the state is derived from Buchanan and Tullock ([1962] 1965); Brennan and Buchanan (1980); Weingast (1990); and North (1990).
11. Beginning with Coase (1937), the modern theory of the firm assumes that there is no theoretical distinction between the market and hierarchies because these institutional arrangements represent alterna-

tive mechanisms for writing and enforcing contracts. The same logic can be applied to the distinction between the market and political institutions. A rational individual will choose one institutional form over another if that institution reduces transaction costs. See Williamson (1975, 1985).

12. For instance, Samuels (1987, 2) examined Japan's energy industry, and concluded: "The Japanese state is a market-conforming player not because . . ., but because in the development of Japanese commerce and industry powerful and stable private actors emerged who established enduring alliances with politicians and bureaucrats. These same actors vigilantly checked market-displacing intervention."

13. This change was, for instance, described by Calder (1988, 150): "Throughout the prewar and wartime periods, for example, the Ministry of Commerce and Industry, predecessor of MITI, had waged a constant struggle with the zaibatsu and the industrial control associations regarding pricing, output, and resource allocation decisions. But SCAP, declaring the zaibatsu responsible for the war economy, banned private cartels and insisted that government officials—that is, technocrats—exercise the powers previously accrued to the control associations. It thus helped reinforce the bureaucratic preeminence in industrial matters—."

14. See Hadley (1970) for zaibatsu dissolution.

15. The reform virtually wiped out the rural landlord class by affecting about 80 percent of all tenancy land. See Calder (1988, 14) who stated: "It undermined traditional conservative mechanisms of social control and significantly increased uncertainty for the conservatives in the Japanese political process."

16. "2,210 officers from 632 zaibatsu corporations and some 2,500 high-ranking officers and large stockholders of other large companies were purged for wartime activities" (Caves and Uekusa 1976, 465).

17. See Muramatsu and Krauss (1987).

18. All of these models are based on the notion that Japanese society is somewhat more controlled by power-elites. See Murakami (1987) for a survey of Japanese models.

19. One should realize that there are at least three types of keiretsu structures in postwar Japan. The first type consists of those groups that are direct descendants of prewar zaibatsu. The second type is made up of those groups that have emerged after World War II. These two types contain main banks at their cores. The last type is comprised of those groups centered around large manufacturing corporations, such as Toyota.

20. See Caves and Uekusa (1976) and Miwa (1990) for a reference.

21. This point was originally made by Naka (1990) and Naka, Brough, and Tanaka (1992).

22. This discussion was based upon a line of argument made by Becker (1983) and Michaels (1988).
23. The power to tax should be interpreted rather broadly. Our use of this term is derived from Brennan and Buchanan (1980, 149–55).
24. According to Calder (1988, 153): "Coupled with the changes in state administrative structure noted above, and the dissolution of the corporatist agricultural association (nokai) in 1947, this proliferation in private-sector interest group formation severely circumscribed the technocratic autonomy of the prewar period in many areas of domestic policymaking."
25. This is a reasonable assumption because the Japanese economy had still not recovered from the devastation of the World War II.
26. The present values of their contracts are increased by creating binding agreements. See Landes and Posner (1975) for the theory of durable political contracts.
27. See Weingast and Shepsle (1981) for the role of the committee system as an enforcement mechanism.
28. For instance, according to Johnson (1982, 199): "The tools in the hands of the economic bureaucrats included control over all foreign exchange and imports of technology, which gave them the power to choose industries for development; the ability to dispense preferential financing, tax breaks, and protection from foreign competition."
29. During the initial phase of the occupation, the Reconstruction Financing Bank (RFB) was established to provide industrial subsidies. Because these subsidies were financed through issuing government bonds, inflation increased. When the Dodge policy was initiated, the activities of the RFB were terminated. See Shiraishi (1983) and Kosai ([1981] 1986).
30. The development of Japan's industrial organization has been examined by many researchers. Recently, new institutional economics has been utilized to analyze Japan's industrial organization. In this respect, see Aoki ([1984] 1990, 1988); Shimokawa (1985); Inoue ([1985] 1986); Horiuchi, Packer, and Fuckuda (1988); Hodder (1988); Miwa (1990); Kawasaki and McMillan (1987); and Asanuma (1989).
31. Former members of executive committees of enterprise-based unions often became corporate board members of Japanese firms. A survey by Nikkeiren (the Japan Management Association) in 1978 showed that 1,012 directors out of a total of 6,457 directors (15.7 percent) at 352 surveyed companies were former executive members of their enterprise-based unions (see Aoki 1988, 92).
32. This encompassing nature of Japanese interest groups was pointed out by Olson (1965, 1982). However, he did not explain why it emerged and how it has been maintained. In this sense, our explanation is an extension of Olson's theory.

33. Casual evidence provided by various researchers shows that industrial policy in Japan rarely has been targeted for aiding narrowly concentrated interests. For instance, Patrick (1986, 13) states: "Japanese industrial policy has been at the industry level, usually rather broadly defined."
34. For instance, upon examining postwar Japan's LDP regime, Calder (1988, 158) asserts: "In a content analysis of political speeches during the 1955 Japanese general election campaign, for example, 'stability' or 'stabilization' (antei) was clearly and consistently used more by the Right than by the Left; this was the only one of twenty-one political terms to show such a clear pattern. This consistent emphasis on stability has continued to the present day."
35. For instance, in 1981, U.S. Congressional staff totaled over 25,000, including 858 staff members at the Library of Congress. By contrast, Japan's Diet employed 3,369 staff members, including 155 Diet Library staff members. The number of secretaries attached to U.S. Congressmen was 11,125, while only 1,526 secretaries were attached to Japanese counterparts. See Sato and Matsuzaki (1986, 83).

References

Aoki, Masahiko. 1988. *Information, Incentives, and Bargaining in the Japanese Economy*, Cambridge: Cambridge University Press, 1988.
———. ed. *The Economic Analysis of the Japanese Firm*. Amsterdam: North-Holland.
Asanuma, Banri. 1989. "Manufacturer-Supplier Relationship in Japan and the Concept of Relation-Specific Skill." *Journal of the Japanese and International Economies* 3: 1–30.
Baerwald, Hans H. 1986. *Party Politics in Japan*. Boston: Allen & Unwin.
Becker, Gary S. 1983. "A Theory of Competition among Pressure Groups for Political Influence." *Quarterly Journal of Economics* 98 (August): 371–400.
Brennan, Geoffrey, and James M. Buchanan. 1980. *The Power to Tax: Analytical Foundations of a Fiscal Constitution*. Cambridge: Cambridge University Press.
Brough, Wayne T., and Shigeto Naka. 1990. "Political Brokers and Political Governance Structures." Unpublished paper presented at the Annual Meeting of the Public Choice Society.
———. "The Role of the American Occupation of Japan." Unpublished paper presented at the Annual Meeting of the Southern Economic Association.
Buchanan, James M., Robert D. Tollison, and Gordon Tullock. 1980. *Toward a Theory of the Rent-Seeking Society*. College Station: Texas A&M University Press.

282 Shigeto Naka, Wayne T. Brough, and Kiyokazu Tanaka

Buchanan, James M., and Gordon Tullock. [1962] 1965. *The Calculus of Consent*, Ann Arbor: The University of Michigan Press.

Calder, Kent E. 1988. *Crisis and Compensation: Public Policy and Political Stability in Japan, 1949–1986*. Princeton: Princeton University Press.

Cargill, Thomas F., and Shoichi Royama. 1988. *The Transition of Finance in Japan and the United States*. Stanford: Hoover Institution.

Caves, Richard E., and Masu Uekusa. 1976. "Industrial Organization," 459–524. In Patrick and Rosovsky 1976.

Coase, Ronald H. 1937. "The Nature of the Firm." *Economica* 4 (November): 386–405.

Crain, Mark W., William F. Shughart II, and Robert D. Tollison. 1988. "Legislative Majorities as Nonsalvageable Assets." *Southern Economic Journal* 55, no. 2 (October): 303–14.

Curtis, Gerald. 1985. "Big Business and Political Influence," 33–70. In Vogel 1985.

———. 1988. *The Japanese Way of Politics*. New York: Columbia University Press.

Friedman, David. 1988. *The Misunderstood Miracle*. Ithaca: Cornell University Press.

Hadley, Eleanor. 1970. *Anti-Trust in Japan*. Princeton: Princeton University Press.

Hamada, Koiichi, and Akiyoshi Horiuchi. 1987. "The Political Economy of the Financial Market," 223–62. In Yamamura and Yasuba 1987.

Hayashi, Fumio. 1986. "Why Is Japan's Saving Rate so Apparently High?" In NBER Macroeconomics Annual 1986.

Hodder, James E. 1988. "Corporate Capital Structure in the United States and Japan," 241–64. In Shoven 1988.

Horiuchi A., F. Packer, and S. Fukuda. 1988. "What Role Has the 'Main Bank' Played in Japan?" *Journal of the Japanese and International Economics* 2: 159–80.

Inoguchi, Takashi, and Tomoaki Iwai. 1987. *'Zoku-Giin no Kenkyu* (A Research on the Tribal-Politicians). Tokyo: Nihonkeizai Shinbunsya.

Inoue, Munemichi. [1985] 1986. "Competition and Cooperation among Japanese Corporations," 139–59. In Thurow [1985] 1986.

Ito, Takatoshi. 1991. *The Japanese Economy*. Cambridge: MIT Press.

Johnson, Chalmers. 1982. *The MITI and the Japanese Miracle: The Growth of Industrial Policy*. Stanford: Stanford University Press.

Kawasaki, Seiichi, and John McMillan. 1987. "The Design of Contracts: Evidence from Japanese Subcontracting." *Journal of the Japanese and International Economies* 1: 327–49.

Klein, Benjamin, and Keith B. Leffler. 1981. "The Role of Market Forces in Assuring Contractual Performance." *Journal of Political Economy* 89, no. 4: 615–41.

Kodansha International Ltd., ed., [1979] 1987. *Politics and Economics in Contemporary Japan*, ed. Murakami Hyoe and Johannes Hirschmeier.

New York: Kodansha International Ltd. Previously published by the Japan Culture Institute.

Koike, Kazuo. 1977. *Shokuba-no Rodokumiai to Sanka* (Labor Unions at Enterprises and Their Participation). Tokyo: Toyokeizai Shinposya.

Komiya, Ryutaro, Okuno Masahiro, and Suzumura Kotaro, eds., 1988. *Industrial Policy of Japan.* Tokyo: Academic Press.

Kosai, Yutaka. [1981] 1986. *The Era of High-Speed Growth: Notes on the Postwar Japanese Economy.* Tokyo: University of Tokyo Press.

Krauss, Ellis S., and Michio Muramatsu. 1987. "The Conservative Policy Line and the Development of Patterned Pluralism," 516–54. In Yamamura and Yasuba 1987.

Landes, William, and Richard A. Posner. 1975. "The Independent Judiciary in an Interest-Group Perspective." *Journal of Law and Economics* 18 (December): 875–901.

Lincoln, Edward J. 1988. *Japan: Facing Economics Maturity.* Washington, D.C.: Brookings Institution.

McCormick, Robert E., and Robert D. Tollison. 1981. *Politicians, Legislation, and the Economy.* London: Martinus Nijhoff.

McCraw, Thomas K., ed. 1986. "From Partners to Competitors: An Overview of the Period since World War II." In *America Versus Japan.* Boston: Harvard Business School Press.

Mackay, R. J., and C. L. Weaver. 1981. "Agenda Control by Budget Maximizers in a Multi-Bureau Setting." *Public Choice* 37, no. 3: 44–72.

Masumi, Junnosuke. 1983. *Sengo Seiji* (The Postwar Politics of Japan), Vol. 1. Tokyo: Tokyo Daigaku Shuppan-kai.

———. [1983] 1985. *Sengo Seiji* (The Postwar Politics of Japan), Vol. 2. Tokyo: Tokyo Daigaku Shuppan-kai.

Matsuzaki, Tetsuhisa, and Seizaburo Sato. 1986. *Jiminto-Seiken* (The Liberal Democratic Regime). Tokyo: Chuo-Koron Inc.

Michaels, Robert. 1988. "The Design of Rent-Seeking Competitions." *Public Choice* 56: 17–29.

Ministry of Finance, ed. 1978. *Syowa Zaisei-shi: Tokei* (Financial History of the Syowa Period: Statistics). Tokyo: Toyokeizai Shinpo-sya.

Miwa, Yoshiro. 1990. *Nihon-no Kigyo-to Sangyo-Soshiki* (Japan's Firm and Industrial Organization). Tokyo: Tokyodaigaku Syuppan-kai.

Munemichi, Inoue. [1985] 1986. "Competition and Cooperation among Japanese Corporations," 139–59. In Thurow [1985] 1986.

Murakami, Yasusuke. "1987. The Japanese Model of Political Economy," 33–92. In Yamamura and Yasuba 1987.

Muramatsu, Michio, and Ellis S. Krauss. 1987. "The Conservative Policy Line and the Development of Patterned Pluralism," 516–54. In Yamamura and Yasuba 1987.

Naka, Shigeto. 1990. "Toward a Public Choice Analysis of the Political Economy of the Postwar Japan." Unpublished Ph.D. diss., George Mason University.

Naka, Shigeto, and Wayne T. Brough. 1991. "The Strucure of Political Resource Allocation in Post-War Japan: A Rent-Seeking Perspective." Paper presented at the Annual Meeting of the Southern Economic Association, Nashville, Tenn., November 24–26.
Naka, Shigeto, Wayne T. Brough, and Kiyokazu Tanaka. 1992. "The Industrial Organization, Rent-Seeking, and the Economic Growth of Postwar Japan." Unpublished paper presented at the Annual Meeting of the Public Choice Society.
Nakatani, Iwao. [1984] 1990. "The Economic Role of Financial Corporate Grouping." 227–58. In Aoki [1984] 1990.
Noguchi, Yukio. 1986. "The Development and Present State of Public Finance," 36–49. In Shibata 1986.
North, Douglass C. 1990. *Institutions, Institutional Change and Economic Performance*. Cambridge: Cambridge University Press 1990.
Okumura, Hiroshi. 1983. *Shin Nihon no Rokudai Kigyo-Syudan* (New Six Enterprise Groupings in Japan). Tokyo: Daiamond Sya.
———. 1990. Hojin Shihonsyugi (Corporate Capitalism). Tokyo: Ochanomizu Syobo.
Olson, Mancur. 1965. *The Logic of Collective Action*. Cambridge: Harvard University Press.
———. 1982. *The Rise and Decline of Nations*. New Haven: Yale University Press.
Ouchi, William. 1984. *The M-Form Society: How American Teamwork Can Recapture the Competitive Edge*. Reading, Mass.: Addison-Wesley.
Ozaki, Robert. 1991. *Human Capitalism: The Japanese Enterprise System as World Model*. Tokyo: Kodansya.
Packman, J., and K. Kaizuko. 1976. "Taxation," 317–82. In Patrick and Rosovsky 1976.
Patrick, Hugh. 1986. "Japanese High Technology Industrial Policy," 3–33. In Patrick and Meissner 1986.
Patrick, Hugh, and Larry Meissner, eds. 1986. *Japan's High Technology Industries*. Seattle: University of Washington Press.
Patrick, Hugh, and Henry Rosovsky, eds. 1976. *Asia's New Giant: How the Japanese Economy Works*. Washington D.C.: The Brookings Institution.
Samuels, Richard J. 1987. *The Business of the Japanese State: Energy Markets in Comparative and Historical Perspective*. Ithaca: Cornell University Press.
Sato, Seizaburo and Tetsuhisa Matsuzaki. 1986. *Jiminto Seiken* (The Liberal Democratic Party Regime). Tokyo: Chuo Koron-sha.
Schaller, Michael. 1985. *The American Occupation of Japan*. Oxford: Oxford University Press.
Shibata, Tokue, ed. 1986. *Public Finance in Japan*. Tokyo: Tokyo University Press.
Shimokawa, Koichi. 1985. "Japan's Keiretsu System: The Case of the

Automobile Industry," *Japanese Economic Studies* 13, no. 4 (Summer): 3–31.

Shiraishi, Takashi. 1983. *Sengo Nihon Tsusyo Seisaku-shi* (Postwar Japan's Public Policy toward Industries). Tokyo: Zeimu Keiri Kyokai.

Shoven, John B., ed. 1988. *Government Policy toward Industry in the United States and Japan.*, Cambridge: Cambridge University Press.

Suzuki, Yoshio. 1986. *Money, Finance, and Macroeconomic Performance in Japan.* New Haven: Yale University Press.

Takahashi, Makoto. 1986. "The Public Sector in the National Economy," 24–35. In Shibata 1986.

Thurow, Lester C., ed. [1985] 1986. *The Management Challenge: Japanese Views.* Cambridge, Mass.: MIT Press.

Trezise, Philip H., and Yukio Suzuki. 1976. "Politics, Government, and Economic Growth in Japan," 753–812. In Patrick and Rosovsky 1976.

Tullock, Gordon. 1980. "Efficient Rent Seeking," 97–112. In Buchanan, Tollison, and Tullock 1980.

Vogel, Erza F., ed., [1975] 1985. *Modern Japanese Organization and Decision-Making.* Tokyo: Charles E. Tuttle.

Weingast, Barry R. 1990. "The Role of Credible Commitments in State Finance." *Public Choice* 66, no.1 (July): 89–97.

Weingast, Barry R., and Kenneth A. Shepsle. 1981. "Structure-Induced Equilibrium and Legislative Choice." *Public Choice* 37: 503–19.

Wildes, Harry Emerson. 1954. *Typhoon in Tokyo: The Occupation and Its Aftermath.* New York: Macmillan.

Williamson, Oliver E. 1975. *Markets and Hierarchies.* New York: The Free Press.

———. 1985. *The Economic Institutions of Capitalism.* New York: The Free Press.

Yakushiji, Taizo. 1987. *Seijika vs Kanryo* (Politicians vs. Bureaucrats). Tokyo: Toyokeizai Shinposya.

Yamamura, Kozo, and Yasukichi Yasuba, eds., 1987. *The Political Economy of Japan: The Domestic Transformation*, Vol. 1. Stanford: Stanford University Press.

V

Market Solutions to
Economic Development

11

Privatization and Development: The Case of Sri Lanka

Manisha H. Perera and Mark Thornton

> What impels every man to the utmost exertion in the service of his fellow man and curbs innate tendencies toward arbitrariness and malice is, in the market, not compulsion and coercion on the part of gendarmes, hangmen, and penal courts; it is self-interest. The member of a contractual society is free because he serves others only in serving himself. What restrains him is only the inevitable natural phenomenon of scarcity. For the rest he is free in the range of the market.
>
> —Mises 1963, 283

Introduction

In the early twentieth century, many development economists and political leaders considered planned development the most direct route to economic progress.* The popularity of development planning was based on the belief that centralized national governments could offer the essential institutional and organizational mechanism for overcoming the major obstacles to development and ensure a high rate of economic growth. The record of development planning in the Third World, like central planning in the former Communist world, did not live up to expectations.[1] The failure of planning has led an increasing number of policy makers to advocate the use of the market mechanism to promote efficiency and economic growth. Privatization, deregulation, and free trade are at the forefront of this market-oriented approach, and are also the key components of the Austrian account of economic development. The focus of this study will be the privatization of public enterprises in Sri Lanka in light of the Austrian approach to economic development.

Austrian Economics and Economic Development

Adam Smith wrote his *Wealth of Nations* explaining the "nature and causes" of the dramatic economic development that had taken place in England. Like Smith, Austrian economics incorporates the subject of economic development and growth into general economic reasoning. Indeed, the Austrian understanding has much in common with the lessons of Adam Smith. This is in sharp contrast to the study of economic development in the twentieth century which has been transformed into a separate and distinct discipline.

The "development economist" is typically a specialist who designs and implements development programs and specific projects for national governments. The Austrian economist operates at a more basic level, examining man and the world as they are in an attempt to understand how the market works and why it sometimes does not. He does not produce grand plans or implement projects as the development economist would.[2] In fact, Austrian economists were among the first critics of development planning. The work of Austrian economist and Nobel Laureate F. A. Hayek represents a concerted attack on this type of constructivist rationalism, the idea that society can and should be engineered and designed for better performance.[3]

Information is a key to understanding the Austrian perspective on stability, growth, and development. Information about the scarcity of resources and the value of goods is carried throughout the economy via the price system. This knowledge can then be used by individuals to perform economic calculations and discover profit opportunities. The perception of profit opportunities spurs on entrepreneurial action, while losses reallocate resources from the unsuccessful to the most alert entrepreneurs—to the extent private property and the rights to profit exist and are maintained in an economy.

Like central planners and bureaucrats, the development planner suffers from an information problem. He has access to more information then he can use, and yet does not have access to enough information to make economic calculations. Development planning appears to work better when it is limited and done with the assistance of a growing market economy. A price system based on private property in conjunction with a well-functioning monetary system reduces the scope of the information problem. Government planning appears less effective when the planning is comprehensive, the projects are large and intrusive, and the economy is primitive.

In the attempt to understand the workings of the market process and government intervention, Austrian economists have established a general conclusion that free markets are efficient and are superior to government intervention or direct government control. This conclusion is well illustrated by past experience. The key element of a free-market economic system is private property. Individuals must have the right to own property and be given the greatest possible control over the use of this property.

The absence of government intervention and the threat thereof allows the market to flourish. The free market is a social system superior to democracy in terms of efficiency.[4] A free-market society must have institutions that protect property rights (especially in capital) and the inequality of economic results. Indeed, this protection and the relative lack thereof is the major difference between the development in the West and the slower development elsewhere.

The start which the peoples of the West have gained over the other peoples consists in the fact that they have long since created the political and institutional conditions required for a smooth and by and large uninterrupted progress of the process of larger-scale saving, capital accumulation, and investment. Thus, by the middle of the nineteenth century, they had already attained a state of well-being which far surpassed that of races and nations less successful in substituting the ideas of acquisitive capitalism for those of predatory militarism. (Mises 1963, 497)

One clear sign of the impact of extensive government intervention in the market is the growth of the informal sector. The growth of informal businesses in Sri Lanka has been quite dramatic and can only be understood as a reaction to the costs of compliance with regulations and taxes. "Informality," which is a result of the market's attempt to circumvent the "bureaucratic model of planning," simply means ignoring and avoiding the negative influence of government (Chickering and Salahdine 1991). The informal sector has made an important contribution to economic growth and the development of the entrepreneurial spirit in Sri Lanka. Policies that remove the distinction between formal and informal business, such as reducing regulations and taxes, should also contribute to the growth and development of both sectors (Sanderatne 1991).

For the Austrian economist, the most sophisticated form of development is the formation and advancement of institutions that are not designed, but that evolve to solve problems, mitigate "felt uneasiness," and stimulate cooperation. Institutions such as language, law, marketplaces (cities), money, the international division of labor, and stock markets are important examples of such institutions. While these institutions may have taken centuries to evolve, undeveloped countries can make great advances by imitating, borrowing, and integrating preexisting institutions from the West, making necessary adaptations and improvements wherever possible.[5] However, the basic requirement for social and economic development is private ownership and relatively unrestricted control of property.

Political History of Sri Lanka

Early Sri Lanka was characterized by a feudal (hegemonic) society. Village ownership was subordinated to the king as sovereign of all the land and he could dispose of it as he saw fit. The Sri Lankan version of feudalism, however, differed significantly from the European, especially the English and French varieties, in that it did not develop large-scale demesne farming, a manorial system, and the military aspects of feudalism. However, there was, in common with European feudalism, an obligation to service as a condition of holding land, whether from secular or religious landlords, but with one vital difference. In Sri Lanka, the nature of that obligation was determined by the caste system (de Silva 1981, 35).

This feudal economic system was modified by the arrival of Portuguese and European commercialism in 1505. Later, Portuguese were displaced by the Dutch and the Dutch by the British. Although Portugal and the Netherlands left their marks on Sri Lanka, the greatest influence over the island was exercised by the British. The changes brought about by the British were set forth with the development of the Colebrooke-Cameron Report (1833). The economic policies of the Colebrooke-Cameron Report helped promote an atmosphere in which private capitalist ventures were viewed with favor. Colebrooke, as a follower of Adam Smith, was against monopolies; as a consequence, the monopoly of the cinnamon trade was eradicated. Other monopolies, such as fish, salt, and other forms of government trading, were also brought to an end. The Colebrooke-Cameron Report also recommended abolition of the centuries-old feudal concept of labor. As a result of the policies introduced by the British, the Sri Lankan economy of the nineteenth century was changed to one of entrepreneurial freedom. By World War I, Sri Lanka (Ceylon) was a classic example of a free and open economy, with a minimum of state intervention. Almost all commercial and business activity was handled by the private sector.

Development Planning in Sri Lanka

The desire to break away from laissez-faire doctrine came to the forefront in the mid-twentieth century. State intervention was advocated on the grounds of bringing about an equal distribution of income and economic opportunity to all classes of citizens. The politicians and nationalists provided the ideological background for intervention. Sri Lankan members of the Legislative Council in the 1920s championed state intervention as a remedy for the economic ills of the island. The early interventionist acts included the establishment of wage boards for plantation labor and the regulation of certain working conditions on the plantations. The increase in unemployment also invited intervention, and the measures adopted included relief work, welfare measures, and poor relief. All politicians, however, did not demand state intervention. Some people with liberal ideas opposed protection and restrictions. In fact, a few legislative members opposed the government system of taxation in 1919, and in 1931 made the opposition to income tax its major platform. The majority of the educated groups, however, thought that the State should initiate all possible economic ventures. As a result, nationalization and public enterprises emerged as the two major forms of state intervention (Warnapala 1988, 27–29).

Nationalization as an instrument of state intervention came to the forefront in 1956. The motivation for nationalization in Sri Lanka, as Joan Robinson stated, was to "throw off the swaddling bands of colonialism and to acquire freedom to control her own economy." Another aim was to push out the foreign businesses.[6] The policy based on such objectives resulted in a number of nationalizations; the nationalization of road transport in 1958 was followed by the nationalization of port cargo handling in 1959. The nationalization of insurance came later in 1960, followed by the nationalization of petroleum distribution in 1962. In 1972, the State fixed a ceiling on the extent of agricultural land that a person could own and in 1975, the government implemented its program of estate nationalization. Also in 1971, the Business Undertaking Acquisition Act was introduced, which was used to acquire private-sector companies (Warnapala 1988, 30–31])

The second form of state intervention was the establishment of public enterprises. The desire to transform the colonial economy led to the creation of public enterprises to engage in commercial and industrial activities. Public enterprises gave the state a predominant role in providing the services essential to the life of the community. These public enterprises fell within the following areas:

1. Industrial and Commercial Enterprises,
2. Cultural, Educational, and Social Service Enterprises,
3. Financial Enterprises, and,
4. Regulatory Enterprises.

Table 1. Number of Public Enterprises, 1958–1977

Sector	1958	1963	1965	1968	1970	1971	1972	1973	1977
Manufacturing	12	18	20	23	24	25	27	29	29
Trading	1	1	2	2	2	10	12	13	13
Agriculture	1	1	1	1	1	1	2	4	4
Service and Other	14	20	22	30	35	45	50	60	61
Total	28	40	45	56	62	81	92	106	107

Source: Karunatilake (1987, 146).

Examples of the above enterprises include: the Sri Lanka Fibre Board, the State Printing Corporation, the Tractor Corporation, the Gem Corporation, the Sri Lanka Transport Board, the Film Corporation, and the Tea Board. This vast network of public enterprises was established on the basis of the Government Sponsored Corporations Act No. 19 of 1955, amended by Act No. 55 of 1957, and the State Industrial Corporations Act No. 49 of 1957. Due to the above legislation, public enterprises grew very rapidly, as shown in table 1. The number of public enterprises grew from 28 in 1958 to 107 in 1977 (Warnapala 1988, 30–33).

Not only did the public enterprises grow in number but the sectors where the state was directly involved in economic activities also increased. These sectors included manufacturing, mining, agriculture, transport, energy, tourism, construction, and research. In agriculture, the public sector owns two-thirds of the total acreage under cultivation, in tea, one-third under rubber cultivation and one-tenth under coconut cultivation. State-owned enterprises in Sri Lanka account for about 40 percent of gross output in manufacturing, over 40 percent of employment in manufacturing, and nearly 60 percent of industrial production. Given the relative importance of the public sector, the performance of the public enterprises have a direct effect not only on the living standards of the people but also on future prospects for the socioeconomic development of the country (Vidanapathirana 1988, 15).

Table 2. Profits/Losses of Selected Public Enterprises
(Rs million)

	1977	1978	1979	1980	1981	1982	1983	1984
State Fertilizer Manufacturing Corp.	—	—	—	—	−679	−161	−25	−302
Ceylon State Hardware Corp.	—	−54	0.8	1.0	−2.4	−10	−19	−27
National Milk Board	−72	−85	−60	−96	(*)			
National Textile Corp.	−17	36	−87	(*)				
Ceylon Steel Corp.	6.5	14	41	28	28	−24	−49	−62
Ceylon Government Railway	−163	−61	−108	−176	−236	−324	−452	−621
Sri Lanka Transport Board	−42	−56	−316	−472	−429	−518	−396	−441

Source: Karunatilake (1987, 158–237).
(*) denotes the year in which the public enterprise was privatized.

Performance of Public Enterprises

The performance of public enterprises under closed-economy policies has been poor. Table 2 illustrates the performance of selected public enterprises in Sri Lanka. This poor performance of public enterprise may be attributed to monopoly power, lack of incentives for workers, lack of managerial expertise, interference in production and prices by the government, and employment policies of the public enterprises.

In 1977 a new government came into power with the promise of liberalizing the economy. The new government announced the closing down of loss-making public enterprises and the handing over of certain key industrial enterprises to the private sector. Poor performance and inefficient management, coupled with the political ideology of the government, led to the conversion of public enterprises into privatized ventures.

Privatization Process in Sri Lanka

The first steps toward privatization were taken in 1977. Many public enterprises, which were not economically viable or could not be made viable, were closed down or sold to the private sector. These public enterprises included the State Fertilizer Manufacturing Corporation, the Tobacco Industries Corporation, the Packaging Materials Corporation, Government Owned Business Undertaking Tile Factories, Minneriya Textiles, the Wellawatte Spinning and Weaving Mills, Ceylon Silks, the Milk Board, and certain units of the Hardware Corporation. The purpose and process of privatizing some of these public enterprises are described below.

State Rubber Manufacturing Corporation (SRMC)

Background

SRMC was established under the State Industrial Corporation Act of 1973. The aim of the SRMC was to provide assistance to small landholders. Before the SRMC was set up, small holders tapped latex from rubber trees, converted it into low-grade ribbed smoked sheets, and sold them to middlemen. With the establishment of the SRMC, the SRMC would buy latex from individual small holders, add value, and export a high-grade rubber. The SRMC is the only corporation providing this service. The SRMC has eight factories, mainly in the rubber-growing districts of the Ratnapura, Kapawalle, and Kelani valleys. The eight factories employ about 250 workers.

Process of Privatization

To free the SRMC from government control and to bring dynamism into its management, the government decided to convert the corporation into a joint-stock company (partial divestiture). On December 31, 1981, the SRMC went into liquidation and was dissolved. In its place, a new limited liability company was formed, valued at 78 million rupees. In the new company, 60

Table 3. Profit Statements of the
State Rubber Manufacturing Co., 1979–1987

Year	Profit (Loss)
1980	(5,801,334)
1981	827,736
1982 January-June	(201,655)
1982/1983	4,325,637
1983/1984	2,912,156
1984/1985	570,516
1985/1986	1,759,642
1986/1987	4,704,317

Source: Nankani (1988, 12).
* Converted July 1982 to Sri Lanka Rubber Manufacturing Company.

percent of ownership was kept by the government and 40 percent was offered to both employees and the public.

Since the formation of the limited liability company the only layoffs were at headquarters, where forty of the total staff of sixty were laid off. Those unemployed were compensated with six months' salary or 20,000 rupees, whichever was less. Table 3 shows that the company has increased profits since divestiture. Workers were also given a bonus of two months' salary a year which compared well with the bonus of less than half a month's salary received by workers in previous years.

The SRMC example shows that public companies can be changed into private companies and perform at a profit. However, for these private companies to work at an optimum level, further steps must be taken to enforce the *independence* of these new companies.

Cooperative Wholesale Establishment (CWE)

Background

CWE is a large state-owned holding company established in 1950 by an Act of Parliament. Like most enterprises set up at the time, the objectives of the CWE were to provide services and employment. CWE has 4,800 employees and annual sales of 2,000 million rupees. In recognition of the need to adopt modern technology and strengthen managerial efficiency, three of CWE's subsidiaries were converted into joint-stock companies. The three subsidiaries were CWE Computer Services, CWE Printers Ltd., and Lanka Milk Foods, Ltd.

CWE Computer Services

This joint-stock company was set up to handle accounting and managerial systems. Seventy-five percent of ownership was held by the parent company (CWE) and employees and allied corporations held 12.5 percent each. As of March 1986, the joint venture had assets worth 2.54 million rupees and 45 employees. Also the company has operated at a profit since the partial divestiture of CWE Computer Services.

CWE Printers Ltd.

The main function of CWE Printers is to provide printing and advertising services to CWE subsidiaries and the Ministry of Trade. Its outmoded machinery, however, could not cope with the increased demand. To inject new capital into this subsidiary, CWE Printers Ltd. was set up as a joint-stock company. Total assets as of March 1986 were 19.1 million rupees. Before the formation of the joint-stock company, CWE Printers were incurring losses. However, since privatization the company is operating profitably, although actual profit statements for CWE Printers Ltd. are not available.

Lanka Milk Foods, Ltd.

Lanka Milk Foods (LMF) was set up to replace the CWE milk powder packing plant that burned down in the early 1980s. LMF was set up as a "private sector" company with government participation in the equity capital. The plant is designed to pack milk powder into triple laminated foil packages without exposure to the atmosphere or to human hands. LMF is said to be modern in

Table 4. Financial Statistics for Lanka Milk Foods, Ltd. (Rs thousand)

Trading Results	1983	1984	1985	1986
Turnover	57,369	527,083	460,611	488,195
Gross Profit	7,564	99,979	145,511	117,776
Profits after Taxation	1,987	(24,228)	65,183	55,401
Dividends	—	—	33,372	36,663

Source: Nankani (1988, 15).

concept and design, and is one of the largest milk powder packaging complexes in the world.

The company has performed profitably since its establishment in 1982 as shown in table 4. Profits before taxes in the quarter ending in March 1987 were 74.4 million rupees, 10 million rupees more than the quarter the previous year. LMF has maintained a tax-free dividend of 12.5 percent since 1985. LMF also does not rely on government subsidies. In 1985 and 1986, the return on assets employed was 25 percent and 18.5 percent, respectively. Given a current interest rate on term loans of 14 percent, LMF can be considered a successful public company.

National Textile Corporation

Background

Prior to 1977, the four state-owned textile mills—Thulhiriya, Pugoda, Veyangoda, and Mattegama—operated together as a virtual monopoly. With the liberalization of the economy in 1977, the mills were predictably unable to compete with foreign and domestic firms due to obsolete machinery and inefficient management. The accumulated losses in the four textile mills exceeded 400 million rupees in 1979.

Process of Privatization and Results

In the case of the textile mills, the method of privatization used by the government was management contracts. The Ministry of

Table 5. Sales of Major Textile Mills,
1982 and 1985 (Rs Million)

Mills	1982	1985
Thulhiriya	255.5	400.0
Pugoda	97.0	335.0
Veyangoda	122.0	281.0
Matlegama	72.9	105.5

Source: Nankani (1988, 19).

Textile Industries arranged to have the three major mills managed by three foreign companies. The medium- and long-term objective of the management contracts was to move toward full divestiture. The management contracts were expected to make the mills viable and attractive to invite equity participation from the public.

According to the Ministry of Textile Industries, there has been a major improvement in the performance of the four mills. Table 5 shows that sales have increased dramatically in the first stage of privatization.

In 1986, for the first time in the history of the mills, they paid a dividend of 10 million rupees to the Treasury. The individual performances of the Thulhiriya, Pugoda, and Veyangoda mills are as follows.

Thulhiriya Textile Mills

Thulhiriya mills are managed by a consortium of three companies, including Bombay Dyeing Manufacturing Co. Ltd, one of the largest composite textile mills in India. Operation of the Thulhiriya Textile Mills under the new management began in 1980, and under the new management arrangement the mills have made profits since 1983. The mills have also earned about 40 million rupees in foreign exchange and the earnings per employee have increased about 30 percent. From table 6, it can be observed that in addition to sales, there has been a significant increase in both profits and employment.

Table 6. Thulhiriya Textile Mills, 1981–1986

	1981	1982	1983	1984	1985	(Jan-Sept) 1986
Net Profit (Loss) (Rs million)	(12.34)	(2.76)	8.33	12.88	56.04	49.57
Employees	2,551	2,845	3,128	3,321	3,802	3,703
Average Earnings per Employee/Month	984	1,140	1,250	1,450	1,502	1,614

Source: Nankani (1988, 19).

Pugoda Textile Mills

Pugoda has been under the management of Lakshmi Textiles of India. Lakshmi, the sixth-largest manufacturer of textile machinery in the world, has been managing Pugoda mills since July 1980. Sales turnover under new management has improved from 89.42 million rupees to 336.37 million rupees, an increase of about 276 percent. With respect to profits, the mills started to show positive results since 1985. Employment in Pugoda mills has also increased since 1981.

Veyangoda Textile Mills

Veyangoda mills are managed by the Tootals Ltd., a UK-based international group. Veyangoda mills made profits in 1986 and also in 1986. There has also been over a 100 percent increase in average employee earnings.

Sri Lanka Telecommunications Department (SLTD)

The inefficiency of SLTD was so glaring and customer frustration so great that there was enormous pressure from the government and the private sector for a major restructuring of services.

Privatization Process

With the decision to privatize SLTD, a Presidential Committee of Inquiry as well as the World Bank were asked to outline broad policy options for its reorganization. Both the Committee of Inquiry and the World Bank arrived at similar conclusions, which included:

1. The creation of a new telecommunications entity (as opposed to a government department),
2. The need to transfer the SLTD into a joint venture with a foreign partner, and
3. The formation of a regulatory body to oversee the telecommunications sector.

A new telecommunications board (TBSL) has been formed to articulate and execute telecommunications policy. Privatization has been broken into two phases. In phase one, the stock would remain government-owned, but in all other respects the company would operate as a "private" commercial enterprise. Phase two involves the actual introduction of private participation and is scheduled to begin in 1992.

Government-Owned Business Undertakings

Tile Factories

There were three major tile factories: Noorani Tiles, Shaw Industries, and Vijaya Tile Works. Noorani Tiles, built in the 1940s, was the largest of its type. In 1960, it was reconstructed and made the most modern tile factory in the country. Situated at the best clay deposit area in Colombo, it produced an average of 25,000 tiles a year, as well as wire-cut bricks and earthenware pipes. It employs about five hundred workers. In 1975, due to labor unrest within the company, the government acquired Noorani Tiles under the 1971 Business Undertakings Act. It was then managed by Ceylon Ceramics Corporation, a government holding company that also managed eighteen other brick and tile companies. The company was placed directly under the Ministry of Industries and a representative of the ministry was appointed to manage the firm.

There is little information on the background of Shaw Industries and Vijaya Tile Works. It is not known when they were established but they were also taken over by the government in the 1980s and managed by a government authority. Shaw Industries and Vijaya Tile Works employed 325 and 200 workers, respectively. The three million rupees in assets owned by Shaw Industries were dwarfed by liabilities of approximately fiften million rupees. Vijaya Tile Works was valued at six million rupees, with six million rupees in liabilities.

By 1982, two factors led to a change in the government's benevolent attitude toward these three tile companies. The public policy of the country had shifted toward privatization and the tile companies posed a continuous drain on the federal budget. The Cabinet therefore decided to sell all three companies. The privatization technique used by the Cabinet was full divestiture through private sale after tendering and transferring of state activity to a new company to be formed by private parties. The final negotiations for all three tile factories were completed in 1988. Unfortunately, the financial results of these new companies were not yet available.

Conclusions

Privatization has attracted much attention in the recent years and it reflects a worldwide interest in reducing the role of the state in national economies, while enhancing the scope of private ownership and the private sector. This movement toward privatization in Sri Lanka and elsewhere is the result of the recognition of the internal inefficiencies of public enterprises. Studies by Davies (1971), De Alessi (1974), Crain and Zardkoohi (1978), Frech and Ginsburg (1981), Davies (1981), and Perera (1992) have clearly illustrated the inefficiencies found in public enterprises.

The inefficiency of public enterprises is predictable from an understanding of the contributions of Austrian economists. Bureaucratic organizations such as public enterprises are rule-guided rather than profit-motivated. These organizations suffer from an information problem that only worsens over time and as more industries are nationalized. The only solution to this problem is privatization.

Privatization has many practical advantages. Privatization can increase the quantity and quality of goods and services available in the market. The profit motive keeps the privatized firms responsive to consumer needs and demands. As the entrepreneurial spirit is released, new techniques are adopted, machines free up labor, and new products are discovered. Through the free-market allocation of resources, privatization over the long term can create more jobs and opportunities for all. Privatization can lead to open, competitive economies that produce high incomes and more permanent jobs. Privatization allows governments to eliminate subsidies to unprofitable state-run enterprises, thereby creating the potential for reduced deficits, inflation, and taxes. Therefore, privatization not only solves the problems of state-run enterprises, it also provides the fuel to further remove government from the economy and thereby promotes further economic development. In short, privatization is the correct procedure to liberate the economies of developing countries from the slow growth and stagnation that have plagued so many for so long.

The limited privatization in Sri Lanka provides an important illustration of the benefits of the Austrian approach to economic development. The first steps toward privatization were taken in 1977, but the actual divestiture of government-owned businesses did not take place till the early 1980s. As shown above, all the privatization ventures thus far have been successful. The State Rubber Manufacturing Corporation, Cooperative Wholesale Establishment, and National Textile Corporation are just a few examples of how through privatization previously public enterprises with large losses are now making large profits.

While successful, privatization in Sri Lanka has been slow, due mainly to the special interests opposed to privatization and to the large-scale communal problems that engulfed the country in the late 1970s. Partial privatization entails partial success. Delaying privatization only delays the success of privatization. While time will provide more facts concerning the success of privatization, there is little doubt that the success so far has helped create the right political and economic environment that promises to expand private ownership within the partially privatized firms, extend privatization to all other public enterprises, and thereby contribute to further economic development.

Notes

* The authors would like to thank Robert B. Ekelund, Jr. and Jeffrey Herbener for their helpful comments and suggestions.
1. See Waterston (1965) for a detailed study on the development planning experience of fifty-five countries.
2. Ludwig von Mises (1963, 869) noted that the "professional economist" was a hindrance to the market economy, referring to them as specialists "instrumental in designing various measures of government interference with business."
3. F. A. Hayek's most famous contribution, *The Road to Serfdom* (1949), clearly showed that planning and extensive interventionism were not "planning for freedom." He discussed the fundamental aspect involved in the failure of planning and indeed, the failure of the economics profession, in his Nobel Memorial Lecture. He concluded here (1989, 7) that

> If man is not to do more harm than good in his efforts to improve the social order, he will have to learn that in this, as in all other fields where complexity of an organized kind prevails, he cannot acquire the full knowledge which would make mastery of the events possible. . . . The recognition of the insuperable limits to his knowledge ought indeed to teach the student of society a lesson of humility which should guard him against becoming an accomplice in men's fatal striving to control society—a striving which makes him not only a tyrant over his fellows, but which may well make him the destroyer of a civilization which no brain has designed but which has grown from the free efforts of millions of individuals.

> Mises (1952; 1963, 285) was also an important early critic of development planning—but in contrast to Hayek, Mises did believe that you could rationally design a successful social order in terms of the general rules and institutions of society.
4. It is also successful in terms of translating individual input into social valuation and in terms of equity and justice. It cannot, however, be said to be superior in these respects because some standards of equity and justice are diametric to other standards and economic analysis cannot determine which standard is superior.
5. From the Austrian perspective, even the planning of simple institutions, such as transportation systems and cities involves an insoluble information problem. This theoretical humility leads many Austrians

to recommend that the government restrict its concerns to protecting property rights and resolving disputes. Even in the judicial realm, the free market is greatly expanding into areas of crime protection, arbitration, and maintenance of prison facilities. Recently, Benson (1990) has argued that well-functioning judicial institutions can develop without a monopoly of force.

6. This type of policy does irreparable harm to a country's connections to the international capital market, the key link for the process of economic development. Sri Lanka became independent in 1948, but it is difficult to link the use of nationalization exclusively to anticolonialism because similar projects were being put into place around the world, including in Sri Lanka's colonial ruler, Great Britain.

References

Alchian, Armen. 1965. "Some Economics of Property Rights." *Il Politico.* (December): 369–82.

Alchian, Armen, and Reuben Kessel. 1962. "Competition, Monopoly, and the Pursuit of Money." *Aspects of Labor Economics* 14.

Barletta, Nicolas. 1987. Preface in *Privatization and Development*, ed. Steve H. Hanke. San Francisco: Institute for Contemporary Studies.

Benson, Bruce. 1990. *The Enterprise of Law: Justice without the State.* San Francisco: Pacific Research Institute for Public Policy.

Chenery, Hollis, and Moses Syrquin. 1975. *Patterns of Development, 1950–1970.*, London: Oxford University Press.

Chickering, A. Lawrence, and Mohamed Salahdine. 1991. *The Silent Revolution: The Informal Sector in Five Asian and Near Eastern Countries.* San Francisco: ICS Press.

Crain, Mark, and Asghar Zardkoohi. 1978. "A Test of the Property Rights Theory of the Firm: Water Utilities in the United States." *Journal of Law and Economics* (October).

Davies, David G. 1971. "The Efficiency of Public versus Private Firms: The Case of Australia's Two Airlines." *Journal of Law and Economics* (April): 149–65.

———. 1981. "Property Rights and Economic Behavior in Private and Government Enterprises: The Case of Australia's Banking System." *Research in Law and Economics* 3.

De Alessi, Louis. 1974. "Managerial Tenure under Private Government Ownership in the Electric Power Industry." *Journal of Political Economy* (May/June): 645–53.

———. 1980. "The Economics of Property Rights: A Review of the Evidence." *Research in Law and Economics* 3, 1–47.

De Mel, Ronnie. 1977. *Budget Speech 1978.* Ministry of Finance and Planning, Republic of Sri Lanka.

308   Manisha II. Perera and Mark Thornton

de Silva, K. M. 1981. *A History of Sri Lanka.* Berkeley, Los Angeles: C. Hurst.
De Soto, Hernando. 1989. *The Other Path: The Invisible Revolution in the Third World.* New York: Harper & Row.
De Walle, Nicholas, "Privatization in Developing Countries: A Review of the Issues," *World Development,* Volume 17, 1989.
Ekelund, Robert, and Robert Tollison. 1981. *Mercantilism as a Rent-Seeking Society.* College Station: Texas A&M University Press.
Finsterwalder, Ottokarl. 1990. "From Marxism to Market: Reforming the CMEA Economics." *Vital Speeches,* May 15, 457–60.
Frech, H. E., and Paul Ginsberg. 1981. "Property Rights and Competition in Health Insurance: Multiple Objectives for Nonprofit Firms." *Research in Law and Economics* 3: 155–72.
Hanke, Steven. 1986. *Privatization: Theory, Evidence and Implementation.* Auburn, Ala.: Ludwig von Mises Institute.
———. 1987. "Introduction in *Privatization and Development,* ed. Steve H. Hanke. San Francisco: Institute for Contemporary Studies.
Hayek, F. A. 1944. *The Road to Serfdom.* Chicago: University of Chicago Press.
———. 1989. "The Pretence of Knowledge." Nobel Memorial Lecture, December 11, 1974, printed in *American Economic Review* 79, no. 6 (December): 3–7.
IMF. 1989. "ADB Attributes Success of Asian Economies to Liberal Policies, Reliance on Market Forces." *IMF Survey,* August 7, 241.
Kaletsky, Anatole. 1988. "Privatization in the Developing Countries." *Central Bank of Sri Lanka News Survey* (March/April).
Karunatilake, H. N. S. 1987. *The Economy of Sri Lanka.* Sri Lanka: Sridevi Printing Works.
McPherson, Peter. 1987. "The Promise of Privatization." In *Privatization and Development,* ed. Steve Hanke. San Francisco: Institute for Contemporary Studies.
Mises, Ludwig. (1920) 1990. *Economic Calculation in the Socialist Commonwealth.* Auburn, Ala.: Praxeology Press.
———. 1952. *Planning for Freedom.* South Holland, Ill.: Libertarian Press.
———. 1963. *Human Action: A Treatise on Economics.* 3d ed., New Haven: Yale University Press.
Nankani, Helen. 1988. "Selected Country Case Studies." In *Techniques of Privatization of State-Owned Enterprises.* World Bank Publication, Technical Paper No. 88.
Perera, Manisha. 1992. "Efficiency of the Public and Private Bus Transport Sectors in Sri Lanka." *Journal of Advanced Transportation* 26.
Sanderatne, Nimal. 1991. "The Informal Sector in Sri Lanka: Dynamism and Resilience." in Chickering and Salahdine 1991.
Vidanapathirana, Upananda. 1988. "Private and State Sectors: Their

Contribution to the Economic Development of Sri Lanka." In *Aspects of Privatization in Sri Lanka*, ed. Gerd Botterweck, 13–21. (Colombo: Friedrich-Eberi-Shiftung).

Warnapala, Wiswa. 1988. "Sri Lanka: Laissez Faire State or Welfare State?" In *Aspects of Privatization in Sri Lanka*, ed. Gerd Botterweck, 22–38. (Colombo: Friedrich-Ebert-Shiftung).

Waterston, Albert. 1965. *Development Planning: Lessons of Experience.* Baltimore: John Hopkins University Press.

12

Financial Reform and Economic Development: The Currency Board System for Eastern Europe

Steve H. Hanke and Kurt Schuler

One of the great debates in economics pitted prominent members of the Austrian School against so-called market socialists in the 1920s and 1930s. When the dust had settled, the Austrians had gotten the best of the socialists on theoretical grounds. That was a well-kept secret in the economics profession for many years. In 1971, however, no less a person than Paul Samuelson crowned the Austrians the victors. He wrote, "It was Hayek, with his point about how the market system brings information to bear upon the outcome, who really won the debate" (Samuelson [1971] 1977, 876). Yet although the economic waste associated with state-owned enterprises and public works projects had been acknowledged for some time by a broad cross section of economists, many still clung to the belief that comprehensive economic planning worked. Notable, for example, were the observations made by John Kenneth Galbraith after a 1984 trip to Russia. He remarked

That the Soviet economy has made great material progress in recent years—certainly in the near decade since my last visit—is evident both from the statistics (even if they are below expectations) and, as many have reported, from the general urban scene. One sees it in the appearance of solid well-being of the people on the streets, the close to murderous traffic, the incredible exfoliation of apartment houses and the general aspect of restaurants, theaters and shops—though these are not, to be sure, the most reliable of indices. (Galbraith [1984] 1986, 270)

Well, by the time the Berlin Wall came down in 1989, it was clear that Galbraith and economists of his ilk literally did not know what they were talking about. Central planning had produced more ruinous results than even the Austrians imagined.

Even though the collapse of socialism has demolished the general case for centralized economic planning, the vogue for planning in certain sectors of the economy remains strong. In particular, most persons have assumed that the issue of currency should be centrally planned, by a government monopolist—the central bank. Plans to reform the economy of the former Soviet Union, such as the Shatalin "500 days" plan, the Harvard "Grand Bargain" scheme, and proposals considered to date by the International Monetary Fund, all stress the importance of controlling the supply of money by granting more independence to central banks (e.g., Allison and Yavlinsky 1991, 41, 89). That flies in the face of both theory and history, which suggest that central banks will not produce stable currencies in Eastern Europe.[1]

Why Central Banking Is Not the Answer

East European nations are trying to become market economies, yet paradoxically they are placing much of the responsibility for doing so on central banks, which are essentially not market institutions.

Marx and Engels wrote in the *Communist Manifesto* that one of the steps for achieving communism was "centralization of credit in the hands of the state, by means of a national bank with state capital and an exclusive monopoly" (Marx and Engels [1848] 1948, 30). Before the revolutions of 1989, East European nations followed Marx and Engels to the letter in this part of the Communist program. They had "monobank" systems, in which no distinction existed between central banking, commercial banking, and subsidizing state-owned enterprises. To try to achieve administrative efficiency, some nations split the functions of the monobank into separate "banks" corresponding to different sectors of the economy (a consumer savings bank, a bank for construction and heavy industry, a bank for foreign trade, and so on). The separate banks were all ultimately subject to control by the same planners at the top, however; they were not independent and did not compete with one another.

East European nations are now trying to split the monobank into its components: a central bank; profit-making, competitive commercial banks; and explicit subsidies to state-owned enterprises through the state budget, separated from the banking system. But as long as they retain central banking, they retain the most important feature of centralized economic planning in money. To kill the principles of central planning embodied in the monobank system, it is necessary to cut off the system's head by abolishing or nullifying the power of the central bank.

The arguments against socialist economic planning developed by the Austrians in the 1920s and 1930s (see Hayek 1935 [1975]) have in recent years been extended to money and banking by William Butos (1986) and especially George Selgin (1988, 64–69, 82–107). Selgin has explained how concentrating reserves in a central bank slows the adjustment of the supply of credit to the demand for credit. Because reserves are more concentrated than they would be in a free market, it takes longer for losses or gains in reserves to affect the behavior of the banking system as a whole. Changes in reserves are signals that indicate to banks whether they have correctly anticipated the public's willingness to grant credit through them. Under central banking, the signals become sluggish or even inoperative for relatively long periods, enabling banks to establish a structure of credits that is not in harmony with the wishes of the public and is hence unsustainable.

So much for the theory of central banking. When we examine the history of central banking, we find that many banking systems have gotten along better without central banks than with them. Central banking is a recent development; most countries did not have central banking until after the First World War, yet many developed sophisticated, stable banking systems well before (Schuler 1992a, 1992b). (Eastern Europe was an exception; the rise of modern banking did not occur in most of Eastern Europe until the late nineteenth century or later, by which time national governments in the region had established central banks.)

The history of central banking in Eastern Europe suggests that central banks are unlikely to provide credible currencies. After all, central banks are responsible for the dire condition of the ruble and the Yugoslav dinar, and for the weak condition of most other East European currencies. We who live in Western nations, most of which have relatively good central banks, tend to forget how rare good central banks are. Western central banks are the star pupils of the class. They produce convertible currencies that depreciate "slowly." However, for most of the ninety-nine nations that the World Bank classifies as low- and middle-income, central banks produce inconvertible, unsound currencies. For example, in those nations, average annual inflation was 16.7 percent from 1965 to 1980 and 53.7 percent from 1980 to 1989 (World Bank 1991, 25).

To issue a fiat currency that functions properly, central banks must possess credibility. That will be difficult in Eastern Europe, especially in the former Soviet Union, where the behavior of the Russian central bank and the newly established central banks in other former Soviet republics has made most citizens distrustful of the ruble and of the new currencies intended to replace it. The ruble zone is now (August 1992) in the early stages of a textbook hyperinflation, with demand for cash outrunning the ability of the printing presses to print notes. Convertibility of the ruble, initially promised to occur on June 1, 1992, has been delayed until at least 1993. None of the currencies issued so far by outlying former Soviet republics to replace the ruble is yet fully convertible.

The poor performance of East European central banks explains why Paul Volcker, the former chairman of the U.S. Federal Reserve System, has indicated that he has little faith that central banks in formerly Communist nations can achieve full currency convertibility. Addressing central bankers in Jackson Hole, Wyoming, in 1990, Mr. Volcker noted that markets developed long before central banks, and stressed that Eastern Europe might actually retard its transition to markets by relying on central banks (Volcker 1990).

Many believe that now that East European countries have joined the International Monetary Fund (IMF), the credibility problem will be solved. That is a false hope. Let us look at recent experience in Yugoslavia, which has been a member of the IMF since 1945. The experience of Yugoslavia prior to the outbreak of civil war shows that, in an environment that has many similarities to that in the former Soviet Union, good behavior, credibility, and sound money have proved elusive (Hanke and Schuler 1991c).[2]

In December 1989 the monthly inflation rate was 50 percent in Yugoslavia, and for the entire year it had been 2,720 percent. Armed with an IMF stabilization plan, Yugoslavia introduced a currency reform in December 1989 that established a "hard" pegged exchange rate of seven dinars per German mark. To maintain the peg under conditions of low credibility, real lending rates were about 40 percent and real deposit rates were about 25 percent per year in most of 1990. Although inflation came down in Yugoslavia during 1990, it remained much higher than in Germany. Hence, the dinar became grossly overvalued and the Yugoslav economy slumped into a deep depression. Eventually, Yugoslavia had to give up on the hard peg and pump massive amounts of credit into bankrupt state enterprises and commercial banks owned by them. At present (August 1992) the official exchange rate of the dinar is 1,200 per mark, while on the black market it is about 1,500 per mark. The government in Belgrade fears that inflation could hit 100,000 percent on an annualized basis by the end of 1992 (Silber 1992).[3]

Eastern Europe appears to have one exception to the pattern of inflation in the mid-double digits or triple digits: Czechoslovakia. That is largely the result of the upright character of its finance minister, Vaclav Klaus. But Klaus has no counterparts elsewhere in Eastern Europe, and instead of relying on luck to produce other Klauses, it would be more prudent to install a monetary system that will be tamper-proof even against imprudent, spendthrift finance ministers. Fortunately, such a system exists. The currency board system is an alternative monetary system well suited for Eastern Europe.[4]

The Currency Board Solution

A currency board is an institution that issues notes and coins convertible into a foreign "reserve" currency or commodity asset at a fixed rate and on demand. It typically does not accept deposits. As reserves, a currency board holds high-quality, interest-bearing securities denominated in the reserve currency (or commodity). A currency board's reserves are equal to 100 percent or slightly more of its notes and coins in circulation, as set by law. (Commercial banks in a currency board system need not hold 100 per cent reserves in reserve-currency assets against their deposits, though.) The board generates profits (seigniorage) from the difference between the interest earned on its reserve assets and the expense of maintaining its note and coin circulation (liabilities). It remits to the government all profits beyond what it needs to cover its expenses and to maintain its reserves at the level set by law. The currency board has no discretion in monetary policy; market forces alone determine the money supply, where the money supply is defined as the public's holdings of notes and coins plus deposits held with the commercial banking system.

The main characteristics of a currency board are as follows:

Convertibility. The currency board maintains unlimited convertibility at a fixed rate of exchange between its notes and coins, on the one hand, and the reserve currency (or commodity), on the other hand. Although the currency board does not convert local deposits denominated in its currency into reserve assets, the exchange rate that it sets will determine the terms of arbitrage between the reserve currency and domestic-currency deposits at commercial banks.

Reserves. A currency board holds reserves adequate to ensure that even if all holders of the board's notes and coins (liabilities) wish to convert them into the reserve asset, the board can do so. Currency boards have usually held reserves of 105 or 110 percent of their liabilities, so that they would have a margin of protection in case the interest-earning securities that they held lost value.

Seigniorage. Unlike securities or most bank deposits, notes and coins do not pay interest. Hence notes and coins are like an interest-free loan from the people who hold them to the issuer. The issuer's profit equals the interest earned on reserves minus the expense of putting the notes and coins into circulation. These expenses are usually less than 1 percent of assets a year. In addition, if the notes and coins are destroyed the issuer's net worth increases, because liabilities are reduced but assets are not. Seigniorage generated by a currency board is significant.

The chief economic difference between using currency issued by a currency board rather than notes and coins issued by a foreign bank (for instance, the U.S. Federal Reserve) is that a currency board captures seigniorage for domestic use, rather than letting it accrue to the foreign bank. A currency board also has the political advantage of satisfying nationalistic sentiment for a local issue of currency.

Monetary policy. By design, a currency board has no discretionary powers. Its operations are completely automatic, consisting only in exchanging its notes and coins for the foreign reserve currency at a fixed rate. Unlike a central bank, a currency board cannot act as a tool of inflationary government finance, nor can it offer state-owned enterprises credit at below-market interest rates to accommodate a "soft budget constraint" because a currency board cannot issue fiduciary money. Under a currency board system, government expenditures can only be financed by taxing or borrowing.

Interest rates and inflation. Given the fixed exchange rate between the local currency and the reserve currency, interest rates and inflation rates for tradable goods in the currency board country will tend to be roughly the same as those in the reserve-currency country.

Record of the Currency Board System

The currency board system is a well-tried system with an excellent record (Schuler 1992b, Hanke and Schuler forthcoming). It has existed in about seventy countries. Most were British colonies or former colonies, but currency boards have also existed elsewhere, including two places in Eastern Europe.

North Russia, the region around Archangel and Murmansk, had a currency board in 1918 and 1919, during the life of an anti-Bolshevik government in the region. The North Russian board was the idea of John Maynard Keynes (Hanke and Schuler 1991a). It issued a very successful, stable ruble currency redeemable at a fixed rate of 40 rubles per £1 sterling. Its currency circulated parallel to the inconvertible, unstable currencies issued by other Russian governments at the time. The board's sterling-backed ruble drove the others out of circulation because it was preferred by inhabitants of the region.

Another East European currency board existed in the free city of Danzig (now the Polish city of Gdansk) in 1923 and 1924. The currency board was established to replace the German mark, which was in the final throes of hyperinflation, with a stable local currency, the gulden. The Danzig currency board was a privately owned cooperative enterprise of banks in the city. It maintained a fixed exchange rate of 25 gulden per £1 sterling. Gulden notes were backed 100 percent by a sterling deposit at the Bank of England. Although the currency board worked well, Danzig replaced it with a central bank because economic theory of the time claimed (incorrectly, in our view) that a central bank was more appropriate for an independent territory (Schuler 1992b, chapter 6).

Economic growth was satisfactory under currency board systems. Foreign investment poured into territories with currency boards because there was no exchange risk with the reserve asset (usually the currency of the largest trading partner) and because property rights were secure. Foreign investment financed the rubber plantations and tin mines of Malaya, the cocoa and peanut plantations of West Africa, and the ports of Hong Kong and Singapore. Because most currency board systems fixed their currencies to stable foreign currencies, inflation was low. As under the gold standard or the gold exchange standard, the supply of reserves was outside the control of the domestic government. Adjustments in the balance of payments took the form of reserve gains or losses or changes in net foreign capital investment. In practice, currency board systems ran current account deficits for decades at a time, while increasing their note issues and bank deposits year after year, because they were able to attract sufficient foreign capital investment.

Despite the success of currency boards, most countries that once had currency boards replaced them with central banks. Economic theory played a role: Keynesians expected wonderful results from discretionary monetary policy. But the main reasons for change were political. Politicians saw central banking as a way of manipulating the money supply to their own advantage. Newly independent nations attached great symbolic importance to central banks as supposed symbols of political maturity. Today, currency boards still exist in Hong Kong, the Falkland Islands, the Cayman Islands, the Faroe Islands, Gibraltar, and (in modified form) Bermuda, Singapore, and Brunei.

Options for Establishing a Currency Board

Currency boards could be established in several ways in Eastern Europe. Most currency boards have been monopoly issuers of currency that used a foreign currency as the reserve asset into which they maintained convertibility of their currency. Some currency boards, however, have been competitive issuers of currency, and some have used gold or a basket of foreign currencies as the reserve asset. Hence the currency board system is compatible with proposals for a gold standard, with or without monopoly issue, and with proposals to allow free banking.

Since we have elsewhere discussed in detail the steps in establishing a currency board (Hanke and Schuler 1991b; Hanke, Jonung, and Schuler 1992), we shall merely summarize them here. The two big decisions in establishing a currency board are whether the board will be a monopoly issuer or a parallel issuer, and what reserve asset it will use.

The currency board may replace the central bank, or it may issue currency in competition with the central bank. Establishing the currency board as the issuer of a parallel currency alongside the central bank may be desirable for political reasons. Entrenched political forces that favor central banking may prevent a nation from abolishing the central bank outright. In a parallel-currency system, the central bank can continue to function with its existing staff and its existing assets; nothing need be taken away from it to give to the currency board. The two currencies will not have a fixed exchange rate unless the central bank also decides to peg its currency to the same reserve currency that the currency board uses. The currency board's notes and coins should be given equivalent legal tender status to those of the central bank. A parallel currency will give the central bank the choice of ceasing to depreciate its currency or withering away as people switch to using the currency board's currency. If the central bank continues its old ways, its currency will eventually be driven out of circulation. Such was the case with the North Russian currency board, whose currency drove currencies of competing issuers, such as those issued by the Bolsheviks and anti-Bolshevik governments, out of use in North Russia.

A currency board need not be the only issuer of a parallel currency. Banks could also be permitted to issue notes and coins, whether convertible into the same reserve asset as the currency board, convertible into a different reserve asset, or fiat money. Their notes and coins would compete with those of the currency board and the central bank, if it still existed. This would be a system of free banking (advocated without a currency board by Annelise Anderson 1991).

Currency boards have issued notes competitively alongside banks in the past, in the Philippines until 1949 and in many British Caribbean colonies from the 1930s to the 1950s. We have no quarrel with free banking—indeed, we would welcome it—but it is important to understand the factors that have historically led to stability or instability for free banking systems. The most important requisite of stable free banking has been strong, competitive banks. Decades of socialism have left Eastern Europe with no real bankers and have bankrupted existing large banks. If free

banking were permitted today in Eastern Europe, it would initially be characterized by feeble competition among poorly capi-
talized local banks, managed by persons with no experience in
banking in a market economy and operating in an environment in
which few people trust local institutions.

At least for several years, then, it is vital that one unquestion-
ably reliable domestic currency should exist. A currency board
can provide such a currency. That will speed the development of a
mature financial system in which sound competitors to the currency board can arise and perhaps eventually displace it. Whether
the currency board would continue to exist after a mature free
banking system developed would depend on whether consumers
wanted to continue holding its notes and coins. If not, the board's
note and coin circulation would decline toward zero as competing
issuers gained circulation. Because the board would have 100
percent foreign assets, it would easily be able to meet competing
issuers' demands to redeem its notes and coins. The board would
fade away after having served as a bridge between central banking
and free banking.

Now that we have considered the role of the currency board as
a monopoly issuer and a parallel issuer, let us consider the other
big decision involved in establishing a currency board: the choice
of a reserve asset. The most logical choices for currency boards in
Eastern Europe are the German mark and the U.S. dollar. The
mark is the de facto reserve currency of Western Europe, which is
Eastern Europe's largest trading partner. Using the mark as the
reserve asset would therefore eliminate currency risk in trade with
Western Europe. The dollar is the most widely used unofficial
currency in parts of Eastern Europe and in the former Soviet
Union. The European Currency Unit (ecu) is another possibility. It
recommends itself as the possible future unified currency of Western Europe. At the moment, though, doubts remain about whether
it will actually make the transition from a currency cocktail to a
currency in everyday use.

Gold is another possible reserve asset. Some economists argue
that to obtain credibility, the Russian ruble should be convertible
into gold or some other commodity (Angell 1989; Wanniski 1990).
A currency board whose reserve asset was gold could lend gold on

the London gold loan market. At present, interest on gold loans is 3 to 4 percent a year. (Rates are quoted daily in the *Financial Times.*) The main disadvantage of gold is that it is not the monetary standard of any of Eastern Europe's trading partners. Establishing gold as the reserve currency would not eliminate exchange-rate risk with any foreign nation, unlike using the dollar or mark. The price of gold in terms of major world currencies has at times been extremely volatile since the end of the Bretton Woods system, although the volatility might be dampened if one or more nations returned to the gold standard. Another disadvantage of gold or other commodities is that nominal rates of interest from gold loans or commodity backing are lower than the rates presently available on securities in the leading hard currencies. This reflects not only a slightly lower inflation rate than most currencies, but higher transactions costs.

Whatever sort of arrangement is adopted for establishing the currency board, and whatever reserve asset the board uses, there should be no restrictions on the use of foreign currencies. People should be free to open bank deposits and make contracts in any foreign currency, or in gold and other commodities. The ability to switch into other currencies will reduce the dependence of the currency board system on the reserve currency. If the reserve currency becomes highly inflationary (as sterling did in the 1970s), people will be able to use more satisfactory currencies instead. Another safeguard against the deterioration of the reserve currency would be for the currency board constitution to include a provision permitting a switch to a less inflationary reserve currency should inflation in the original reserve currency exceed predetermined limits (see Hanke and Schuler 1991b, Appendix).

Advantages of the Currency Board System for the Economic Development of Eastern Europe

The currency board system has a number of advantages for East European nations. The foremost is that it depoliticizes the money supply by requiring 100 percent foreign reserves against government note and coin issue. The fixed, binding reserve requirement leaves the supply of notes and coins to be determined by market forces alone. The supply can expand only if people come to the currency board with additional supplies of the reserve asset for conversion into notes and coins. The supply contracts when people decide that they would like to hold fewer currency board notes and coins. (As we explained above, this does not mean that the supply of notes and coins is rigidly linked to the current account balance.) The currency board is passive: it responds to the public's demand, but does not initiate changes in the supply of notes and coins of its own volition.

Most currency board systems have not required banks to hold any particular ratio of reserves against deposits; instead, they have left banks to decide what reserve ratio was appropriate. If the government imposes no reserve requirements, or at least does not vary reserve requirements in an attempt to influence bank credit, the deposit component of the money supply is also determined by market forces alone.

Depoliticizing the supply of money makes hard budget constraints effective on the government, on state enterprises, and on private persons. A currency board generates an amount of seigniorage compatible with low inflation, but it cannot be used as a tool of inflationary finance. The government must raise money by explicit taxation or by borrowing; it cannot use inflation as a hidden tax. That puts pressure on the government to reform its finances by reducing the most unproductive activities in the economy: the military, loss-making state enterprises, certain price subsidies for consumers. Because it enforces a hard budget constraint, the currency board system should, in our opinion, be established early in the sequence of economic reform measures. Hard budget constraints are not a precondition for the currency board system; rather, they can be the result of the currency board system.

Another advantage of the currency board system is that it is transparent. The people of Eastern Europe have been fed lies systematically for years under socialism—lies about the competence of political institutions, about the economy, about their own well-being. The last thing they want now is more muddying of the waters. A central bank is a guarantee of a monetary policy lacking transparency. To achieve its desired effects, a central bank must surprise market participants, which frequently means hiding its intentions. Because it is so transparent, a currency board is far more easily held accountable to its goals than a central bank, and accountability in economic policy making is a very desirable thing to encourage in Eastern Europe now.

The currency board system is easy to maintain because it is simple to operate. Few East European countries, and none of the former Soviet republics, have sufficient trained personnel to run a central bank adequately. The currency board system requires no fine judgments and years of experience; its main work is a counting-house routine that can be easily taught and supervised.

To ensure that the advantages brought by the currency board system remain, a currency board constitution could combine features used by past currency boards. A properly designed constitution will forestall attempts at government manipulation. The constitution could specify, for instance, that a majority of the currency board's directors be foreign nationals, chosen by private institutions in their home countries. Important decisions could require a supermajority. The currency board could be incorporated in a safe-haven country such as Switzerland, with ownership of the board's assets remaining with the board itself, not with the government. We have discussed these measures elsewhere (Hanke and Schuler 1991b).

We have spoken of the advantages of establishing currency boards. What is the monetary cost? Surprisingly, it is modest. The real supply of domestic currency is small in Eastern Europe, especially in the former Soviet Union. Years of high inflation and currency restrictions have induced people to hold real assets and hard foreign currency in preference to domestic financial assets and domestic currency. At present market rates of exchange the reserves necessary for currency boards would range from $70 million in Albania to no more than $6 billion in Russia. The experience of currency board systems shows that after currency stabilization with a currency board, the inflows of foreign capital necessary to expand the supply of currency will be readily forthcoming, provided that rights to private property are secure.

The currency board system is a well-proven one that is more compatible than central banking with the transition from socialism to a market economy. The question remains, will a currency board solution see the light of day? Until recently, it received little more than dismissive comments in official circles. But that has changed in recent months. In early May 1992, Thomas Dawson, the U.S. Executive Director of the IMF, told the Senate Foreign Relations Committee that the IMF was seriously considering the currency board system for Russia (Hitt 1992). In July, Senator Phil Gramm successfully introduced an amendment to the Russian aid bill (called the Freedom Support Act) to encourage currency boards. The amendment allows American funds supplied to the IMF's ruble stabilization fund to be used to establish a currency board (or boards) in any of the former Soviet republics (Hanke and Gramm 1992). In Russia, a group from the Tyumen region, in the eastern Ural mountains, has established the framework for a regional currency board.[5] The group has printed "Ural franc" notes and has been incorporated in Liechtenstein. The currency board could be up and running within weeks of receiving permission from Moscow. After all, it took Keynes just eleven weeks to establish the currency board of North Russia.

Notes

1. For the sake of convenience we use "Eastern Europe" in an extended sense, to include all of the former Soviet Union.
2. Steve Hanke observed the recent Yugoslav experience firsthand as the personal economic advisor to Mr. Zivko Pregl, deputy prime minister of Yugoslavia (1990 to June 1991).
3. For information about the scandals afflicting the National Bank of Yugoslavia, see Sudetic (1991) and World Bank (1989).
4. Other economists who have recently voiced support for currency boards in the former Soviet Union and Eastern Europe include Milton Friedman (1991), Daniel Gressel (1989), Robert Hetzel (1990), Jerry Jordan (1991), Allan H. Meltzer (1991), and Sir Alan Walters (1991).
5. Steve Hanke has advised the group.

References

Allison, Graham, and Grigory Yavlinsky. 1991. *Window of Opportunity.* New York: Pantheon Books.

Anderson, Annelise. 1991. "Free Banking Can Solve the Ruble Problem." *Wall Street Journal Europe*, October 16.

Angell, Wayne D. 1989. "Monetary Policy in a Centrally Planned Economy: Restructuring toward a Market-Oriented Socialist System." Unpublished manuscript, Federal Reserve System Board of Governors, Washington, D.C.

Butos, William. 1986. "The Knowledge Problem under Alternative Monetary Regimes." *Cato Journal* 5, no. 3 (Winter): 849–71.

[Friedman, Milton.] 1991. "Milton Friedman m fl: 'Precis vad Estland behöver.' " *Dagens Industri* (Stockholm), December 17, 9.

Galbraith, John Kenneth. [1984] 1986. *A View from the Stands*, ed. Andrea D. Williams. Boston: Houghton Mifflin.

Gressel, Daniel. 1989. "Soviet Macroeconomic Imbalances during Perestroika." Unpublished manuscript, GT Capital Management, San Francisco.

Hanke, Steve H., and Phil Gramm. 1992. "U.S. Hard Currency Plan for Former Soviet Union." *Financial Times*, July 7.

Hanke, Steve H., Lars Jonung, and Kurt Schuler. 1992. *Monetary Reform for a Free Estonia: A Currency Board Solution*. Stockholm: SNS Förlag.

Hanke, Steve H., and Kurt Schuler. 1991a. "Ruble Reform: A Lesson from Keynes." *Cato Journal* 10, no. 3 (Winter): pp. 655–66.

———. 1991b. "Currency Boards for Eastern Europe." Washington. D.C.: Heritage Foundation.

———. 1991c. *Monetary Reform and the Development of a Yugoslav Market Economy*. London: Centre for Research into Communist Economies.

———. Forthcoming. *Currency Boards and Economic Development*.

Hanke, Steve H., and Alan A. Walters. 1991. *Capital Markets and Development*. San Francisco: Institute for Contemporary Studies Press.

Hayek, Friedrich A., ed. [1935] 1975. *Collectivist Economic Planning*. Clifton, N.J.: Augustus M. Kelley.

Hetzel, Robert. 1990. "Free Enterprise and Central Banking in Formerly Communist Countries." *Federal Reserve Bank of Richmond Economic Review* 76, no. 3 (July): 13–19.

Hitt, Greg. 1992. "IMF Weighs 'Currency Board' to Anchor CIS Monetary Systems." Dow Jones newswire, May 15.

Jordan, Jerry. 1991. "Fiscal and Monetary Policies during the Transition from Socialism to Capitalism." Unpublished manuscript, First Interstate Bancorp, Los Angeles.

Marx, Karl, and Friedrich Engels. [1848] 1948. *The Communist Manifesto*. New York: International Publishers.

Meltzer, Allan H. 1991. "Inflation and Money in Brazil." Unpublished manuscript, The World Bank, Washington, D.C.

Samuelson, Paul A. [1971] 1977. "Liberalism at Bay." In *The Collected*

Scientific Papers of Paul A. Samuelson, vol. 4, ed. Hiroaki Nagatami and Kate Crowley, 865–80. Cambridge, Mass.: MIT Press.

Schuler, Kurt. 1992a. "Overview: The World History of Free Banking." In *The Experience of Free Banking*, ed., Kevin Dowd, 7–47. London: Routledge.

———. 1992b. "Currency Boards." Ph.D. diss., George Mason University.

Selgin, George A. 1988. *The Theory of Free Banking: Money Supply under Competitive Note Issue*. Totowa, N.J.: Rowman and Littlefield.

Silber, Laura. 1992. "Yugoslavia Devalues Dinar by 57%." *Financial Times*, April 13.

Sudetic, Chuck. 1991. "Financial Scandal Rocks Yugoslavia." *New York Times*, January 10.

Volcker, Paul. 1990. "The Role of Central Banks." In *Central Banking Issues in Emerging Market Economies: A Symposium Sponsored by the Federal Reserve Bank of Kansas City*. Kansas City: Federal Reserve Bank of Kansas City.

Walters, Alan. 1991. "A Hard Ruble for Boris." *London Evening Standard*, November 22.

Wanniski, Jude. 1990. "Save Perestroika with Monetary Deflation." *Wall Street Journal*, May 16, 20.

World Bank. 1989. *Yugoslavia, Financing Restructuring: Policies and Priorities*, vol. 1. Washington, D.C.: World Bank.

———. 1991. *World Development Report 1991: The Challenge of Development*. Oxford: Oxford University Press.

Contributors

George B. N. Ayittey is Associate Professor of Economics at the American University, Washington, D.C. Dr. Ayittey is the author of *Indigenous African Institutions* (Transnational Publishers, 1991) and *Africa Betrayed* (St. Martin's, 1991).

Peter J. Boettke is Assistant Professor of Economics at New York University. Dr. Boettke is the author of *The Political Economy of Soviet Socialism: The Formative Years, 1918–1928* (Kluwer, 1990) and *Why Perestroika Failed: The Politics and Economics of Socialist Transformation* (Routledge, 1993).

Wayne T. Brough is Director of Research at the Citizens for a Sound Economy Foundation in Washington, D.C. He received his Ph.D. in economics from George Mason University, specializing in industrial organization and public choice. Dr. Brough has previously worked at the Office of Management and Budget, the Agency for International Development, and in the research branch of an investment bank, where he covered U.S. domestic policies.

Young Back Choi is Assistant Professor of Economics and Finance at St. John's University. Dr. Choi is the author of *Paradigms and Conventions: Uncertainty, Decision Making, and Entrepreneurship* (University of Michigan, 1993).

Steve H. Hanke is Professor of Applied Economics at John Hopkins University. Dr. Hanke also serves as Chairman of the MERIT Group, Inc., in Baltimore, as underwriting manager for special risk programs, and as a Lloyd's of London Correspondent, and as Vice President of FCMI Financial Corporation in Toronto, currency traders and international money managers.

Steven Horwitz is Assistant Professor of Economics and the Flora Irene Eggleston Faculty Chair at St. Lawrence University. Dr. Horwitz specializes in monetary economics, comparative economic systems and the history of economic thought. He is the author of *Monetary Evolution, Free Banking, and Economic Order* (Westview, 1992), as well as numerous articles in professional journals.

Shyam J. Kamath is Professor of Economics at California State University at Hayward. Dr. Kamath is the author of *The Political Economy of Suppressed Markets* (Oxford, 1992) as well as numerous articles in professional journals such as *Public Choice* and *Economic Development and Cultural Change.*

Shigeto Naka is Assistant Professor of International Studies at Hiroshima City University, Japan. Dr. Naka received his Ph.D. in economics from George Mason University and specializes in public choice, industrial organization, and the political economy of Japanese development.

David Osterfeld is Professor of Political Science at St. Joseph's College. Dr. Osterfeld's most recent work is *Prosperity Versus Planning* (Oxford, 1992).

Manisha H. Perera is received her Ph.D. in economics from Auburn University. Dr. Perera previously taught at the University of Northern Colorado and is now a private economic consultant in San Jose, California.

Jan S. Prybyla is Professor of Economics at Pennsylvania State University and author of, among other books, *Reform in China and*

Other Socialist Economies. He was Visiting Professor of Economics at Nankai University Tainjin in 1987–88.

Ralph Raico is Professor of History at State University of New York College at Buffalo and author of numerous articles on the history of European liberalism.

Kurt Schuler is Postdoctoral Fellow at Johns Hopkins University in Baltimore. Dr. Schuler received his Ph.D. from George Mason University and is the author of numerous articles in monetary economics. He is the coauthor (with S. H. Hanke and Lars Jonung) of *Russian Currency and Finance* (Routledge, 1993).

Parth J. Shah is Assistant Professor of Economics at University of Michigan at Dearborn. Dr. Shah received his Ph.D. from Auburn University and specializes in monetary economics.

Kiyokazu Tanaka has been Professor of Economics at Sophia University, Japan, since 1983. Dr. Tanaka specializes in public choice.

Mark Thornton is the O. P. Alford III Assistant Professor of Austrian Economics at Auburn University and the Director of Academic Programs at Auburn University for the Ludwig von Mises Institute. Dr. Thornton is the author of *The Economics of Prohibition* (Utah, 1991), as well as numerous professional articles.

Index

Agarwala, Ramgopal, 246
agency problem, 271
Ajibola, Bola, 167
Ake, Claude, 158
Alexander Committee, 110
American Occupation (of Japan), 256,
  263, 266, 276; reverse course of, 266,
  270, 271, 272
Arndt, H. W., 5
Austrian School of Economics, 8, 9, 10,
  15, 17, 222, 290, 291, 304, 310
authoritarian political rule, 250
Ayres, Robert, 195

Baechler, Jean, 39
balance of payments, 206
banking system, 17, 104
Barro, Robert, 242
Bauer, P. T., 37, 38, 43, 46, 52, 53, 178,
  223
Becker, Gary, 263, 276
Berman, Harold, 44
Bhagwati, J., 102, 109
Bohm-Bawerk, E., 23
Bolshevik Revolution, 2, 3, 93, 94
Buchanan, James, 131
Buddhism, 234
Butos, William, 312

calculation, economic problem of, 290
capital, 9, 17, 101, 103, 200, 260

Carlyle, A. J., 45
central banking, 311–14
Chang, Prime Minister (Korea), 243
Christianity, 234
Chun, President (Korea), 249
Clark, J. B., 23
Colebrooke-Cameron Report (Sri
  Lanka), 293
colonial rule (Japanese over Korea),
  234–35
common law, 19
Companies Act, 106
Conable, Barber, 198
Confucian legacy (in Korea), 234
Conquest, Robert, 7
contract law, 16
Cooperative Wholesale Establishment
  (of Sri Lanka), 298
corporatist economic system, 215–16
Cowen, Tyler, 218, 223
credibility (of central banks), 313–14
currency board system, 314–15
current account deficit, 205

Davidson, Basil, 170
depoliticizing policy, 321–22
deregulation, 290
Desai, P., 102
devaluation policy, 202
development, 9, 25, 31, 90
direct foreign investment, 79

discovery, as economic procedure, 125, 290
division of labor, 1, 20
Dodge, Joseph, 266, 271, 273
Domar, Evsey, 5
Dutch experiment, 48

Eberstadt, Nicholas, 217, 219, 224
Economic Cooperation Administration, 217
Economic Stabilization Board, 266
education, 242
Eisenhower, Dwight, 236
enabling environment (for development), 206, 207
encompassing interest, 232, 242, 243, 247, 268
entrepreneurship, 28, 63, 82, 124, 128, 130, 131, 290
equilibrium theory (in economics), 2
Essential Commodities Act, 104
European "miracle," 38
European Recovery Program, 210
Export Credit Guarantee Corporation, 113
external account debt, 204
externalities, 131, 148

Fair Price Shops, 105
Faith, Roger, 131
Farley, Hugh, 243
federalism, 215
feudalism, 292
financial intermediation, 17, 24, 25, 27, 31; as creative endeavor, 26, 30
financial markets, 82
fixed exchange rate system, 316, 319
Ford Foundation, 216
foreign aid, 9, 149, 159, 200, 236
foreign capital, 323
Foreign Exchange Regulation Act, 111
foreign investment, 317
formalism in economics, 2–4
Forson, Kwame, 164
free trade, 290

Galbraith, John Kenneth, 310
Gandhi, Rajiv, 118, 123

General Agreement on Tariffs and Trade, 186
Gerschenkron, Alexander, 240, 242
gold (as monetary standard), 320
government failure theory, 124
Great Depression, 4, 97
growth theory: Harrod-Domar model of, 5, 24; neoclassical, 5, 9

Hancock, Graham, 187
hard budget constraint, 322
Hayek, F. A., 2, 16, 124, 212, 222, 290
Hicks, John, 39
Hogan, Michael, 214, 220
Houphouet-Boigny, Felix, 151, 164
Hughey, Ann, 191

ideology, 3, 211
import licensing, 107–8
indigenous institutions, 169, 170, 177
Industrial Credit and Investment Corporation of India, 104
Industrial Development and Regulation Act, 105
Industrial Development Bank of India, 104
Industrial Finance Corporation of India, 103
industrial policy, 232, 239, 240, 251, 252
informal sector, 292
institutions (as key determinant in development), 1, 9, 10, 19, 38, 40, 42, 49, 62, 65, 75, 92, 119, 221, 222, 257, 262, 277, 291, 292
International Bank for Reconstruction and Development, 187
International Development Association, 187
International Monetary Fund, 185, 311, 314
international trade, 186
investment (private), 196
Irwin, Michael, 198

Johnson, Lyndon, 192
Jones, E. L., 53

Kaunda, Kenneth, 152
Keidanren, 275
keiretsu structure, 260, 267, 268, 273, 275, 277
Kendall, Leon, 178
Keynes, John Maynard, and Keynesianism, 2, 4, 5, 8, 24, 217, 223, 324
Khanin, Grigory, 7
Killick, Tony, 147, 154, 160
Klaus, Vaclav, 314
kleptocrats, 165
Knight, Frank, 2, 23
knowledge (problem of), 9, 16, 124, 125, 126, 128, 130, 212, 222, 290
Kodan, 266, 267
Kolko, Gabriel, 215
Krauss, Melvyn, 192
Krishna, Raj, 114
Krueger, Ann, 110

Lal, Deepak, 27, 124
land reform (Japan), 265
Landes, David, 40, 41
Lange, Oskar, 2
Laski, Harold, 94
Lavoie, Don, 220
Law for the Elimination of Excessive Concentration of Economic Powers, 265
Lee Dynasty, 234
Lenin, Vladimir, 3, 65
liberalism, 1, 50, 206, 222
linkages (in development), 148
Louw, Francis, 178

Mabogunje, A., 154
MacArthur, Douglas (General), 258
Mao, Chairman, 66, 68, 69
market failure theory, 148
Marshall Plan, 210, 214
Marx, Karl, 51, 94, 311
McKinnon, Ronald, 24
McNamara, Robert, 191
Menger, Carl, 23
military aid, 236
Milward, Alan, 220
minimum wage laws, 105

Ministry of International Trade and Industry, 268
Mises, Ludwig von, 212, 289
monetary system, 1, 9, 20, 22, 222
Monopolies and Restrictive Trade Practices Act, 107
moral hazard problem, 272, 273
Mugabe, Robert, 169
Multilateral Investment Guarantee Agency, 187

Nardo, Japheth M. M., 154
National Industries Development Corporation of India, 103
national resources, 234
National Textile Corporation (Sri Lanka), 300
nationalization of industry, 266, 294
Nehru, Jawaharlal, 93, 94, 95, 125; socialist vision of, 96
Neo-Institutionalist School of Economics, 9–10
neo-Stalinist model of planning, 68
New Deal policies (U.S.), 215
New Economic Policy (Soviet Russia), 3
N'Gouabi, Marien, 152
Nixon, Richard, 192
Nkala, Enos, 169
Nkrumah, Kwame, 150, 153, 171
Nove, Alec, 4
Nyerere, Julius, 150, 152, 154

Office of the Chief Controller of Imports and Exports (India), 112
Olson, Mancur, 232, 243; theory of encompassing interest, 232, 242, 243, 247, 268

Park, President (Korea), 237, 238, 239, 240, 243, 244, 249, 250
Parliament (Japanese Diet), 266, 270, 272
Pirenne, Henri, 43
Pisani, Sallie, 216
planning, 16, 90, 98, 124, 211, 213; central, 265; comprehensive, 213, 310;

planning (*continued*)
discretionary, 2; noncomprehensive, 217
political environment, economic impact of, 66
positivist revolution in science (impact on economic science), 2, 3
private enforcement mechanisms, 273
privatization, 75, 290, 297
Progressive Era (U.S.), 215
property rights, 1, 16, 19, 41, 52, 66, 75, 77, 127, 130, 222, 291, 292
public choice theory, 124, 257, 261, 262
public enterprises, 304
public ownership, 90

Ramadou, Amina, 159
rent-seeking, 249, 257, 262, 268, 269, 270, 275
Reserve Bank of India, 111
Rhee, Syngman, 237, 243
Robinson, Joan, 294
Rosenberg, Nathan, 51
Rostow, W. W., 52
ruling elites, 251

Samuelson, Paul, 310
Schoeck, Helmut, 46
Schumpeter, Joseph, 2, 29–30
Sekyi, Kobina, 178
Selgin, George, 28, 312
Selyunin, Vasily, 7
Senghor, Leopold, 152
Shenoy, B. R., 124
Smith, Adam, 1, 3, 9, 19, 63, 65, 290, 293
socialism, 8, 64, 93, 94, 151; Fabian model of, 93, 94
soft budget constraint, 316
Soviet socialism, 63, 94, 97

Special Economic Zones (China), 70
special interest groups, 247, 305
Sri Lanka Telecommunications Department, 302
Srinivasan, T. N., 109
Stalinist model of planning, 4, 8, 73
State Rubber Manufacturing Corporation (Sri Lanka), 297
state-owned enterprises, 197

tariff system, 120
tax rates, 129, 177
Third World, 4, 195, 197, 199, 200, 201, 289; debt crisis of, 202
time-horizon, 276
Toure, Sekou, 153
transaction costs, 273
transparency (of law), 322

unions (labor), 106, 273
United Trust of India, 104

Viner, Jacob, 45
vision: as influence on public policy, 91–92, unconstrained, 96–97, 125
Volcker, Paul, 313

Wade, Robert, 232
War Communism (Soviet Russia), 3, 65
Waters, Alan, 201
Webb, Sidney and Beatrice, 94
Weinstein, Joel, 215
Wexler, Immanuel, 216
Wiebe, Robert, 215

Xiaoping, Deng, 69, 70

Yaw, Amoafo, 166

Zaibatsu, 264, 265

Printed in the United States
By Bookmasters